THE HIST
VEGETARIA
COW-VENERATION
IN INDIA

For the first time, this influential study by Ludwig Alsdorf is made available to an English speaking audience, translated by Bal Patil. It focuses on two of the most pertinent issues in Indian religion, the history of vegetarianism and cow-veneration, and its historical approach remains relevant to this day.

With reference to significant brahminical texts, such as key chapters of the *Book of Manu,* the book centres on the author's analysis of the role of Jainism in the history of vegetarianism. The author explores the history of meat-eating in India and its relationship to religious thought and custom, and searches for solutions to the problem of cattle veneration. Besides a comprehensive translation of the original German manuscript 'Beiträge zur Geschichte von Vegetarismus und Rinderverehrung in Indien', four important articles directly related to Alsdorf's work by Kapadia, Heesterman and Schmidt are made available in this new edition.

These additional contributions and careful notes by the editor Willem Bollée add a modern perspective to a study that remains a key reference for students and scholars of Religious Studies, Asian Studies and History.

Ludwig Alsdorf (1904–1978) was one of the most influential Indologists of his generation. He had wide range of interests and worked on Prakrit, Apabhramsha and Pali literature, in particular on Jaina universal history and prosody. His pioneering metrical analyses of ancient Indian literature prepared the ground for great advances in the dating of texts and the reconstruction of the history of Indian philosophy. One of his most influential studies is the present work.

Willem Bollée is Professor Emeritus at the University of Heidelberg, Germany.

Bal Patil is an independent researcher, journalist and Chairman of the Jain Minority Status Committee, Dakshin Bharat Jain Sabha, a century old Jain organization in India. He is the co-author of Jainism (1974, with Colette Caillat and A.N. Upadhye), and his English translation of Ludwig Alsdorf's *Les Etudes Jaina, Etat Present et Taches Futures,* edited by Willem Bollée was published in 2006. His translation of Hiralal Jain's *Jainism Through the Ages* from Hindi into English is due for publication.

ROUTLEDGE ADVANCES IN JAINA STUDIES

Series Editor: Peter Flügel

School of Oriental and African Studies

Jain Studies have become an accepted part of the Study of Religion. This series provides a medium for regular scholarly exchange across disciplinary boundaries. It will include edited collections and monographs on Jainism.

STUDIES IN JAINA HISTORY AND CULTURE
Disputes and Dialogues
Edited by Peter Flügel

HISTORY, SCRIPTURE AND CONTROVERSY
IN A MEDIEVAL JAIN SECT
Paul Dundas

THE HISTORY OF VEGETARIANISM AND
COW-VENERATION IN INDIA
Ludwig Alsdorf
Edited by W. Bollée

THE HISTORY OF VEGETARIANISM AND COW-VENERATION IN INDIA

Ludwig Alsdorf

Translated from German by Bal Patil
Revised by Nichola Hayton

Edited with additional notes, a bibliography and four appendices by
Willem Bollée

Routledge
Taylor & Francis Group
LONDON AND NEW YORK

Title of the German original:
Beiträge zur Geschichte von Vegetarismus und Rinderverehrung in Indien.

Akademie der Wissenschaften und der Literatur. Abhandlungen der Geistes- und Sozialwissenschaftlichen Klasse Jahrgang 1961 – Nr. 6.

Published by: Verlag der Akademie der Wissenschaften und der Literatur in Mainz in Kommission bei Franz Steiner Verlag GmbH. – Wiesbaden, 1962.

First published in German in 1962 as 'Beiträge zur Geschichte von Vegetarismus und Rinderverehrung in Indien' by the Verlag der Akademie der Wissenschaften und der Literatur, Mainz, Germany

First published in English in 2010
by Routledge
2 Park Square, Milton Park, Abingdon, Oxfordshire OX14 4RN

Simultaneously published in the USA and Canada
by Routledge
711 Third Avenue, New York, NY 10017

Routledge is an imprint of the Taylor & Francis Group, an informa business

First issued in paperback 2011

Typeset in Taj by
Florence Production Ltd, Stoodleigh, Devon

British Library Cataloguing in Publication Data
A catalogue record for this book is available from the British Library

Library of Congress Cataloging in Publication Data
Alsdorf, Ludwig, 1904–1978.
[Beiträge zur Geschichte von Vegetarismus und Rinderverehrung in Indien. English]
The history of vegetarianism and cow-veneration in India/
Ludwig Alsdorf; translated by Bal Patil; revised by Nichola Hayton; edited by Willem Bollée.
p. cm. – (Routledge advances in Jaina studies; 3)
First published in German in 1962 as 'Beiträge zur Geschichte von Vegetarismus und Rinderverehrung in Indien' by Verlag der Akademie der Wissenschaften und der Literatur, Mainz, Germany.
Includes bibliographical references and index.
1. Vegetarianism – Religious aspects – Jainism. 2. Cows – Religious aspects – Jainism. 3. Jainism – History.
4. Vegetarianism – India – History. I. Patil, Bal, 1932–.
II. Bollée, Willem B. III. Title.
BL1375.V44A5813 2010
294.5'48693 – dc22 2009031560

ISBN13: 978-0-415-54824-3 (hbk)
ISBN13: 978-0-415-53360-7 (pbk)
ISBN13: 978-0-203-85959-6 (ebk)

CONTENTS

ABBREVIATIONS

Amg.	Ardhamāgadhī
Āp.	Āpastamba
Baudh.	Baudhāyana
BKBh	Bṛhatkalpabhāṣya
Dasav	Dasaveyāliya
Mbh	Mahābhārata
MW	Monier Williams, *Sanskrit-English Dictionary*
PE	Pillar Edict
PSM	Pāia-sadda-mahaṇṇavo
PW	Böhtlingk und Roth, *Sanskrit-Wörterbuch*
RE	Rock Edict
Sa.	Sanskrit
Vāj.	Vājasaneya
Vas.	Vasiṣṭha
Yājñ.	Yājñavalkya

INTRODUCTION

The subjects of this essay, sparing living beings, which gradually led to vegetarianism, and the veneration of cattle, which has no direct relation to it, were not new to indologists when Alsdorf took them up, but no one had strictly applied the historical method to them. The fact that new publications with references to his study keep being published, such as Scherfe 1993 ṁṁ 164–168, amply shows its continuous actuality and justifies an English version at a time when the knowledge of German in our discipline is no longer obvious.

Originally *ahiṃsā* – non-violence (to living beings) – had nothing to do with vegetarianism as it was, in Alsdorf's opinion, based on (but not explained by) a 'magico-ritualistic' dread of destroying life, this being part of an all-Indian religious development. In the Vedic period people ate meat of ritually killed animals, specially cattle, because killing to sacrifice was not discredited. Later, *ahiṃsā* more and more limited meat consumption. As early as Kauṭilya, before the Manusmṛti that is, *ahiṃsā* was propagated as an ideal for all people, but at the time of the Manusmṛti brahmanic renouncers still ate meat, for religions are conservative and the mendicants, brahmin as well as Jain and Buddhist, according to Alsdorf are still continuing the nomadic stage of the Indians when they entered the subcontinent.

The greater part of the treatise is dedicated to an analysis of the three strata of the juridical literature, viz. Dharmasūtras, Dharmaśāstras (beginning with Manu) and contemporary texts such as Yājñavalkya and relevant parts of the Mahābhārata (stories of Tulādhāra and Vicakhnu; connection between vegetarianism and Vaiṣṇavism), and finally the independent commentaries to the old texts and the Kṛtyakalpataru and other Nibandhas. Alsdorf stresses the contradiction in the juxtaposition of old and new in Manu (after the example of the levirate). In an excursion the relation between

Vasiṣṭha and Manu is dealt with. Summarizing he states that there is little ground for Bühler's assumption of a lost Mānava-Dharmasūtra as a source of Manu, and that Vasiṣṭha comes between the older Dharmasūtras and the Manusmṛti. The essential difference between brahmanism and the reformatory religions is that in the latter the new ideal of *ahiṃsā* did not clash with the great hindrance of the traditional sacrificial cult and other customs at which animals were killed.

This is illustrated in the Uttarajjhāyā 12 and 25 by the ancient story of the Jain monk asking at a brahmanical sacrifice for alms which is refused. In the following discussion the monk does not protest against the killing of the victim, but against mystified ritual practices in a language not understood by the common people, and brahmanical arrogance. The word *ahiṃsā* hardly plays a role in the ancient text. The opposition of the Jains to the brahmanical sacrifice was, at least in the beginning, only part of their opposition against brahmanic religion and haughtiness. Jainism (Jinism) and Buddhism participate in a pan-Indian spiritual movement which is to be taken into account for the interpretation of the famous historical testimonies for the ancient Indian vegetarianism in Aśoka's inscriptions.

In the emperor Aśoka's edicts, too, *ahiṃsā* is evidenced as non-Buddhist. Aśoka participates in a common Indian movement of thought and is a religiously tolerant monarch; his Buddhism only favours his *ahiṃsā*.

A summary of views on *ahiṃsā* was given in the English Abstracts of the Tenth World Sanskrit Conference in Bangalore (1997: 374–76) by H.W. Bodewitz, who takes *ahiṃsā* to originally be an alternative to Vedic sacrificial ritual. Some later publications have been inserted into the Bibliography of the present translation of Alsdorf's text.

The last quarter of Alsdorf's essay is dedicated to the problem of cattle veneration to which he does not know a solution. He ascribes it, first reluctantly – and aware of the fact that for Indologists 'it is a most convenient catchall and a dignified academic way of saying "I don't know"' (Doniger O'Flaherty 1980: 244) – to the Indus Valley Civilisation, but then, after discovering cattle bones, gave up the idea again, whereas Professor Doniger seems to seek a solution in a psychoanalytical direction.

Regarding the appendices to Alsdorf's treatise, it was thought to be of interest to add J.C. Heesterman's review of it, as well as H.-P. Schmidt's articles 'The Origin of Ahiṃsā' and 'Ahiṃsā and Rebirth', with the kind permission of the authors and their publishers.

Heesterman objects to Alsdorf's taking the contradictions in texts such as Manu as chronological successions and would rather parallel the monk, who can only lead a sinless life thanks to the layman's killing his food and water, to the *yajamāna*, the person who pays for and profits from the sacrifice, enabled to partake of the meat by the Vedic priest who kills the victim. Thus the cycle of life and death can only be broken by renouncers who avoid death by *ahiṃsā*. This would explain the juxtaposition of contradictions and also point to the problem of the origin of *ahiṃsā*.

As to this problem, Schmidt in his first paper 'Origin of ahiṃsā' (1962, reprinted here) thinks Alsdorf 'lost sight of the difference between ahiṃsā and vegetarianism' (last para but one of p. 626) and would himself imagine the latter to be a popularized version of the former doctrine. To that end he is searching 'for the specific motives on which the rule of ahiṃsā for the brahmanic renouncer is based' (last para of ch. I). He then establishes that in Vedic texts *ahiṃsā* is not expected of the common man, but a brahmin 'following the *ahiṃsikā vṛtti* accepts only food ... killed by others' (last para but one of p. 635) and a Vedic student has to keep the vow of *ahiṃsā* which is a means of penance. Thus the idea of *ahiṃsā* may have 'originated among world renouncers, was adopted by the Brāhmaṇas and finally considered to be a rule for the whole society' (first para of ch. III) for which the brahmins were the social example.

From the Bhṛgu-legend Schmidt deduces that the ritualists were animists who put plants and animals on a par with man and animals and thus wanted to eliminate the evil consequences of killing and hurting them. The verb 'to kill' is replaced by 'to appease'. Schmidt then emphasizes the similarity of the Vedic and Jain animistic Weltanschauung, and the connection of *ahiṃsā* and belief in reincarnation. Absolute renunciation may lead to final release from transmigration, but 'the ethical motivation of non-violence is secondary: the original motive was fear resulting from the breakdown of magico-ritualistic world-conception' (last sentence of p. 655).

In Schmidt's second appendix here he continues his study of *ahiṃsā* and reincarnation, the ideas the three Indian religions share and which thus in his view may also have a common source. Salvation from transmigration is only possible for renouncers, those that is, who strictly practise *ahiṃsā*, as against the loose *ahiṃsā* of the laity (which Śvetâmbaras of course disagree with). Schmidt further argues with Wezler who thinks magico-ritual fear of destroying life in any form is not the only ground of *ahiṃsā*, but does not suggest other causes.

At the author's request the last paragraph of ch. VII, and ch. VIII were put at the end of ch. VI. In it he once more rejects the view of Alsdorf and Chapple who looked for the origin of *ahiṃsā* and vegetarianism in the Indus civilization in favour of a development inside the Vedic culture. For Schmidt vegetarianism has become the cornerstone of *ahiṃsā*, because one can abstain from meat but not from vegetal food.

The article now ends with a refutation of Heesterman' theses, first, that the obsessive concern about ritual undoing of the injury (to victims) points to the impending collapse of the violent sacrifice. The replacement of the Ṛgvedic decapitation by strangulation does in Schmidt's opinion not mean a progressive decline of violence, but another attitude towards blood which is offered to the demons and therefore must stay outside the place of sacrifice. Schmidt also rejects Heesterman's opinion 'that the typical fusion of ahiṃsā and vegetarianism arose from brahminical ritual thought, while Buddhists and Jains originally had no particular use for vegetarianism' (second para of p. 227). On the contrary, the Jains have become the strictest vegetarians whereas not all believers in the brahmanical revelation (*śruti*) are vegetarians, nor even all brahmins.

It is of course only fair to also give the Jains a chance to explain their view on vegetarianism and thus Kapadia's article 'Prohibition of Flesh-eating in Jainism' of 1933, because it contains a letter of Jacobi, which was inserted as representative of many others such as Upadhye or Malvania, the titles of some of whose articles can be found in the bibliography.

The publication in the Routledge series required many notes and the addition of this Introduction; misprints have been silently corrected. References to Indian texts follow the way of quotation in Monier Williams' *Sanskrit-English Dictionary*, the *Critical Pāli Dictionary* and *Schubring's Doctrine of the Jainas.*

Tantus labor non sit cassus.

The editor

CONTRIBUTIONS TO THE HISTORY OF VEGETARIANISM AND COW-VENERATION IN INDIA

[3] *Two commandments which, also to the Hindus themselves, belong to the most characteristic features of Hinduism and rightly form the foundation of their religion, are: *ahiṃsā*, which literally means 'non-violence' (English in the original [WB]) and signifies the practical extension of 'you shall not kill' to the animal world; and the other, apparently inherent in the first, but factually to be treated as distinct, is the veneration of or, as the Indians prefer to say, 'the protection of cows'. To the modern observer both appear to be deeply embedded in the Indian soul. Both played a central role in the life and teaching of Mahātmā Gandhi, appearing as the well-known 'renunciation of violence', i.e. non-violence raised from the magical-ritual sphere to a mystic-ethical plane. Both have almost incalculable economic consequences which can only be alluded to in passing here. One may smile about the fact that around Cambay in Gujarat, the peasant folk disregard the official rules for getting rid of the strays, which are rampant; on the contrary, every household donates a *roti* on a daily basis for these useless curs. A minister of agriculture, however, was in no mood for smiling when he lamented in the press a few years ago that the Kathiawar peasants refused to kill the locusts and would rather transport them by cart to the next village and set them free there.

The most conspicuous and economically far-reaching effect of *ahiṃsā* is, however, the widely practised renunciation of meat, fish

---

* The pages of the German original are inserted in square brackets. References in the text pertain to these pages. Editor's notes are indicated by (WB).

and frequently eggs. By no means are all Hindus vegetarians,[1] indeed not even a majority are, but vegetarianism established by the religion of such a significant and influential section of people as in India has scarcely any parallel elsewhere in the world. We can again refer to Gandhi here. The extraordinary significance which vegetarianism had for him will have strongly impressed every reader of his autobiography, which appeared a few months ago, finally also in German.[2] **[4]** In addition to that, the sanctity of cattle (by no means only the cow!) precludes even most non-vegetarians from the consumption of beef, and this considering the fact that the prohibition of cattle killing has plainly made India, the country most abounding with cattle in the world. Millions of cattle which are no longer of service at all are robbing the others of their fodder: it is scientifically verifiable that the available supply of nourishment does not suffice for the rest of cows.[3] This chronic crisis of nutrition could probably alone be solved if the cattle population of India were halved. It is the sacredness of the cattle which presents one of the toughest problems to the Indian economy.

The frequent question about the origin or source of so characteristic and vital a feature of the Indian culture as *ahiṃsā* and 'cow-veneration' has not been answered satisfactorily to this day. From the start, we should well exclude rationalistic responses such as the prohibition of cattle killing as a wise protection of an absolutely essential agricultural aid from destruction in times of famine, or vegetarianism as a climatic measure of hygienic precaution. On the other hand, the question of the origin of the veneration is even more taxing in view of the fact that in Indian antiquity the situation was quite different from today: the Aryans, whose immigration during the middle of the second millennium BCE is the crucial event in Indian history, are presented in their ancient literature as meat-eaters, who certainly did not shrink from slaughtering and consuming their numerous cattle.

It is beyond the scope of the present investigation to conclusively answer the question, nor is it possible or intended to write a complete history of *ahiṃsā* and cattle protection based on a collection

1 About 1990, G.-D. Sontheimer reckoned 70% of Hindus to be non-vegetarians (private communication (hereafter p.c.) to WB).

2 Gandhi 1960.

3 Alsdorf 1955: 132 – This is not the case any more, see e.g. Harris quoted in Chapple 1993: 137 (p.c. from Chapple) (WB).

of material widely scattered throughout the entire literature.[4] It will merely be attempted to trace through observations, especially in the 'legal texts', the gradual emergence and assertion of vegetarianism and cattle-protection, and thus, perhaps, to approach an answer to our question. Two methodical remarks must be made in advance.

Firstly, it should once more be stated clearly that vegetarianism and a cattle-taboo must be distinguished despite all relatedness: millions of Hindus, **[5]** it is true, eat fish, chicken and goats, but on no account beef.[5] The ban on cattle-killing prevails also in places where, perhaps in the service of the goddess Kālī, or in religious festivals especially in Nepal, streams of goat- and buffalo blood flow, and any tourist to India has experienced that even in English-run hotels they are served chicken or what is called mutton (which in reality is goat) at every meal, but very rarely beef. The cattle-taboo is, therefore, to be treated as distinct from vegetarianism, or in addition to it.

Secondly, Indian vegetarianism is unequivocally based on *ahiṃsā*; this is clearly expressed in a stanza of the most famous and authoritative of the so-called Indian legal texts, the Manu-smṛti:

'One cannot obtain meat without injuring living beings, but the killing of living beings does not lead to heaven; therefore, one must do without meat.'[6]

Yet so logical a conclusion: no flesh without animal slaughter, therefore, no *ahiṃsā* without renunciation of meat consumption – appears inevitable only to us and to the majority of *modern* Indians. By no means, however, is it drawn everywhere even today, as a quote from T. Hagen's book on Nepal, one of many examples, illustrates[7]: 'For the Sherpas the [Buddhist] religion prohibits the killing of animals, but they love meat nevertheless. Therefore butchers are invited to come from Tibet every year in order to slaughter a few yaks.'

---

4 Much has been compiled in Om Prakash 1961.

5 Some, especially brahmins, are said to eat beef stealthily because it is cheaper than goatmeat bought by many people (p.c. Sontheimer to WB).

6 5, 48: *nâkṛtvā prāṇināṃ hiṃsāṃ māṃsam utpadyate kvacit / na ca prāṇi-vadhaḥ svargyas, tasmān māṃsaṃ vivarjayet.* A Mahābhārata stanza expresses the same thing more drastically (13, 115, 26): 'For flesh is certainly not produced from grass, wood or stone! Flesh comes from the killing of creatures, therefore it is a sin to eat it' (*na hi māṃsaṃ tṛṇāt kāṣṭhād upalād vâpi jāyate / hatvā jantuṃ tato māṃsaṃ, tasmād doṣas tu bhakṣaṇe*). – See also, e.g. Zimmerman 1987: ch. VII 'Vegetarianism and Nonviolence' (WB).

7 Hagen 1960: 76.

The same 'moral principle', according to which it suffices not to do the killing oneself while one can unscrupulously profit from the killing done by others, held good originally and for a long time in ancient India. This is shown by an inquiry into the two great reform religions, Buddhism and Jainism, arising in the sixth century BCE.[8] They have both played a role in the history of *ahiṃsā* and vegetarianism, a role which has usually been largely misunderstood.

It is right that both particularly stress *ahiṃsā*. Nevertheless it is, to begin with, absolutely certain that the Buddha was not a vegetarian and did not forbid meat-eating to his monks either. As to this, it is quite irrelevant whether eating the *sūkara-maddava* **[6]** which, according to the canonical report[9] causes the Master's death, was 'juicy pork' (which appears fairly certain) or whatever else for there is no doubt that the Master and his disciples, as the texts report, ate also meat on numerous occasions when they were invited to the houses of the laity.

The monks in Burma, who follow and guard the ancient injunctions and teachings with particular purity and austerity, nowadays also accept meat as alms from the laity without more ado and consume the same.[10] They are thus in full accord with the oldest code of the rules of the Order, the Vinayapiṭaka of the Pali canon. In it, meat-eating by the monks and the Buddha is often mentioned and everywhere presumed,[11] and meat and fish, along with rice boiled in milk, groats and barley flour, form the solemn and oft-repeated list of the 'five (basic) foodstuffs'.[12] Not only that, but vegetarianism is explicitly discarded or declared unnecessary under certain conditions.

It is related in Cullavagga 7, 3, 14f. (Vin II 197, 4ff.), how the wicked Devadatta planned to bring about a schism by proposing to

8 Probably rather in the fifth century, see Dundas 2002: 24 (WB).

9 Franke 1913: 222 note 4, and Waldschmidt 1939: 63ff.

10 According to the information passed on by word of mouth by leading Burmese monks, but a quotation from Tinker 1957:171 may be added: 'For instance, Buddhism abhors the taking of life and, with its ancient Hindu associations, particularly objects to the killing of cows for meat. Within recent years a vegetarian movement has gained ground among leading exponents of Buddhism in which Ū Nu is particularly prominent. The Prime Minister has disavowed any intention by those in power to prohibit the killing of animals for food, nevertheless this practice is definitely becoming increasingly restricted . . . In Lower Burma the sale of beef has ceased entirely, owing to restrictions.'

11 Cf. the indexes to Horner 1949–66 under 'meat' and 'flesh'.

12 *bhojanīyaṃ nāma pañca bhojanāni: odano kummāso sattu maccho maṃsaṃ.*

the Buddha five intensifications of the rules of the Order: the monks must live for life only in the forest and not go into the villages, live only on alms and not accept invitations, wear only rags from rubbish-heaps and not let themselves be presented with clothes, live only under trees and not under a roof, and finally, eat neither flesh nor fish; infringements of these injunctions would have to be counted as transgression.[13] The rejection of these proposals, which **[7]** Devadatta expected, then followed quite promptly. The Buddha left it to the monks, whether to dwell in the forest or in the vicinity of a village, whether to beg for alms or to accept invitations, whether to wear rags or to accept donations of clothes, and he permitted an eight months' stay (outside the rainy season that is!) under a tree. As to the last proposal, however, he declared: 'Fish and meat are pure under three conditions: when (the monk) has not seen, nor heard and has no suspicion (that the animal was killed on purpose for him).'[14]

The bracketed supplement follows inter alia from a story narrated in the Mahāvagga (76, 31, 12–14; Vin I 237, 24ff.). The general Sīha in Vesāli has obtained a lot of meat for the Buddha and his monks, who had accepted his invitation to a meal. While this is being consumed, the Jains run through the streets and shout:

> Today the general Sīha killed a big animal and prepared therefrom a meal for the ascetic Gautama. The ascetic Gautama eats this meat although he knows that it was especially killed for him (*uddissa kataṃ*), that the killing was (done) for his sake (*paṭicca-kammaṃ*).[15]

---

13 *sādhu, bhante, bhikkhū yāvajīvaṃ āraññakā assu, yo gām'-antaṃ osareyya, vajjaṃ naṃ phuseyya; yāva jīvaṃ piṇḍa-pātikā assu, yo nimantanaṃ sādiyeyya, vajjaṃ naṃ phuseyya; yāvajīvaṃ paṃsu-kūlikā assu, yo gahapati-cīvaraṃ sādiyeyya, vajjaṃ naṃ phuseyya; yāvajīvaṃ rukkha-mūlikā assu, yo channaṃ upagaccheyya, vajjaṃ naṃ phuseyya; yāvajīvaṃ maccha-maṃsaṃ na khādeyyuṃ, yo maccha-maṃsaṃ khādeyya, vajjaṃ naṃ phuseyyā ti.* – This would presuppose that many laypeople would inhabit the jungle (WB).

14 *tikoṭi-parisuddhaṃ maccha-maṃsaṃ: a-diṭṭhaṃ a-ssutaṃ a-parisankitaṃ ti.*

15 *ajja Sīhena senā-patinā thūlaṃ pasuṃ vadhitvā samaṇassa Gotamassa bhattaṃ kataṃ, taṃ samaṇo Gotamo jānaṃ uddissa kataṃ maṃsaṃ paribhuñjati paṭicca-kammaṃ* (Horner: '. . . the recluse Gotama makes use of this meat, knowing that it was killed on purpose (for him), that the deed was (done) for his sake'). The expressions *uddissa kataṃ* and *paṭicca-kammaṃ*, of which the first, as we shall see, has a parallel with the Jains,

The general, to whom these reproaches are reported, rejects the same as a calumny and protests that he would not even for his life's sake deliberately deprive any living being of its life.[16]

In fact, he neither slaughtered the same nor let it be slaughtered, but had only sent out a servant with the customary formula: 'Go, my dear, and see, if there is meat.'[17] At the end of the meal the Buddha announces to his monks:

> One should, monks, not eat meat when one knows that it has been killed especially for him (*uddissa kataṃ*) . . . I permit you, monks, fish and **[8]** meat, which are pure in a three-fold respect: (when namely the monk) has not seen, nor heard, nor cherished a suspicion . . .[18]

For the Buddha and his monks, therefore, abstinence from meat and fish belonged to the nonsensical, and hence objectionable tightening and overstraining of the monastic rules.[19] The essential condition for eating meat is, however, that the consumer has neither killed the animal himself, nor had it killed especially for him, so that the responsibility for the killing does neither directly nor indirectly fall upon him. We shall see that a similar condition, but even more strictly conceived and hedged in, also holds good for the Jains.

Today the Jains, laymen as well as monks, are the strictest of all vegetarians, and *ahiṃsā* represents to them as the highest command of their religion (*ahiṃsā paramo dharmaḥ*): they extend it even to vermin; I have myself witnessed how a poisonous centipede (*kankhajūrā*), which had bitten a monk, was put in a brass pot and set free in a field. That Jain monks may have ever partaken of meat is inconceivable and unacceptable to modern orthodox Jains.[20]

---

in connection with 'flesh' could be euphemisms; as to this we can render them only with 'killed particularly for . . .' and 'killed for his sake'.

16 *na ca mayaṃ jīvita-hetu pi sañcicca pāṇaṃ jīvitā voropeyyāma.* – This seems an odd utterance for a general (WB).

17 *gaccha, bhaṇe, pavatta-maṃsaṃ jānāhi!* (Horner: 'Go, good fellow, find out if there is meat to hand').

18 *na, bhikkhave, jānaṃ uddissa kataṃ maṃsaṃ paribhuñjitabbaṃ . . . anujānāmi, bhikkhave, tikoṭi-parisuddhaṃ maccha-maṃsaṃ: a-diṭṭhaṃ a-ssutaṃ a-parisankitaṃ.* – Seyfort Ruegg 1980:240 refers with the wrong page number (53) to this passage in Alsdorf (WB).

19 As regards the later battle against meat-eating in some Mahāyāna books cf. Waldschmidt 1939: 80ff.

20 See Kapadia's article further down (WB).

Nevertheless, it ensues incontestably, as Schubring points out (2000, § 154) from passages in two of the oldest canonical texts. Here, in the long list of alms which the monk should not accept, also appear 'meat with many bones and fish with many fishbones'.[21] The reason given for the prohibition, in a stanza **[9]** which recurs identically in both texts, is that more of such alms would be thrown

---

21 Āyāranga II 1, 10, 5 *bahu-y-aṭṭhiyaṃ vā maṃsaṃ macchaṃ vā bahu-kaṇṭagaṃ;* Dasaveyāliya 5, 1, 73 *bahu- aṭṭhiyaṃ poggalaṃ aṇimisaṃ vā bahu-kaṇṭagaṃ.* It is quite obvious that here, in the midst of the *prose* of the Āyāra, an old *śloka*-line in its original form is contained, the metre of which, just in the *metrical* chapter of the Dasaveyāliya, was grossly violated by the secondary substitution of *maṃsa* by *poggala* and of *maccha* by *aṇimisa.* For *aṇimisa* 'not blinking' in Sanskrit, too, the meaning 'fish' is attested, but for *pudgala* the meaning 'meat' is otherwise never and nowhere known. It is easy to show how it has come about in our passage through a misconception. In the continuation of the Āyāra-passage to be quoted subsequently, *poggala* – literally 'mass, matter'– is used to indicate the *quantity* of meat and could be conceived as a designation of the sheer meat in contrast to the bones; on it the further generalizing substitution of *maṃsa* through *poggala* in the Dasaveyāliya is based. – (Sūyagaḍa 2, 1, 16 *se jahā nāmae kei purise maṃsāo aṭṭhiṃ abhinivvaṭṭittāṇaṃ uvadaṃsejjā: ayaṃ, āuso, maṃse, ayaṃ aṭṭhī* 'just as when someone draws a bone out of meat and shows (it with the words) "This, venerable Sir, is the meat, that, the bone"' and Samavāya 34 *pacchanne āhāra-nīhāre a-disse maṃsa-cakkhuṇā* '(the Jina's) eating and defecating is secret; no flesh (i.e. human) eye can see (it)' clearly show the normal meaning of *maṃsa* in the canon. Later, as in Tiloyapannatti IV 899, Jinas seem not to eat at all: *bhoyaṇa-uvasagga-parihīṇā* – an attempt to stop the recollection of the opposite in some ancient texts? – See also Dundas 1985 and 1997: 12; Cottam Ellis 1991: 91; Jaini 1993 [WB]).

That, however, even in this text, the normal words *maṃsa* and *maccha* are at all substituted by *poggala,* which in fact has a quite different meaning, and by the far-fetched *aṇimisa,* and that by a gross disregard for the metre, should be understood only as a kind of euphemism in which the later disapproval of meat and fish is suggested. Compare the subsequent exposition of the later reinterpretation of the words and the canonical references for the condemnation of meat-eating to be dealt with further down. – Cf. Deo 1956: 172 (> Jha 2004: 85 note 95). In PSM *poggala* is given the sense of *māṃsa* in two places: Hemacandra, *Prākṛtavyākaraṇa* I 116 and Nemicandra II (until 1270 C.E.), *Pravacanasārôddhāra* [Bombay, 1922] 421b 9 [*dvāra* 268, vs 64] *tiri-pañc'indiya davve khette satthi-hattha poggalâiṇṇaṃ,* with the scholiast Siddhasena's explanation 421a 10 *tairaścena paudgalyena māṃsena* ... The oldest meaning of Sa. *pudgala* seems to be 'body, a man's material appearance' from which the meaning 'flesh' would seem an easy development, cf. *piṇḍa* 'body; meat' and *medaskṛt* 'body, flesh' (MW) (WB).

away than could be eaten, hence the greater part would be refuse.[22] Should now, Āyāranga II 1, 10, 6 continues, someone offer the monk meat with many bones or fish with many fishbones, he should answer: 'Your Reverence, or Sister, I am not permitted to accept meat with many bones: give me as much (*poggala*, body, mass) as you like, but no bones.' If, however, he should have inadvertently accepted meat with many bones or fish with many fishbones (certainly that means: if he should find out after accepting the alms that it contains too many bones or fishbones), he should not offend the donor through a brusque return, but should go away with it and *eat the meat and fish* in a ritually pure (i.e. free from living beings) place, a garden or a lodging, and then deposit the bones or fishbones in a suitable place with the precautionary measures assigned for such cases.[23]

---

22 *appe siyā bhoyaṇa-jjāe, bahu ujjhiya-dhammie;* literally: 'Little would belong to the category of edibles, much would have the characteristic of what has to be thrown away.' (In Āyāra II 1, 10, 4 the same verse-line serves immediately before to substantiate the ban on accepting sugarcane; in the Dasaveyāliya, sugarcane, meat, fish and other things are combined into one *śloka*). Jacobi, Leumann (1892: 621) and Schubring incorrectly print *bahu-ujjhiya-dhammie* as one compound, and Schubring translates: 'would be an alms small in quantity, but a great prostitution of the dharma.' It seems certain to me that Jacobi's translation 'so that only a part of it can be eaten and the greater part must be rejected' has chosen the right meaning; it rests on Śīlâṅka's quite correct explanation of the Āyāra passage: *atrâivaṃ-bhūte parigṛhīte 'py antarikṣv-ādike 'lpam aśanīyaṃ bahu paritya-jana-dharmakam iti matvā na parigṛhṇīyāt.*

23 *siyā ṇaṃ paro bahu-aṭṭhieṇa maṃseṇa vā maccheṇa vā uvanimantejjā: āusanto samaṇā, abhikankhasi bahu-aṭṭhiyaṃ maṃsaṃ paḍigāhettae? etappagāraṃ nighosaṃ soccā nisamma se puvvām̲ eva āloejjā: āuso ti vā bhaiṇī ti vā, no khalu kappai me bahu-aṭṭhiyaṃ maṃsaṃ paḍigāhettae; abhikankhasi me dāum jāvatiyaṃ, tāvatiyaṃ poggalaṃ dalayāhi, mā aṭṭhiyāiṃ ... se ya āhacca paḍigāhie siyā, taṃ no hi tti vaejjā, no aṇaha* [? read: *ahaha?*] *tti vaejjā. se ttam̲ ādāya egantam̲ avakkamejjā 2 ttā ahe ārāmaṃsi vā ahe uvassayaṃsi vā app' aṇḍe jāva saṃtāṇae maṃsagaṃ macchagaṃ bhoccā aṭṭhiyāiṃ kaṇṭage gahāya se ttam̲ āyāe egantam̲ avakkamejjā ahe jhāma-thaṇḍilaṃsi vā jāva pamajjiya 2 pariṭṭhavejjā*. (Jacobi's translation 'he should not say: "No, away, take it!"' conveys the expected sense, but is not to be reconciled with his text: *taṃ no tti vaejjā, no ha tti, no haṃdaha tti vaejjā*. The above text is based on a collation by Schubring, according to whose kind information *no handaha tti vaejjā* 'he must not say: "there, take it"' is to be deleted as not being in the text, though in itself it would fit well. The Cūrṇi says: *so ya puṇa saḍḍho saḍḍhī vā pharusaṃ na bhaṇejjā*, which can only signify: 'but he must not speak rudely to the layman or laysister (accusative!).'

In the Dasaveyāliya the same rule is found in a **[10]** somewhat later passage, thus separated from the ban to accept meat and fish with many bones and fishbones, and extended to indigestible foreign bodies in the food; 5, 1, 84ff:

> Thereby while eating it may happen that he hits on a bone, fishbone, a piece of straw or wood, a small stone or something similar, but he must not, after he has taken it out, throw it away, neither (should he) spit it out of his mouth; he must take it in his hand, go away, find a spot free of living beings, carefully put it down and then return.[24]

In his *ṭīkā* on the Āyāranga, finished in 872 CE, Śīlâṅka does not comment on the words *maṃsa* and *maccha*, because, evidently, he held these completely unequivocal and normal words to need no explanation. That he understood these phrases in their ordinary sense one can very well conclude from the remark he added to his explanation of the above verses *appe siyā bhoyaṇa-jjāe:* he gives this explanation where the verse appears for the first time, namely at the prohibition to accept sugarcane, and points to the following 'meat-*sūtra*' with the words *evaṃ māṃsa-sūtram api neyam* – a designation. This could scarcely have been his choice if by *māṃsa* he had wished a vegetable substance to be understood. It is different for the classical commentator of the Dasaveyāliya, Haribhadra (writing in the middle of the eighth century CE); the peculiar expressions *poggala*

24 *tattha se bhuñjamāṇassa aṭṭhiyaṃ kaṇṭao siyā / taṇa-kaṭṭha-sakkaraṃ vā vi annaṃ vā vi tahā-vihaṃ // taṃ ukkhivittu na nikkhive, āsaeṇa na chaḍḍae / hattheṇa taṃ gaheūṇaṃ egantaṃ avakkame // egantaṃ avakkamettā a-cittaṃ paṭilehiyā / jayaṃ pariṭṭhavejjā, pariṭhappa paḍikkame.* Schubring translates: '. . . it might happen that he meets with a bone, a thorn, a bit of grass . . .' It appears certain to me that *aṭṭhiyaṃ kaṇṭao* signifies 'bones or fishbones' here, too. – Here also Ohanijjutti 482 may be mentioned where the monk is ordered to remove bones and fishbones, etc. from his alms: *gara, visa, aṭṭhiya, kaṇṭaga . . . vigiñcejja,* cf. Mette 1974: 102 (text on p. 195); 126 (OhaBh 277). Abhayadeva's contemporary Droṇa gives no explanation in his commentary, thus showing that for him the words in question have their common meaning, but Bṛhatkalpabhāṣya 5870, which depends on ON 482, replaced *aṭṭhi* by *(maya-)macchi* (*mṛta-makṣika* 'dead fly') and gave *kaṇṭaga* the sense of 'thorn'; see further Mette, op. cit., p. 102 note 97. A still later witness is Kṣemakīrti who finished his commentary on the Bṛhatkalpabhāṣya in 1275 CE. On BKBh 1239 *māṃsa-phala-puppha-bhogī* he writes the scholion: *'māṃsa' tti yatra durbhikṣe samāpatite māṃsena kālo 'tivāhyate'* (WB).

and *aṇimisa* implicity required an explanation, and he renders them without prejudice as *māṃsa* and *matsya*, adding that others thought them to be the names of two fruits with a consistency similar to that of meat and fish, because they stand in a section otherwise dealing with plants.[25]

This explanation as fruits with hard seeds or stalks, or the like, is the only generally recognized explanation today. In 1932 a new edition and translation of the Dasaveyāliya produced by Schubring was printed in Glückstadt through the munificence of one of the Ahmedabad businessmen,[26] **[11]** and then it was sent to India. When one found out there that in 5, 1, 73 *maṃsa* and *maccha* were translated by 'meat' and 'fish', the whole edition was shelved; up to this day it has not been delivered, and a Bombay solicitor explained to me that there *could* be no question of meat and fish in the text, as it would go against the preaching of *ahiṃsā* by the founder of the religion, Mahāvīra. The Jains lodged a protest with the editor of the 'Sacred Books of the East', Max Müller, against Jacobi's translation of the Āyāra-passage, and the high priest of the Bombay Jain community sent Jacobi the following elucidation of the passage: 'A monk or a nun on a begging tour is prohibited from receiving a conserve of fruits containing a large portion of bark or an exterior covering of a fruit.'[27]

---

25 *anye tv abhidadhati: vanaspaty-adhikārāt tathāvidha-phalâbhidhāne ete iti.*

26 'Ahmedabad: The Managers of Sheth Anandji Kalianji' – in Schubring 1932: 210, the incriminated words *meat and fish with many bones* in vss 73 and 84 have been replaced by a series of crosses. This, and the reason for it, ought of course have been mentioned in the editor's Preface (WB).

27 Cf. Kapadia 1933: 232ff. In his long letter addressed to Motilal Ladhaji dt. 14/2/1924 and reproduced there, Jacobi, by virtue of two passages in the Mahābhāṣya and in Vācaspatimiśra's Nyāyasūtra Commentary, meets the Jains halfway through the proposal to understand the phrases 'meat with many bones' and 'fish with many fishbones' as 'metaphorical' designations, which became proverbial for 'an object containing the substance which is wanted in intimate connection with much that must be rejected': 'The meaning of the passage is, therefore, that a monk should not accept as alms any substance of which only a part can be eaten and a great part must be rejected.'

It is needless to refute in detail Jacobi's argumentation (not completely cited here); an impartial reading of the Āyāranga section should be enough to convince the reader that the question is of real meat and fish. Should 'meat with many bones' metaphorically stand for all, of which only a small part is edible and the greater discardable, it would be inexplicable that the verse *appe siyā bhoyaṇa-jjāe* in the Āyāranga would

Now, in addition to the two passages discussed, there comes yet another famous canonical testimony for the use of meat by the founder[28] of the religion himself. In Viyāhapannatti, Śataka 15, (685b *sūtra* 557; Suttāgame I 731, 26 [WB]) the seriously sick Mahāvīra sends one of his disciples to tell the laywoman Revaī in Meṇḍhiyagāma:

> You have prepared for me the bodies of two pigeons which I do not need; (but) besides, you have something else, a leftover from yesterday (*pāriyāsiya*) of cock-meat killed ('done') by a cat. Bring that; that is what I need.[29]

The disciple carried out the instructions and after eating the cock-meat Mahāvīra soon recovered. **[12]**

---

be adduced *first* as the basis of the prohibition of sugarcane and then once again for *maṃsa* and *maccha*; even less could in the Dasaveyāliya meat ('*poggala*') and fish ('*aṇimisa*') have been brought together with several vegetable objects into one list which then is followed by the substantiating *appe siyā* . . . – Moreover, such a metaphor sounds rather unexpected when used by vegetarians, but cf. *amiṣa* 'meat' > 'anything comestible' put before the Jina image as *agra-pūjā* (Williams 1963: 223) which seems to point to meat as a common dish (WB).

Bothra's paraphrase in Amar Muni's *Illustrated Daśavaikālika sūtra* 5, 1, 73f. runs: 'If an ascetic is offered fruits with many seeds, scales, thorns, asthik, tinduk and bilva fruits, sugar-cane slices, pods or other such fruits or vegetables with little to eat and much to throw, he should refuse and tell the donor that he is not allowed to accept such fruit' (1997: 144; p.c. Dr P. Flügel). Suzuko Ohira adopts Schubring's translation in her thesis 1994: 18f. (§§ 56ff.), where also the other passages about meat-eating in the canon are dealt with, but appears not to have seen Alsdorf's present work. Bones, as in contrast to meat, are inauspicious (Thurston 1912: 57; Abbott 1974: 419) (WB).

28 Meant is reformer, if the 23rd Fordmaker Pāsa was a historical person (Dundas 2000: 19; Schubring 2000: 29 [§ 16]) which is denied by Bhaṭṭ (Jaina Studies 4: 6; see also Bollée 2008a: 2). According to Bhaṭṭ, the *cāujjāma* doctrine ascribed to Pāsa is not earlier than the first or second century BCE. Its unknown originator, whose father may have happened to be called Aśvasena, then was made the son of the king of snakes of that name in the Mbh, because all Jinas are princes, and thus became a mythological character (WB).

29 *taṃ gacchaha naṃ tumaṃ, Sīhā, Meṇḍhiyagāmam nagaraṃ Revaīe gāhāvaiṇīe gihe, tattha naṃ Revaīe gāhāvaiṇīe mamaṃ aṭṭhāe duve kavoya-sarīrā uvakkhaḍiyā, tehiṃ no aṭṭho. atthi se anne pāriyāsie majjāra-kaḍae kukkuḍa-maṃsae, taṃ āharāhi, eeṇaṃ aṭṭho.* – The passage and Alsdorf's discussion of it is also dealt with by Wezler 1978: 101. Forest ascetics are allowed to eat of the rest of animals killed by predators (WB).

The little story bears such ideosyncratic features that one cannot help considering it historical.[30] Apart from that, it fits remarkably well with what we have learnt from the Buddhists. In it, too, the phrase 'meat done' in the sense of having been killed by somebody appears; and it agrees exactly with the rule the Buddha passed, that Mahāvīra declines to accept pigeons prepared *for his sake* (*mama aṭṭhāe*) and instead requests a cock killed not by man but by an animal: there could not be a more certain guarantee, therefore, that the cock was not slaughtered for Mahāvīra, on his account – in this case even the lay sister is free from any responsibility for the killing.[31]

The commentator of the Viyāhapannatti, Abhayadeva, lived in the second half of the eleventh century. On the 'pigeon bodies' and the meat of the cock 'done (in)' by the cat he remarks: 'For these expressions "some" assumed the normal meaning (*śrūyamāṇam evârtham*), "only the sense heard", but others explained the pigeon bodies to be pumpkins, called so after their pigeon colour'; the 'cat' would either be a certain (body) wind[32] and *mārjāra-kṛta* would mean 'done in order to subside this (wind)', or *mārjāra* becomes a plant known as 'cat' and *mārjāra-kṛta* means 'mixed therewith' (? *bhāvita*); finally, according to the opinion of the former 'some', *kukkuṭa-māṃsa* would mean something like *bījapūra-kaṭāha* ('lemon pot'?).[33]

---

30 Ohira 1994: 203 (§ 546) thinks 'it is a fiction made up in relation to Gosāla's prophecy; therefore its historicity can well be doubted'. Ibid., p. 18 (§ 57) Ohira wonders that 'there is hardly any other direct reference (beside Ācār and Sūy II 2, 38 [WB]) forbidding monks receiving flesh in the earlier canonical texts' ... (§ 58) 'It seems that Pūjapāda is the first author who criticized this point (viz. consumption of meat by monks [WB]) in his Sarvārthasiddhi VI 13 ... It is thus feasible to assume that the rigid vegetarianism of the present day Jainas commenced at such a later time, most probably after the mass exodus of the Jainas from Mathurā ... (§ 59) Receiving meat from the laity was thus understood not touching upon *hiṃsā* on the part of the monks at that time' (WB).

31 Apart from this, the flesh of animals killed by beasts of prey (*kravyâda*) is also pure according to the brahmanic doctrine, cf. Manu 5, 131; Yājñ. 192 etc., but especially Vas. XIV 27: *mārjāra-mukha-saṃspṛṣṭaṃ śuci eva hi tad bhavet*.

32 Deo 1956: 172f. makes thereof 'a kind of gas'!

33 *duve kavoyā ity ādeḥ śrūyamāṇam evârthaṃ kecin manyante; anye tv āhuḥ: kapotakaḥ pakṣi-viśeṣas, tadvad dve phale varṇa-sādharmyāt; te kapote kūṣmâṇḍe, hrasve kapote kapotake te ca śarīre ca vanaspati-jīva-dehatvāt kapota-śarīre. atha vā kapota-śarīre iva dhūsara-varṇa-sādharmyād eva kapota-śarīre kūṣmâṇḍa-phale eva ... majjāra-kaḍae ity āder api kecic chrūyamāṇam evârthaṃ manyante,*

Here, too, even in the eleventh century, the correct explanation has survived, in addition to the vegetarian reinterpretation, which – a fitting pendant to the attempt to turn the pork eaten by the Buddha into a mushroom dish, or something similar (see p. [6]) – has gained universal acceptance to this day,[34] whereas the correct translation meets with fierce indignation. **[13]** Kapadia cites one such correct translation in Gujarati by G.J. Patel[35] and observes:

> This translation was greatly resented by Jains, especially when Mr G.J. Patel's article *'Mahāvīr swāmi no māṃsāhār'* (the meat-eating of the Lord Mahāvīra) was published . . . Several articles were written as a rejoinder by some of the Jain *sādhus* and others. There they have pointed out that the words *kavoya, majjāra* and *kukkuḍa* do not signify a pigeon, a cat and a cock, but stand for *kūṣmâṇḍa, vāyu-viśeṣa* or *virālikā* (a kind of *vanaspati*) and *bīja-pūraka*, respectively. They have further supported their view by quoting Nighantus and Suśrutasaṃhitā.

As little as we can agree with these vegetarianist reinterpretations (it is typical enough that for *majjāra-kaḍae* two quite different ones were given!), as little can it be denied, on the other hand, that other canonical passages, at least for monks, disapprove of meat-eating, if not condemn it outright. Kapadia has collected these passages in his article of 1933. Although in a quotation from Ṭhāṇanga IV, Viyāhapannatti VIII, 9 and Uvavāiya 56 (Leumann 1883: 62 last line) we should not translate *kuṇimâhāra*, which is threatened

---

anye tv āhur: mārjāro vāyu-viśeṣas, tad-upaśamanāya kṛtaṃ saṃskṛtaṃ mārjāra-kṛtam; apare tv āhur: mārjāro virālikâbhidhāno vanaspati-viśeṣas, tena kṛtaṃ bhāvitaṃ yat tat tathā. kiṃ tad ity āha: kukkuṭa-māṃsakaṃ bījapūra-kaṭāham. – See Jha 2004: 86 note 102 and Deleu 2007: 106 with reference to Balbir 1984: 30f. (WB).

34 Cf. Deo 1956: 172f.

35 *tũ Meṇḍhik nagar mã Revatī gṛhapatnī che, te ne tyã jā, teṇe māre māṭe be kabūtar rāndhīne taiyār karyā che, paṇ te ne kaheje ke māre tem nū kām nathī; paraṃtu gai kāle bilāḍāe mārelā kūkḍā nū māṃs teṇe taiyār karelū che, te māre māṭe lai āv*, 'In the town of M. is a housewife R., go to her. She has cooked and prepared two pigeons for me. But tell her that I do not need these. However, she has prepared the meat of a cock killed by a cat yesterday; bring me that' (Kapadia 1941: 128). – No discussion about taking away the animal's legitimate food (WB).

with punishment in hell, as 'eating meat', we may be allowed to understand it literally as 'eating carrion'. But in Dasaveyāliya 12, 7 it belongs to the proper qualities of the good monk that he is *a-majja**-*maṃsâsi amaccharī ya* (Schubring: '[he should] not [drink] liquor nor eat meat, and [he should] not [be] envious [of any one who does so]'), and in Sūyagaḍa II 2, 72 in a similar context monks are called *a-majja-maṃsâsiṇo*. In Uttarajjhāyā 5, 9 and 7, 5–7 consuming alcohol and meat appear in two partly verbatim congruous lists of the gross sins of ignorant worldlings.[36]

Finally, in chapter 19 **[14]** of the same text, a youth justifies his resolution to renounce the world by depicting to his parents, who want to dissuade him from renouncing worldly life, the torments of hell which he had endured in former births for the sins of worldly life; thereby he says in vs 69f.:

> You like flesh in pieces and roasted: I was forced (in hell) to eat again and again my own fire-coloured (i.e. bloody raw) flesh.
> You like to drink brandy, rum, spirits and (like to eat) honey:
> I was forced (in hell) to drink blazing hot fat and blood.[37]

Here, too, the consumption of meat and alcohol are put together and repaid by infernal punishments accordingly.

Jain tradition itself states that the editing and recording of the canon did not take place until a full millennium after the death of the founder of the religion, namely in the beginning of the sixth century, at the Council of Valabhī. It has long been known and

---

* In the German original wrongly: *amaccha* (WB).

36 5, 9: *hiṃse bāle musāvāī māille pisuṇe saḍhe / bhunjamāṇe suraṃ maṃsaṃ seyam eyaṃ ti mannaī* (Jacobi: 'An ignorant man kills, lies, deceives, calumniates, dissembles, drinks liquor, and eats meat, thinking that this is the right thing to do'). 5, 9[a]= 7, 5[a]; 5, 9[c]= 7, 5[c]! 7, 7: *aya-kakkara-bhoī ya tundille* [so! Charpentier wrongly writes: *tuṇḍille*] *ciya-lohie / āuyaṃ narae kankhe jahāesaṃ va elae*, (Jacobi: 'He eats crisp goat's meat, his belly grows, and his veins swell with blood – but he gains nothing but life in hell, just as the ram is only fed to be killed for the sake of a guest').

37 *tuham piyāī maṃsāī khaṇḍāiṃ sollagāṇi ya / khāvio mi sa-maṃsāī aggi-vaṇṇāi 'negaso // tuhaṃ piyā surā sīhū merao ya mahūṇi ya / pāio mi jalantīo vasāo ruhirāṇi ya*. Jacobi's translation 'poisoned meat' rests on the wrong reading *visamaṃsāiṃ*. Charpentier prints *khāvio misamaṃsāiṃ* and gives in his commentary long elucidations on *misa*, which can be disposed of by correct word-separation. A glance at the parallel *pāio mi* of vs 70 should have shown him that *mi* = *asmi* (and consequently *samaṃsāim* = *sva-māṃsāni*).

acknowledged that in the Jain canon ancient and very old sections stand side by side with young and very recent ones. Indeed, more than a few parts of the canon date far back to the time when, as we shall soon see, vegetarianism had to a large extent asserted itself also among the Hindus. The passages just presented which condemn meat-consumption can in no way shake the testimony of the three dealt with at the very beginning, in which we may rather see very important testimonies from the oldest period of the Jain tradition, – testimonies whose credibility is substantially supported by Buddhist parallels. Yet this is not all; indeed the consistency, reduced to absurdity, with which the Jain monk tries to practise *ahiṃsā*, allows us to understand particularly clear the apparent inconsistency of his flesh-eating.

Jainism teaches what one could call a total animism: all of nature is animated; not only animals and plants, but also the elements earth, water, fire and air consist of countless elementary individual souls.[38] As for the monk *ahiṃsā* is extended to these, for example, the prohibitions on **[15]** splashing and heating water, handling fire, and using a fan, which would hurt the arial souls.[39] It goes without saying that the acceptance and consumption of every animated (*sa-citta*) nourishment is prohibited to him. 'Someone else must therefore,' as Schubring strikingly puts it, 'have first taken away its life.'[40] This holds good even of water which the monk does not heat himself, but may only drink when it is made lifeless by boiling.[41]

The rule observed even today makes it easier for the Indologist, for example, who visits Jain monks in remote regions, to get boiled drinking water than elsewhere in India. The monk can thus eat or drink practically nothing, unless by its killing a layman has violated *ahiṃsā*, and then there is indeed no fundamental difference between the use of water boiled by others, plants cooked by others or the flesh of animals killed by others. In view of this, the above (p. [7f.]) cited condition of the Buddha concerning flesh and fish certainly holds good quite universally: the Jain monk may accept nothing at all as alms which has been purchased, fetched, prepared, etc. for him alone. The alms prepared 'for him personally who is expected'[42] is called *uddesiya,* which exactly corresponds to the Buddhist *uddissa-*

38 Schubring 2000 § 104f.
39 Dasaveyāliya, ch. 3 and 4.
40 Schubring 2000 § 154.
41 It is called then *udaga-viyaḍa,* i.e. 'water modification'.
42 Schubring 2000 § 154.

kataṃ. Through an exhaustive casuistry of conditions, the non-observance of which makes the offering unacceptable, the monk is thus safe-guarded against any ever so indirect and remote participation in the taking of life.

At the same time, the essential nature of *ahiṃsā* becomes quite clear here: originally it has nothing to do with ethics, as we understand it, but is a magic-ritualistic taboo on life which should not be destroyed in any form whatsoever.[43] That this is largely valid even nowadays also for Hinduism, as is shown in Katherine Mayo's famous book 'Mother India', where the modern practice (amply depicted and condemned by Gandhi in the sharpest of terms) in which strict vegetarianism and the outraged refusal to shorten the most horrible mortal agony of a cow can be mixed with abominable cruelty to animals on an everyday basis[44] and with the most miserable dairy farming. When a Jain monk lives sinlessly merely as a result of the transgression of the layman, it is after all the same egoism which in ancient Buddhism concentrates the whole energy of a monk on working on his own emancipation and makes the **[16]** behaviour of the monk towards his fellow human beings subordinate to the viewpoint of promoting his efforts towards his own deliverance, in other words, the egoism against which Mahāyāna Buddhism later sets its altruistic ideal of deliverance for all of mankind. The fact that it was only important for the Jain monk not to offend *ahiṃsā* himself, while profiting from the transgression by others without a second thought, has modern parallels too, not only those in the practice of Sherpas and Burmese Buddhist monks outlined above (p. [5f.]). So, we may not be outraged so easily or mock, when the pious Hindu, often without any scruples, sells his cow to the Muslim butcher.

Now let us turn from Buddhists and Jains to the brahmins. With regard to them, the gradual rise of *ahiṃsā* and its vegetarian

---

43 Schmidt 1968: 627 remarks that Alsdorf does not explain this (WB).

44 For instance by overloading beasts of burden through greed of grain (Williams 1973. 67f. [*atibhārâropaṇa*], [*atibhāra-vahana*] and 288–90. Hemacandra, *Tri*° X 3, 60 describes ascetics hitting with sticks cattle which eat the grass of their huts: *tāpasās te gās tā yaṣṭibhir atāḍayan*; at X 3, 89ff. villagers starve a bull, and at X 3, 329 at a chariot race bulls are urged on with a goad with iron spikes: *prājanârābhir īrayan . . . a-kṛpas tāv avāhayat*. See also Mette 1991: 126f. = 2009: 141f.; Bruhn 2007: 64 and Bollée 2006: 59ff. 'In religious practice and scriptural sources, there was failure to prohibit outright abuse of animals' (Sridhar and Bilimoria 2007: 316); and Balbir 2009a: 812 *et passim*. As early as ṚV X 85, 43f. Sūryā is urged to love animals (WB).

consequence is particularly well illustrated in the pertinent section of the 'Lawbook of Manu'. In reading this, it is to be borne in mind that, in this most authoritative code of Indian customs and laws, a fundamental change of view and custom has found expression to the effect that the old and new are, not infrequently, simply placed in juxtaposition to, or rather after, each other, regardless of the flagrant contradictions resulting from it. A well-known example is perhaps that of the rules for conduct in the levirate,[45] the custom familiar also outside India, attested to in the Indian epics, amongst other texts, according to which the brother of a man who died in childless wedlock begets by his sister-in-law the offspring which is so necessary for the sacrifices to the fathers.

The changed view, whereby a wife is not permitted to have intercourse with a man after the death of her husband, from which came the well-known prohibition of widow-remarriage and, as extreme, the practice of widow-burning, to such a view the levirate became offensive in the highest degree. One dares not, however, simply do away with the old rule. It is faithfully imparted in Manu 9, 59; then again follow four stanzas (60–63) which manifestly try to limit the custom and make it less offensive: it is determined that after the procreation of *one* son, intercourse with the sister-in-law has to be broken off and that, when it is pursued out of sensuality, both partners forfeit their caste. According to a later passage (9, 143f.) the second son begotten in this way is even disinherited. Then five stanzas follow abruptly (9, 64–68), which condemn the levirate in the sharpest of tones and bluntly prohibit it. It is a custom fit for cattle, **[17]** which does not find any support in the sacred texts, and had catastrophic consequences when practised by humans in ancient times.

Considered critically and historically, the apparently juxtaposed and contradictory regulations become successive stages of historical development and exactly the same holds true of the section on meat-eating in Manu.

The stanzas 5–25 in chapter 5 give the numerous and complex regulations regarding forbidden and permitted foods, which in every lawbook take a significant place. Vegetables, especially leek, garlic, onions and mushrooms, also belong to the dishes forbidden not only under specific circumstances (slightly sour or stale, mixed with impure substances, etc.), but forbidden at all. Above all there

45 Cf. Bühler's translation in 1886: xciv.

is a long list of animals which cannot be eaten; it varies considerably with the different authors. Such an enumeration naturally implies that other animals could indeed be eaten, and this is emphasized by the fact that general prohibitions are restricted by explicit permission to eat certain species of animals. The most important example is an old stanza which permits the consumption of five five-clawed animals. Heinrich Lüders has followed it through the entire legal literature, the epics and the Buddhist Pali literature.[46] Here it is only about the distinction between 'kosher' and 'non-kosher' meat; the consumption of meat as such is presumed as self-evident.[47] Still there is no question of vegetarianism.[48] **[18]**

Just as with the levirate, a second stage of conflict follows this first stage of the still undisputed old views, one of compromises between old and new. Here, too, the newly arising opinions confront the strong powers of inertia of tradition; indeed they are, in this case, in actual fact wholly invincible, since in the brahmanic religion bloody animal sacrifices play a central role. To its fully correct and only thus magically effective execution belongs not only the killing of the sacrificial victim but also the ritual enjoyment of its flesh.

---

46 Lüders 1940: 175ff.

47 A misconception occurring time and again up to this day is when, for example, Jolly 1896: 157, perceives in the determinations of kosher and non-kosher animals 'remnants of a laxer interpretation of *ahiṃsā* which declares certain animals to be edible'. Accordingly the triumphal procession of *ahiṃsā* had consisted in a gradual extension of the ban on killing from only some to more and more species of animals. With this the historical development is wholly misunderstood. For *ahiṃsā* there cannot be any fundamental distinction between particular species of animals. Conversely, we do find regulations regarding the purity and impurity of animals among many peoples (e.g. the Jews), who know nothing at all of *ahiṃsā*. The distinction between pure and impure animals and the ban on killing based on *ahiṃsā* have originally and historically nothing at all to do with each other. Inevitably, however, these were (and from that stems, in part, the misconception) later combined with one another by the Indians, whereby the old rules on pure and impure and the new ones totally banning killing, or restricting it to ritual occasions, as will be shown soon (p. [19]), were brought into line with each other in such a way as to also restrict the consumption of meat still conditionally permitted to 'kosher' animals. – Hemacandra calls Manu's lawbook a *hiṃsā-śāstra* (Williams 1963: 70; WB).

48 Of *ahiṃsā* only indirectly in *one* passage (Manu 5, 22) which permits (or prescribes) the brahmins the killing of kosher animals and birds for offering and for the sustenance of relations; the passage will concern us later (p. [27]).

We note only provisionally that it was precisely cattle which were considered the most important traditional offering.

Moreover, it was not only about the sacrifice, but also, for example, about the sacred ancient rule according to which an ox or goat is to be slaughtered for a brahmin or a noble guest:[49] so familiar and solemn a rule that the expression *go-ghna* 'cow-killer' is transmitted to us as a synonym of the words for 'guest'.[50] Therefore, because it was now impossible to question the ancient sacrifices, it only remained to postulate that the ban on killing and meat-eating did not hold true in all cases where the ritual requires both; this was made easier, as we shall see, by the ancient doctrine that killing for sacrifice is not killing.

Exactly this is found in another section in Manu, of 18 stanzas (5, 27–44), the unsystematic arrangement, repetitions and inconsistencies of which clearly characterizes it as a compilation of disparate materials. That this section cannot at all be actually **[19]** reconciled with the preceding is shown by the illogicality of a transitional verse (5, 26), patched in between, which announces that after the 'completely imparted' (!~) rules on permitted and forbidden dishes, now the ones on allowed and prohibited meat-eating will follow[51] – as if meat had not also been a dish and as if it had not previously time and again been about forbidden meat.

With varying shifts of accent in the new section, the fact of meat-eating being permitted at ritual occasions is again and again

---

49 ŚpBr. 3, 4, 1, 2: *atithir vā eṣa etasyâgacchati yat somaḥ krītas, tasmā etad yathā rājñe vā brāhmaṇāya vā mahôkṣaṃ vā mahâjaṃ vā pacet*. Ait.Br. 3, 4, 6: … *ātithyaṃ kriyate. 'gniṃ manthanti some rājany āgate. tad yathâivādo manuṣya-rāja āgate 'nyasmin vârhaty ukṣāṇaṃ vā vehataṃ vā kṣadanta, evam asmā etat kṣadante yad agniṃ manthanty; agnir hi devânām paśuḥ*. Vasiṣṭha IV 8: *athâpi brāhmaṇāya vā rājanyāya vâbhyāgatāya mahôkṣāṇaṃ vā mahâjaṃ vā paced, evam asyâtithyaṃ kurvantîti*. Śāṅkh. gṛhyas. 2, 15, 1: *ṣaṇṇāṃ ced arghyānām anyatama āgacched, go-paśum ajam annaṃ vā yat samānyatamaṃ manyeta, tat kuryān; nāmāṃso 'rghaḥ syāt* (!~). Yājñav. 1.109: *mahôkṣaṃ vā mahâjaṃ vā śrotriyā yôpakalpayet*. Cf. further Āśv. gṛhyas.1, 24, 30ff.; Pāraskaragṛhyas. 1, 3, 26f. – Both parallels cited from ŚpBr. and Ait.Br. can hold good as confirmation of Thieme's finding in 1957: 90, corroborated by other materials, that 'through all the essential particulars of its form and its process' the Vedic sacrifice is 'defined as a stylistic banquet'. (Cf. Schlerath 1960: 129ff.) Thus, historically considered, the slaughter of a cattle for the guest was the model for the cow sacrifice.

50 Pāṇini 3, 4, 73.

51 *etad uktaṃ dvijātīnāṃ bhakṣyâbhakṣyam a-śeṣataḥ / māṃsasyâtaḥ pravakṣyāmi vidhiṃ bhakṣaṇa-varjane.*

confronted with its reprehensiveness under other circumstances.[52] As to this, we read with special interest in vs 32 that meat-eating at sacrifices for deities and fathers is not a transgression, no matter whether the meat was bought, slaughtered by oneself or donated by someone:[53] unmistakenly an argument with the Buddhist and Jain views about qualified permission to eat meat which we have come across above (p. [7]). The categorical contention that killing for sacrifice is not killing appears twice: 5, 44 'One should regard the injury to moving and immovable creatures, which the Veda has prescribed for certain occasions, as non-injury,'[54] and vs 39: 'Svayambhū himself created the animals for the sake of sacrifice; the sacrifice serves the welfare of the whole world; therefore, killing for sacrifice is not killing.'[55]

In order to ensure the correct execution of important ceremonies which are threatened by *ahiṃsā*, stanza 35 even threatens heavy punishment for the rejection of ritually prescribed flesh-eating: the concerned in question will be reborn twenty-one times as **[20]** a sacrificial animal.[56] On the other hand, doubts are appeased by the doctrine that a high rebirth be ensured to the sacrificed animal as well as to the sacrificer.[57] In one stanza (37) a substitute animal appears out of ghee or flour.[58]

---

52 Vs 31: Meat-eating for the purpose of sacrifice is divine custom, otherwise it is a demonic (*rākṣasa*) one; 33: except in times of emergency (*āpadi*), flesh-eating is only permissible according to precept (*vidhinā*); he who eats meat not in keeping with the regulations will after death be eaten by the animals killed by him; 34: extra-ritual flesh-eating is punished after death more severely than animal-killing out of greed; 36: a brahmin must and is allowed to eat only sacrificial animals consecrated with mantras; 38: whoever kills an animal other than for the purpose of sacrifice will be killed in future rebirths as many times as the animal had hair; 41: animal-killing is exclusively permissible when entertaining a guest (!) and at sacrifices for the gods and fathers; 43: in none of the three stages of life (student, householder, forest-dweller) nor in emergencies should one commit an injury not sanctioned by the Veda.

53 *krītvā svayaṃ vâpy utpādya parôpahṛtam eva vā / devān pitṝṃś cârcayitvā khādan māṃsaṃ na duṣyati.*

54 *yā veda vihitā hiṃsā niyatâsmiṃś carâcare / ahiṃsām eva tāṃ vidyāt.*

55 *yajñârthaṃ paśavaḥ sṛṣṭāḥ svayam eva Svayaṃbhuvā / yajño 'sya bhūtyai sarvasya, tasmād yajñe vadho 'vadhaḥ.*

56 *niyuktas tu yathânyāyaṃ yo māṃsaṃ nâtti mānavaḥ / sa pretya paśutāṃ yāti saṃbhavān ekaviṃśatim.*

57 40: *oṣadhyaḥ paśavo vṛkṣās tiryañcaḥ pakṣiṇas tathā / yajñârthaṃ nidhanaṃ prāptāḥ prāpnuvanty ucchritīḥ punaḥ;* 42: *eṣv artheṣu paśūn hiṃsan veda-tattvârthavid dvijaḥ / ātmānaṃ ca paśūṃś câiva gamayaty uttamāṃ gatim.*

In addition, just at the beginning of the section, the partaking of meat is permitted, apart from ritual occasions, when someone's life is endangered as well as in the case of feeding brahmins.[59] Then follow three stanzas, which proclaim, somewhat out of context, what we would call the natural right of mankind to partake of meat: the divine order of creation has destined all animate and unanimate nature to be nourishment for the breath of life[60] (28); the inanimate is nourishment for the animate; animals without fangs are nourishment for those with fangs, as are those without hands for those with hands; the timorous for the brave (29).[61] The eater who eats edible beings every day does not commit an offence, because the creator himself has created living beings to eat and be eaten (30).[62]

Then in complete contradiction, not only to these stanzas but also to everything preceding them, follows a third section of eleven stanzas (44–55), which explicitly appeals to the rule of *ahiṃsā*, and unconditionally brands *any* partaking of meat as immoral, and praises the merit of a total commitment to vegetarianism in the highest terms. Here is the stanza already cited in the beginning (p. [5]), which states that no flesh can be obtained without violence to living beings, wherefore meat is to be shunned; and – like a polemic against the above-mentioned vs 32 (flesh consumption in connection with a sacrifice to gods and fathers **[21]** is not an offence, no matter if the meat is purchased, slaughtered by oneself or given as a gift) – vs 51 reads 'The one sanctioning (the killing), the carver, slaughterer, buyer, seller, cook, servant and consumer – they are all killers.'[63]

As if to weaken, at least to some extent, the all too glaring inconsistencies between these requirements of uncompromising

58 *kuryād ghṛta-paśuṃ saṅge kuryāt piṣṭa-paśuṃ tathā /na tv eva tu vṛthā hantuṃ paśum icchet kadācana.* – '(Images of) animal pairs out of flour' (*mithunānāṃ ca yathôpapādaṃ piṣṭasya* . . .) Śāṅkh. Gṛhyas. 4, 19; cf. Oldenberg 1878: 156.

59 *prokṣitaṃ bhakṣayen māṃsaṃ brāhmaṇānāṃ ca kāmyayā / yathā-vidhi niyuktas tu prāṇānām eva câtyaye.*

60 *prāṇasyânnam idaṃ sarvaṃ Prajāpatir akalpayat / sthāvaraṃ jangamaṃ câiva sarvaṃ prāṇasya bhojanam.*

61 *carāṇām annam a-carā, daṃṣṭriṇām apy a-daṃṣṭriṇaḥ / a-hastāś ca sa-hastānāṃ, śūrāṇāṃ câiva bhīravaḥ.*

62 *nâttā duṣyaty adann ādyān prāṇino 'hany ahany api / dhātrâiva sṛṣṭā hy ādyāś ca prāṇino 'ttāra eva ca.*

63 *anumantā viśasitā nihantā kraya-vikrayī / saṃskartā côpahartā ca khādakaś cêti ghātakāḥ.*

ahiṃsā vegetarianism[64] and the preceding discussion, there finally follows one last stanza (56), which testifies, alone through the inclusion of the themes of alcohol and sexuality, that, properly speaking, it belongs to another context: 'There is no offence in the consumption of flesh, intoxicating beverages and sexual intercourse; that is in fact the (natural) conduct of living beings; however, abstinence brings great rewards!'[65]

The Manusmṛti is not only the most esteemed but also the oldest of the classical metrical lawbooks, the so-called Dharmaśāstras, which form the second layer of Indian law literature and whose origin is fixed approximately from the second century BCE until a few centuries CE. Prior to these legal textbooks is the oldest stratum of scriptures in prose with verse insertions, the so-called Dharmasūtras and they are followed by the commentaries and the great medieval collections, the Nibandhas, whose number is occasionally augmented by the learned pandits even today.

If we now first look back from Manu to the Dharmasūtras, it becomes apparent that, in these branches of Vedic literature from the three stages which we ascertained in Manu, essentially only the first is represented. Everywhere in the context of the detailed and complicated rules for permitted and forbidden meals appear lists of edible and non-edible animals, and in many places, meat eating is clearly presumed to be normal.[66] By contrast, not only is the third stage of the demand for uncompromising vegetarianism missing, but also even the second confrontation **[22]** between *ahimsā* and animal-sacrifice.[67] This applies without restriction to the very probably pre-Buddhistic *sūtras* of Baudhāyana and Āpastamba.[68]

---

64 Only vs 52 does strictly speaking not belong here, but to the previous section, because the assertion that there is no worse offender than the one who tries to augment his own flesh by means of that of someone else is weakened by the addition: 'without worshipping fathers (or) gods' (*an-abhyarcya pitṝn devān*), which, of course, again exempts the sacrifices.

65 *Na māṃsa-bhakṣaṇe doṣo . . . nivṛttis tu mahā-phalā*. The stanza is quoted by Hemacandra 141, 58f. on Malliṣeṇa vs 23 and referred to by Balbir 2009. In Schmidt 1968: 628 this stanza is added to put the discussion into the proper context – that of the renunciatory way of life which is the ideal of the brahmin (WB).

66 Cf. Baudh. II 4, 7; 6, 2; 11, 15 (forest ascetics can live on flesh torn by beasts of prey, in addition III 3, 6); 12, 8; III 1, 13, and 4, 1 (no flesh in case of a special vow); Āpast. I 17, 15 and 19; II 17, 26–18, 3; Vas. XIV 12.

67 See also Baudh. II 17, 29; 18, 2; III 3, 19 from which follows that *ahiṃsā* belongs to the special rules respectively to the vows for ascetics and forest hermits, and therefore is demanded only for them.

Matters are somewhat but only apparently different in the case of Vasiṣṭha. Illustrating this requires a closer investigation of several passages in the text.

Excursus: Vasiṣṭha and Manu

In Vas, numerous stanzas are found which stand in similar or only slightly deviating form in our Manu text[69] without being shown as citations from Manu.[70] Alongside these, 'Manu' or 'the Mānava' is again explicitly quoted eleven times and some of these citations, but by no means all, reappear in our Manu. As is well-known, Bühler took this as proof that the Manusmṛti did, as Max Müller had mooted, originate from an old, not preserved Mānavadharmasūtra. The principal and essential proof of this is the passage Vas. IV 5–8.

After in IV 4, truth, angerlessness, generosity, *ahiṃsā* and procreation have been enumerated as required by all the four Varṇas (*sarveṣāṃ satyam a-krodho dānam ahiṃsā prajananaṃ ca*) the text continues:

5 *pitṛ-devatâtithi-pūjāyām apy eva paśum hiṃsyād iti Mānavam.*
6 *madhu-parke ca yajñe ca pitṛ-daivata-karmaṇi*
atrâiva ca paśuṃ hiṃsyān nânyathêty abravīn Manuḥ.
7 *nâkṛtvā prāṇināṃ hiṃsāṃ māṃsam utpadyate kvacit,*
na ca prāṇi-vadhaḥ svargyas, tasmād yāge vadho 'vadhaḥ.
8 *athâpi, brāhmaṇāya vā rājanyāya vâbhyāgatāya mahôkṣāṇaṃ vā mahâjaṃ vā paced; evam asmā ātithyaṃ kurvantîti.*

The Mānava says: Only in the reverence of ancestors, gods and guests may one violate an animal.

[23] At a *madhu-parka* (i.e. in hospitality), in sacrifices and during rites in honour of ancestors – only on such occasions may one violate an animal, otherwise not, so said Manu.

---

68 The same is true for Gautama's *sūtras*, which indeed, provided Meyer 1927: VII and 253ff. is right, would be placed much later, long after Manu.

69 Bühler (SBE XIV, p. XX notes 1 and 2) counts 41 such stanzas; the list in note 1 (in which II 10 should read II 30, and XXV should be XXVI) could be completed by parts of stanzas.

70 On the whole, the majority are not recognisable as quotations, but a number of them is preceded by the customary remark *athâpy udāharanti*, or they are at least followed by an *iti* which does not occur in the Manu text.

> One does not obtain flesh without injuring living beings, but the killing of living beings does not lead to heaven; therefore, the killing for sacrifice is not killing.
>
> Moreover, one must cook a big ox or a big goat for a Brahman or Kṣatriya coming (on a visit); in this way one shows hospitality to him.

Bühler comments on this passage:[71]

> All the four *sūtra*s must be taken as a quotation, because the particle *iti*, 'thus', occurs at the end of IV, 8, and because the identity of *sūtra* 6 with Manu V, 41, as well as the close resemblance of *sūtra* 7 to Manu V, 48, shows that the quotation is not finished with *sūtra* 5. If we accept this explanation, we have in our passage the usual arrangement followed in the Dharma-sūtras. First comes the prose rule, next the verses which confirm it, and finally a Vedic passage on which both the rule and the verses rest ... If it is thus necessary to admit that Vasiṣṭha's quotation is taken from a Mānava Dharma-sūtra, the agreement of the doctrine taught in the quotation and of a portion of the text with those of our Manu-smṛti shows further that this Dharma-sūtra must have been the forerunner of our metrical law-book.

To this it has to be said in the first place that the *iti* after *sūtra* 8 cannot in any way prove that the Manu citation is complete up to there; indeed one must rather regard the *iti Mānavam* of vs 5 as a distinct mark of the end of the quotation, and the *ity abravīn Manuḥ* of vs 6 as the concluding mark of another quotation, while the *iti* of vs 8 marks the end of a third citation, whether it deals now (as I believe) with an inaccurate quotation of the passages mentioned above p. [18] note 1 from ŚpBr. and AiBr. or, as Bühler (*SBE* XIV, p. XIX) presumes, with a (more precise) citation from a 'hitherto unknown Brāhmaṇa'. There is no clue at all that Vasiṣṭha also quotes this citation from the 'Mānava'.

If one further holds the *sūtra*s 5 and 6 side by side, one cannot doubt that the second is a versification of the first; one may rather

---

71 *SBE* XXV, p. xxxi; cf. also *SBE* XVIII–XX, 26 note 5; *SBE* XXV, p. XXII; Jolly 1896: 12, 17; Winternitz III, 2 1965: 585f.

doubt that the author or compiler of the Mānava himself has let his own *sūtra* be followed by a self-quoting versification. Altogether one sees that this stanza is not only accommodated in our Manusmṛti but also in Śānkh. gṛhyas. 2, 16, 1 – there in similar connection to the one in Vasiṣṭha; thus one may hold it at least **[24]** much more probable that Vas. does not quote this stanza from the 'Mānava', but, if not from either of the two already mentioned sources, then from the stock of popular *dharma*-stanzas.

Even more informative is a comparison of Vas. IV 7 with Manu 5, 48. Not only Bühler (*SBE* XIV 27 note) but also Jolly (1896: 157) assume without any ado that the closing *pāda* of Vas. 'therefore, killing for sacrifice is not killing' becomes s u b s t i t u t e d in Manu 5, 48 by the *pāda* 'therefore, one must forgo flesh', 'to suit the *ahiṃsā* doctrines of the compilers of the metrical smṛtis' [English in the original] as Bühler says. It is astonishing that neither he nor Jolly are scandalized by the crass illogicality of the Vas. verse: Certainly the second half of the stanza only lets itself be logically justified – if at all – p r o v i d e d one makes a quite essential addition to the text, which is not, in itself, foreseeable: 'killing of living beings does not lead to heaven – but, as is well-known, sacrifice does – hence, killing for sacrifice is not killing.' This somewhat entangled argumentation[72] could apply if, in the first half of the verse, something about the necessity of the sacrifice, or even a mention of sacrifice were included; yet instead of that, the text says: 'No meat is obtained by one anywhere without injuring living beings.' It is very clear that after the interpolation 'but killing animals does not lead to heaven', the only logical conclusion is the one from Manu 5, 48: 'Therefore must one forgo meat.'

It appears to me that Manu 5, 48 is undoubtedly the genuine, original form of the stanza – with the most radical, most advanced *ahiṃsā* standpoint! – whereas Vas. IV 7 – a vindication of animal-sacrifice! – is a secondary, meaning inverting distortion. When one sees that the *pāda* 'therefore killing for sacrifice is not killing' is likewise to be found in Manu, and as an indeed quite meaningful conclusion of the stanza 5, 39, discussed previously (p. [19]), the conjecture can hardly be dismissed that the Vas. stanza is taken directly from our Manu text, and represents a clumsy conglomerate

72 Meyer 1927: 46 'Yet indeed killing for sacrifice is not killing, because the killing does not lead the killer to heaven, but leads the sacrifice to heaven. Hence see, e.g. Vas. IV 7; Manu V 39–44 . . .' – See also Doniger 1976: 96 quoting Raghavan 1962: 356; Hiltebeitel 2001: 203 (WB).

of 5, 48 and 5, 39. Citation from our Manu text is, therefore, not improbable for Vas. IV 6, too. The numerous common Vas. and Manu stanzas and stanza-parts should be once again examined in the light of these suppositions. Already now it may be shown at least in two cases, that our Manu text is clearly more correct or older than that of Vas. **[25]**

1. In Manu 8, 98, dealt with by Lüders (1917 = 1940: 439), Vas. reads *kanyânṛte* instead of *paśv-anṛte*, which, as Lüders (1940: 444) confirms, is unoriginal against *paśv-anṛte*.
2. Ibid., p. 441 Lüders writes:

> Although it is certain in general ... that the versified text-books are later than those composed in prose, it appears to me to be certain that the authors of the *sūtras* have often refashioned old memorial verses into prose ... In numerous cases, the original metrical character of the sūtras still distinctly gleams through; in others it results from the content or by comparison with aphoristic literature.[73]

If, in recollection of these sentences, one reads in Vas. VIII 4f.: *sāyam āgatam atithiṃ nâparundhyāt/nâsyân-aśnan gṛhe vaset*, then one can easily suppose that these two *sūtras* are nothing more than one *śloka*, of which the third *pāda* and the last four syllables of the second (perchance '*kadācana*'?) have been omitted. This supposition is confirmed by the Manu verse (3, 105) corresponding to the content, in which the *sūtra* Vas. VIII 5 appears as the last *pāda*: *a-praṇodyo 'tithiḥ sāyaṃ sūryôḍho gṛha-medhinā/kāle prāptas tv a-kāle vā nâsyân-aśnan gṛhe vaset*. At the same time, we can with greatest probability take from this stanza the missing third *pāda* between Vas. VIII 4 and 5, since a little later we read as *sūtra* 8 the *śloka*: *nâika-grāmīṇa atithir vipraḥ sāṃgatikas tathā/kāle prāpto a-kāle vā nâsyânaśnan gṛhe vaset*. Bühler translates this thus:

73 'So gewiß im allgemeinen ... die versifizierten Lehrbücher jünger sind als die in Prosa abgefaßten, so gewiß scheint es mir zu sein, daß die Sūtra-Verfasser so und so oft alte Memorialverse in Prosa aufgelöst haben ... In zahlreichen Fällen schimmert der ursprünglich metrische Charakter von Sūtras noch deutlich durch, in anderen ergibt er sich aus dem Inhalt oder durch Vergleich mit der Spruchliteratur' (WB).

> A Brāhmaṇa who lives in the same village (with his host) and a visitor on business or pleasure (are) not (called) guests. (But a guest), whether he arrives at the moment (of dinner) or at an inopportune time, must not stay in the house of a (householder) without receiving food.

But for the completion '(but a guest)' there is no occasion or justification at all; the only possible translation is rather: 'A fellow villager is not a guest, and neither is a *sāṃgatika* brahmin. Whether he comes on time or untimely, he must not spend the night in his house without eating.'

That two absolutely incompatible stanza-halves are brought together here is corroborated by the stanza Manu 3, 103: *nâika-grāmīṇam atithiṃ vipraṃ sāṃgatikaṃ tathā/upasthitaṃ gṛhe vidyād bhāryā yatrâgnayo 'pi vā*,[74] 'One must not consider as a guest a fellow villager or a *sāṃgatika* brahmin who has turned up in the house, or where(else) are wife and fires.' Thus we have in Vas. VIII 8 a *śloka* **[26]** whose two halves are not compatible with each other; however, they fit perfectly to the respective other halves of two Manu *śloka*s, 3, 103 and 105, but the last *pāda* of the Vas. *śloka* appears once again there where it is really pertinent – Vas. VIII 5 – and where also the third *pāda* would be pertinent and can be found in Manu. (Moreover, one should note that in Vas. 8 the transposition of the accusative into the nominative has led to the false *sandhi*: *grāmīṇa atithir,* which therefore proves the originality of the Manu text, while reciprocally in Manu, the abnormal *sandhi*: *prāpto a-kāle*[75] has evidently been smoothed out secondarily to *prāptas tv a-kāle*.) The circumstances here are not unlike those in the case of Vas. IV 7, only rather more complicated, and it is difficult not to believe in a rather awkward performance on the part of a Vas.-compiler or, more probably, an interpolator having worked with our Manu text.

We observe a similar distortion as in Vas. VIII 8 again in stanza Vas. XI 34, concerning our theme:

> *niyuktas tu yatiḥ śrāddhe daive vā māṃsam utsṛjet*
> *yāvanti paśu-romāṇi tāvan narakam ṛcchati.*

---

74 The *śloka* appears again in Śāṅkh. gṛhyas. 2, 16, 3 with the variant *viproṣyâgatam eva ca* instead of *vipraṃ sāṃgatikaṃ tathā*.

75 Führer wrongly prints: *prāpte*.

To begin with, the first line is no doubt corrupt. It is nonsensical that the determination of the penalty for the refusal to eat meat at an ancestor sacrifice or one to the deities ought to pertain precisely and only for a *yati*; and, above all, the first line must certainly be either a relative or conditional clause. As a matter of fact, it begins in Kṛtyakalpataru III 7 (*GOS* CXI p. 318), where the stanza from 'Yama' is cited, with the words: *āmantritas tu yaḥ śrāddhe*. One can then confidently correct the Vas. text in *niyuktas tu yadi śrāddhe*.

We now find an equivalent of the first line in Manu 5, 35:

niyuktas tu yathânyāyaṃ yo māṃsaṃ nâtti mānavaḥ
sa pretya paśutāṃ yāti saṃbhavān ekaviṃśatim,

but we read a counterpart of the second in Manu three stanzas later (5, 38):

yāvanti paśu-romāṇi, tāvat-kṛtvo ha māraṇam
vṛthā-paśu-ghnaḥ prāpnoti pretya janmani janmani.[76]

[27] Yājñ. 1, 180 corresponds to it as regards the contents:

vaset sa narake ghore dināni paśu-romabhiḥ
saṃmitāni durācāro yo hanty a-vidhinā paśūn.

Yājñ. thus confirms that the punishment according to the number of animal hairs belongs to the animal-killing outside the sacrifice, not (as with Vas.) to the refusal to eat meat on ritual occasions. One may conclude, therefore, that the Vas.-stanza represents a later insertion, in any case does not fit to the present context, because in Vas. it appears in a long section which exclusively concerns itself with the *śrāddha*, while in the stanza the text talks about the refusal to eat meat not only at the sacrifice offered to the dead but also at that to the deities (*daive*).

There remains a last Vas. passage on the theme of meat which indeed gives no cause for doubt that it is the direct source of two stanzas of our Manu text. Chapter XIV begins its exposition about permitted and forbidden foods (*bhojyâbhojya*) with numerous and

---

76 The Kṛtyakalpataru cites a contamination of this and the previous stanza from Hārīta: *niyuktas tu yathā śrāddhe yas tu māṃsaṃ na bhakṣayet / yāvanti paśu-romāṇi tāvan narakam ṛcchati.*

involved rules as to from whom one may or may not accept food. It says: 14. *na mṛgayor iṣu-cāriṇaḥ parivarjyam annam.* 15. *vijñāyate hi: Agastyo varṣa-sāhasrike sattre mṛgayāṃ cacāra. tasyâsaṃs tara-samayāḥ puroḍāśā mṛga-pakṣiṇāṃ praśastānām:*

> The food (given) by a hunter hunting with arrows is not to be refused for it is taught (in the Veda): During a thousand years' Soma sacrifice, Agastya went on a hunt. He had sacrificial cakes consisting of the meat of kosher animals and birds.

It is clear that Manu 5, 22f. is versification hereof:

> *yajñârthaṃ brāhmaṇair vadhyāḥ praśastā mṛga-pakṣiṇaḥ*
> *bhṛtyānāṃ câiva vṛtty-artham, Agastyo hy ācarat purā.*
> *babhūvur hi puroḍāśā bhakṣyānāṃ mṛga-pakṣiṇām*
> *purāṇeṣv api yajñeṣu brahma-kṣatra-saveṣu ca.*

> Brahmins are allowed to kill kosher animals and birds for sacrifice and for the subsistence of their dependents; indeed Agastya proceeded (thus) in the past. There were also sacrificial cakes prepared from edible animals and birds at the sacrifices of antiquity and those of brahmins and *kṣatriyas*.

The versification is exceedingly clumsy and not understandable at all without the Vas. text. The disappearance of Agastya's hunt could be connected with the fact that in Manu 4, 212 the *mṛgayu* is explicitly listed among those people from whom one may not accept food. However, the strange and factually false insertion **[28]** of the *pāda*: *bhṛtyānāṃ câiva vṛtty-artham* is clarified with a glance at the *śloka* (XIV 13) immediately preceding in Vas.:

> *gurv-arthaṃ dāram ujjihīrṣann arciṣyan devatâtithīn*
> *sarvataḥ pratigṛhṇīyān, na tu tṛpyet tataḥ svayam.*

> For the Guru (or) to support wife (and child) or to honour gods and guests, one may accept (something) from somebody, but one must not satiate oneself therefrom.

This stanza appears in the correct context, namely, under the prescriptions as to from whom one may accept something, in Manu

4, 251, to which the Vas. *pāda*s b–d literally correspond, but *pāda* a has the following form: *gurūn bhṛtyāṃś côjjihīrṣan*. It is a two-fold improvement of the Vas. text: the metrical irregularity of the nine-syllabled *pāda* is removed, and *dāram* standing as *pars pro toto* is replaced by the more comprehensive *bhṛtyān*.

The appearance of the full stanza Manu 4, 251 emphasizes that the removal of 'for Guru, wife (and children)' from Vas. XIV 13, and the change of the stipulation granting permission to accept from any giver to the permission to slaughter kosher animals is secondary. For the rest it is to be noted that the Vas.-passage neither discusses on *ahiṃsā* – quite the contrary! – nor does it belong to the discussion on bloody sacrifice. Only in the two Manu stanzas does the new problematic gently emerge (yet without any polemic!); but significantly enough they are not found in the section on discussion of sacrifice (5, 27–44), but in that on kosher and non-kosher foods and especially on animals.

To summarise:

1 From Bühler's showpiece, there remains only the short beginning, the citation Vas. IV 5 above, as evidence of a lost Mānava-Dharmasūtra as the source of our Manu, so that, in particular, the proof is lacking 'that the author of the Vasiṣṭha Dharma-sūtra knew a treatise attributed to a teacher called Manu which, like all the other Dharma-sūtras, was partly written in aphoristic prose and partly in verse'. Whether Bühler's hypothesis, which Jolly 1896: 17f. has already described as fundamentally questionable, can still be maintained after the removal of this vital support would have to be clarified through a new examination of the relation between Vas. and Manu.

2 Uncompromising vegetarianism is nowhere mentioned in Vas.; the passages which point to an argument between *ahiṃsā* and sacrifice are nearly all suspicious of being later insertions. It remains as the only point **[29]** the commandment, in IV 4 (alongside others), of *ahiṃsā* for all four social classes; then, in the subsequent *sūtra* of the Mānava citation, the *ahiṃsā* keyword occurring here is followed by the justification of animal-killing through ritual motives – yet indeed without any polemical note; it is Manu 5, 41 which first introduces the intensifying *atraiva–nânyathā*.

I certainly cannot give up the – naturally not strictly provable – suspicion that Vas. IV 4 could have originally been a *śloka* line;

something like: *sarveṣāṃ satyam a-krodho dānam prajananaṃ tathā; ahiṃsā* would then have been later inserted in a transposed prose form: the *sūtras* 5–8 would then have followed this subsequently inserted keyword. The suspicion is further nourished by the fact that, on the one hand, of the four virtues remaining after the elimination of *ahiṃsā*, each is especially characteristic of one of the four *varṇas*: *satya* for the brahmins,[77] *a-krodha* for the warriors, *dāna* for the Vaiśyas, *prajanana* for the *śūdras*, the 'proletarians'; while, on the other hand, *ahiṃsā* is rather conspicuous as a demand on all the four classes, at least in olden times as that. Above all, however, what best corresponds to this suspicion and confirms it further is that we have recognised the distorting citations above in IV 6 and 7 of our Manu text.

However, even if we accept that *ahiṃsā* and the discussion of sacrifice, which are completely absent in Baudh. and Āpast., are noticeable in first traces in Vas., then it supports well the common presumption which places Vas. between the oldest Dharmasūtras and the Manusmṛti;[78] Meyer (1927: VII) dates Vas. in about the 4th century BCE.

If we now turn again to Manu in order to direct the view ahead on the contemporary and later legal texts, we notice straight away a work that indeed does not properly belong to the law texts but can and must be nevertheless counted in a certain sense as belonging to it, and whose close connection with the Manusmṛti is well-known:[79] the Mahābhārata.

To be sure, the particularly rich material which the epic offers us can only be used **[30]** chronologically to a very limited degree since, as is well-known, in it pre-Buddhist, later and very late works stand alongside each other and, strictly speaking, the age of each of the countless building stones of the monstrous, labyrinthine and gigantic construction, differing by many hundreds of years, must be determined separately.

For our purposes, we may content ourselves with Oldenberg's statement[80] that the Manusmṛti apparently dates from approximately the same time as large sections of the Mahābhārata. With

77 Cf. the rule cited by Lüders 1951: 408 from the Mahābhārata for the brahmin to always speak the truth (*ṛta-vādī sadā ca syāt*) and ibid., p. 410 making the *ṛta* and *satya* equal to the Brahman.

78 Cf. Jolly 1896: 6; Winternitz III 1963–5: 578f.

79 Cf. Bühler 1886: LXXIV–XC; Winternitz 1963–5: 587f.

80 Oldenberg (see 1903 entry) 1923: 187.

these considerations, we can state that in the didactic portions of the epic[81] the debate between animal-sacrifice and *ahiṃsā*, between meat-eating and vegetarianism is at a peak, which testifies to its topicality. It is neither possible nor necessary to present the entire material: naturally, the same arguments and formulas known to us from Manu are repeated many times over. Hence a selection should suffice which, above all, takes into account what is suitable to supplement that which is already known to us.[82]

In Vanaparvan (III 199), the 'pious hunter' (*dharma-vyādha*), a professional wildgame dealer makes a 38 stanzas-long plea for animal-killing and meat-eating to a brahmin. He initially clarifies that his really awful (*ghora*) profession is karma-ordained fate; similarly predestined is the killing, the killer being only the executing instrument.[83] Moreover, the animals killed and sold in their turn acquire religious merit in that they feed gods, guests, fathers, etc. with their flesh. Thus King Śibi also earned his way to heaven through the gift of his own flesh, and King Rantideva (well-known through Kālidāsa's Meghadūta 45) who had 2,000 small livestock and 2, 000 cows slaughtered daily attained matchless glory through his donations of meat-dishes. Beyond this, the Veda also lays down that plants, like animals, are designated to be food for the world[84] – consequently, the appeal to natural law and the order of creation, **[31]** which we already know from Manu 5, 28–30.

Only after that does the appeal to animal-killing for the sacrifice prescribed by the Veda appear, whereby the sacrificial animal gains entry to heaven. Without the animal sacrifice no one would ever have chanced upon meat-eating![85] Meat-eating in ritual is not only sinless, it is to be looked upon as non-meat-eating, just as sexual

81 That in the *old* parts, the epic legend proper, hunting and meat-eating by the heroes are a completely unproblematic matter hardly needs to be emphasized. On this and on meat-eating in the Mbh. in general see Hopkins 1901: 377ff.

82 In the following, passages from Mbh. III and XII are cited according to the critical Poona edition, from XIII and XIV, for which this has not yet come out, according to the Bombay edition, occasionally corrected with the help of the Calcutta edition.

83 Vs 3: *vidhinā vihite* (v. l. *hi hate*) *pūrvaṃ nimitto ghātako bhavet*. – Cf. Biardeau/Malamoud 1976: 136 (WB).

84 Vs 5: *oṣadhyo vīrudhaś câpi paśavo mṛga-pakṣiṇaḥ / annâdya-bhūtā lokasya, ity api śrūyate śrutiḥ.*

85 Vs 10: *yadi nâivâgnayo, brahman, māṃsa-kāmâbhavan purā / bhakṣyaṃ nâiva bhaven (v.l. naivābhavan) māṃsaṃ kasyacit.*

intercourse with one's wife during the time of *ṛtu* ('fertility') is not a breach of chastity.[86] Once again, the *dharma-vyādha* returns to the fateful karmic conditionality of his profession: as a consequence of a curse, King Saudāsa had devoured even men. Giving up a karma-determined profession is sin, its continuance merit. Yet one can remove and mitigate bad karma through generosity, honesty, obedience and hospitality to brahmins (and the *dharma-vyādha* tries to do this).

Then follow at last longer expositions which show the impossibility of consistent *ahiṃsā*. Cultivation is counted as 'good' (*sādhu*), but the plough destroys living beings to a great extent.[87] Seeds are also alive, e.g. rice grains,[88] as well as plants and trees, which one cuts without much ado – the whole world is filled with living beings, which feed on each other.[89] Knowingly or unknowingly, everyone kills living beings at every step; no one can avoid *hiṃsā*; the zealous ascetic even can only curtail it at most.[90] These last stanzas really read like an attempt to make clear to the Jain monks the absurdity of their exaggerated efforts for *ahiṃsā*.

What is, however, particularly worth noting, in this whole unsystematic, disorderly and not always logical sequence of arguments, is that no objection by the brahmin nor any refutation from the standpoint of *ahiṃsā* follows. One has the impression that the justification of the *dharma-vyādha* reflects a relatively early phase of the **[32]** *ahiṃsā* discussion and that agrees with the fact that we find

---

86 Vs 12: *a-māṃsâśī bhavaty evam, ity api śrūyate śrutiḥ / bhāryāṃ gacchan brahmacārī ṛtau bhavati brāhmaṇaḥ.*

87 Vs 19: *kṛṣiṃ sādhv iti manyante, tatra hiṃsā parā smṛtā / karṣanto lāṅgalaiḥ puṃso ghnanti bhūmi-śayān bahūn / jīvān anyāṃś ca bahuśas, tatra kiṃ pratibhāti te?* Just as XII 254, 44: *bhūmiṃ bhūmi-śayāṃś câiva hanti kāṣṭham ayo-mukham.*

88 Cf. on this below, p. [39f.].

89 Vs 23f.: *sarvaṃ vyāptam idaṃ, brahman, prāṇibhiḥ prāṇi-jīvanaiḥ / matsyā grasante matsyāṃś câiva, tatra kiṃ pratibhāti te? // sattvaiḥ sattvāni jīvanti bahudhā, dvija-sattama, / prāṇino 'nyonya-bhakṣāś ca, tatra kiṃ pratibhāti te?*

90 Vs 28f.: *ke na hiṃsanti jīvān vai loke 'smin, dvija-sattama? / bahu saṃcintya, iha vai nâsti kaścid ahiṃsakaḥ // ahiṃsāyāṃ tu niratā yatayo, dvija-sattama, kurvanty eva hi hiṃsāṃ te, yatnād alpatarā bhavet.* – Schmidt 1968: 626 finds that in concentrating his attention on the history of vegetarianism Alsdorf has lost sight of the difference between *ahiṃsā* and vegetarianism and does not attempt to fix the point at which and the reason why vegetarianism became the main-stay of the *ahiṃsā*-doctrine, of which, according to Schmidt, vegetarianism is a popularized form (WB).

ourselves in the Vanaparvan on the whole in one of the older parts of the epic.

Conversely, this corresponds to the fact that the most detailed treatment of the theme of *ahiṃsā* and vegetarianism is located in a notoriously very recent part of the Mbh., a tract of 157 stanzas in the Anuśāsanaparvan (XIII 113–116; cr. ed. 114–117 [WB]) is clearly more advanced in its development towards the absolute recognition of *ahiṃsā*. Certainly there is here still less of an orderly and systematic structure or inner logic of the whole than in the defence of the *dharma-vyādha*; the squalid text is an entangled mess with contradictions and, in part, multiple also literal repetitions (besides a few more or less literal agreements with Manu). Yet it champions almost always the standpoint of uncompromising vegetarianism which also rejects the use of sacrificial meat. At the beginning of ch. 115, Yudhiṣṭhira indeed explicitly requests clarification of the contradiction between the *ahiṃsā* doctrine and the command of meat-use in the sacrifice for the ancestors (*śrāddha*), but in his answer thereon Bhīṣma does not at all respond, and instead begins an enthusiastic eulogy of complete renunciation of meat.

There are not more then a scanty dozen stanzas scattered incoherently in different places which allow the generally restricted meat-eating on specific occasions.[91] The Agastya story already known to us from Vas. and Manu appears twice here: in 115, 59f. it says:

> Out of consideration for the well-being of creatures, the high-minded Agastya has, through his *tapas*, consecrated the wild animals to all the gods; in this manner, the rites related to the gods and the fathers are not left out, and the fathers pleased by being downright saturated with meat.[92]

In 116, 15ff., however, Agastya becomes like an Indian St Hubert in that his consecration of wild animals serves to vindicate hunting as the general custom of the *kṣatriya*s, who do not, therefore, sin

---

91 In Mbh. XIII 115, 45 meat-eating is signified as a pardonable offence: *prokṣitâbhyukṣitaṃ māṃsaṃ tathā brāhmaṇa-kāmyayā / alpa-doṣam iha jñeyaṃ, viparīte tu lipyate* (cf. Manu 5, 27 ab; *alpa-doṣa*, however, can really also mean 'sinless'.

92 *prajānāṃ hita-kāmena tv Agastyena mahâtmanā / āraṇyāḥ sarva-daivatyāḥ prokṣitās tapasā mṛgāḥ // kriyā hy evaṃ na hīyante pitṛ-daivata-saṃśritāḥ / prīyante pitaraś câiva nyāyato māṃsa-tarpitāḥ.*

through the consumption of flesh obtained through their valour; as a very characteristic further vindication is added that hunting is always connected with the risk of one's life, and that the animal also has a chance to kill the hunter.[93] **[33]**

This piece of genuine *kṣatriya*-ethics operates as an extraneous body in the ever-new, exaggerated eulogy of *ahiṃsā* (the close of ch. 116 is really a hymn to it!); the threats of punishment for meat-eating, the promises of reward for meat-abstinence. Immediately after the vindication of the use of meat at the *śrāddha* through Agastya's consecration of wild animals follows in 115, 61ff. a section on the reward of even temporally limited meat-renunciation beginning with the guarantee that one year of meat-abstinence equals a hundred years of hardest asceticism; the core is comprised by a list of forty-six pre-historic kings who gained heaven and stay in glittering splendour in Brahmaloka as a reward for meat-abstinence during the bright half of the month of Kārttika. As a conclusion of the chapter, there follows a bombastic *Śravaṇaphala* ('benefit of hearing' [WB]). It is precisely this utterly arbitrary and senseless stringing together of names from mythology and legend – even Rantideva is again to be found here! – that is taken by the author of the Kṛtyakalpataru as worth quoting.[94]

When we stated above (p. [15]) that *ahiṃsā* has essentially nothing to do with ethics in our sense of the word but is a magical-ritualistic taboo on life, it is naturally not contradictory that the Indians, nevertheless, soon attributed to it the ethical foundation valid

93 *ksatriyāṇāṃ tu yo dṛṣṭo vidhis, tam api me śṛṇu / vīryeṇôpārjitaṃ māṃsaṃ yathā bhuñjan na duṣyati / āraṇyāḥ sarva-daivatyāḥ sarvaśaḥ prokṣitā mṛgāḥ //16// Agastyena purā, rājan, mṛgayā yena pūjyate / nâtmānam a-parityajya mṛgayā nāma vidyate //17// samatām upasaṃgamya bhūtaṃ hanyati hanti vā / ato rājarṣayaḥ sarve mṛgayāṃ yānti, Bhārata //18// na hi lipyanti pāpena na câitat pātakaṃ viduḥ.* The passage is cited in Kṛtyakalpataru III 313f. Thereby the offensive passive *hanyati* in 18a is eliminated through the meaning-impairing reading *bhūtaṃ hanyeta mānavaḥ*.

94 In III p. 324f. he cites, with numerous deviations from the concurrent text of the Bombay and Calcutta editions, the vss 62–79 inclusive of vs 71, which is not at all appropriate here and thus clearly interpolated, and 79 which again extols the life-long entire abstinence from meat and honey. – Because the citations from the Mbh. are not identified in the *GOS* edition, the occurrences unmentioned so far are here specified (they all originate from XIII 115f.): p. 317:115, 52f.; 45; 116, 22c, d; 14 a, b; p. 324, first vs quoted:115, 16.

even to this day. Little of it is to be sensed in Manu; it is all the more prominent in our Mbh. tract. Its chief guiding principle is *ātmâupamya*, to-respect-others-as-oneself; this yields our 'what you don't want others to do to you', or as 113, 8 expresses it: 'One should not do to others what one abhors oneself.'[95] The greater part of Adhyāya 113 deals with this theme, while **[34]** we find it furthermore modified in that there is nothing in this world one loves more than one's life. Therefore, one must exercise compassion towards others as with oneself.[96] But whoever exercises compassion towards all creatures, on him will be bestowed compassion from them also: consistent *ahiṃsā* guards against each and every hazard.[97]

The critically decisive point of the *ahiṃsā* problem and the real stone of contention, however, remains, viz. the animal sacrifice. The Mokṣadharma and the Anugītā[98] show us the discussion on this in a succession of examples which run through the entire gamut of possibilities, so to speak, from successful defence of the Vedic tradition to its reinterpretation and its daring explicit rejection.

We find a full justification of the bloody offering, and one no longer refuted by its opponent, in Gokapilīya 'the story of Kapila and the cow'.[99] On seeing a cow which is tethered to be slaughtered[100] for a guest doubts about the Veda dawn in the Ṛṣi Kapila. In order to dispel these, the Ṛṣi Syūmaraśmi possesses the cow and begins a debate with Kapila. On his question of whether, beyond the written

95 *na tat parasya saṃdadhyāt, pratikūlaṃ yad ātmanaḥ.*

96 Mbh. XIII 116, 12: *na hi prāṇāt priyataraṃ loke kiṃcana vidyate / tasmād dayāṃ naraḥ kuryād yathâtmani tathâpare.* Similarly previously 115, 21: *prāṇā yathâtmano 'bhīṣṭā bhūtānām api vai tathā*; further 116, 26: *prāṇa-dānāt paraṃ dānaṃ na bhūtaṃ na bhaviṣyati / na hy ātmanaḥ priyataraṃ kiṃcid astîha niścitam.*

97 *a-bhayaṃ sarva-bhūtebhyo yo dadāti dayā-paraḥ / a-bhayaṃ tasya bhūtāni dadatîty anuśuśruma // kṣataṃ ca skhalitaṃ câiva patitaṃ kliṣṭam āhatam / sarva-bhūtāni rakṣanti sameṣu viṣameṣu ca // nâinaṃ vyāla-mṛgā ghnanti na piśācā na rākṣasaḥ / mucyate bhaya-kāleṣu mokṣayed yo bhaye parān.* Just as previously 115, 28f.: *kāntāreṣv atha ghoreṣu durgeṣu gahaneṣu ca / rātrāv ahani sandhyāsu catvareṣu sabhāsu ca // udyateṣu ca śastreṣu mṛga-vyāla-bhayeṣu ca / a-māṃsa-bhakṣaṇe, rājan, bhayam anyair na gacchati.*

98 The translation of both in 'Vier philosophische Texte des Mahābhāratam' further quoted as 'Deussen'.

99 Mbh. XII 268 cr. ed. [WB]; Deussen 1922: 440ff. – See Schreiner (1979: 301 note 20) who does not fully agree with Alsdorf (WB).

100 Thus Nīlakaṇṭha explains by quoting the passage Ait.Br. 3, 4, 6 reproduced above on p. [18] note.

tradition, there is something higher than *ahiṃsā* he extols the sacrifice and holds a discourse on its composition to which – just like daily nourishment (!) – all the animals and plants, beyond that, the entire world belong; everything is created for the sacrifice (29: *yajñârthāni hi sṛṣṭāni*); but whoever sacrifices believing that the sacrifice must be brought about without desire for reward 'injures nothing, kills nothing and does not hurt any one'.[101]

It was stated in vs 24 before that:

> 'Animals and men, trees and herbs desire for **[35]** heaven and no heaven is to be gained except by sacrifice,' which Nīlakaṇṭha comments thus: 'And thereby there is no sin in killing (*hiṃsā*); on the contrary, (sacrifice) is for the sacrificial animals, etc. aspiring to heaven a support according to the text of the mantras (ṚV. 1, 162, 21): "Truly, thou diest not thereby, thou dost not come to grief. Thou goest to the gods by the wonted way." '[102]

We will examine the Ṛgveda stanza addressed to the sacrificed horse again below (p. [67]). The Rṣi speaking out of the cow closes with a confident assertion that one should sacrifice and allow sacrifice without worry; on the basis of Vedic authority heaven will be bestowed on the sacrificer, neither this nor the other world to the non-sacrificer. The discussion then turns to another question.

The same conclusion, in spite of its somewhat different course, has the concern of a conversation between a sacrificing priest (*adhvaryu*) and an ascetic (*yati*), who accuses him of *hiṃsā* in the sacrifice of a ram (Mbh. XIV 28, Deussen 1922: 927ff.). The *adhvaryu* retorts promptly that the ram is not ruined but, according to the Veda, participates in heavenly bliss;[103] its component parts will enter into the corresponding elements, the sun, etc., its life into heaven (cf. note below). The *yati* asks sarcastically if the sacrifice takes place for the good of the ram, then what purpose might it still have for the *adhvaryu*? Moreover, he should first of all go to the brother, father, mother and friend of the ram and obtain their consent

---

101 *na hinasti hy ārabhate (v.l. nârabhate) nâbhidruhyati kiṃcana / yajño yaṣṭavya ity eva yo yajaty a-phalêpsayā.*

102 *na câtra hiṃsā-doṣo 'sti, pratyuta svargârthināṃ paśv-ādīnāṃ 'na vā u etan mriyase na riṣyasi devām id eṣi pathibhiḥ sugebhiḥ' iti mantra-varṇād ayam upakāra eva.*

103 Vs 8: *nâyaṃ chāgo vinaśyati / śreyasā yokṣyate jantur yadi śrutir iyaṃ tathā.*

for the killing.[104] Finally he will, after the killing, only have the soulless body, like firewood without fire. In contrast to this, the *yati* energetically advocates the principle of *ahiṃsā* towards all beings (*bhūta*) and the realization thereof **[36]** here on earth (*pratyakṣam*), not in a life hereafter (*parokṣam*).

The answer of the *adhvaryu* could be directed to a Jain; it leads the *ahiṃsā* of the *yati* ad absurdum in that it employs the word used by him for 'being' in its other common meaning, i.e. 'element':

> You eat the olfactory qualities of the earth; you drink the flavours made from water; you see the colours of light; you feel the properties emerging from the air; you hear the tones stemming from the ether; you think thoughts with the mind – and you have (to be sure, indeed) the notion that all these elements are life. You have renounced the taking of life (but) you live in *himsā*! There is no activity (no life) without *hiṃsā* – don't you think so, brahmin?[105]

The *yati* counters with explanations on the intransitory-transitory double nature of the *ātman*, which do not appear to fix as a rejoinder

---

104 Vs 12f.: *atra tvāṃ manyatāṃ bhrātā pitā mātā sakhêti ca /. . . evaṃ evânumanyeraṃs, tān bhavān draṣṭum arhati / teṣām anumataṃ śrutvā . . .* This mocks the taking seriously the declared wish in the *adhrigu-praiṣa* ('call of the *hotar* upon the *āgnīdhra* and other priests to start the sacrifice' [WB]) before the killing in a sacrifice: 'His mother, his father, his full brother must agree with him (i.e. his killing), as likewise his friend belonging to the same herd' (Ait.Br. 2, 6, 7 among others: *anv enam mātā manyatām anu pitânu bhrātā sa-garbhyo 'nu sakhā sa-yūthyaḥ*). Cf. Schwab 1886: 102; Kane II/2 1974: 1121f. The preceding contentions of the *adhvaryu* about the entrance of the components of the ram into the elements etc. were cited from the direct continuation of the *adhrigu-praiṣa*.

105 vs 19–21: *bhūmer gandha-guṇān bhuṅkṣe, pibasy āpomayān rasān / jyotisāṃ paśyase rūpaṃ, spṛśyasy anila-jān guṇān // śṛṇoṣy ākāśa-jān śabdān, manasā manyase matim /sarvāṇy etāni bhūtāni prāṇā iti ca manyase // prāṇâdāne nivṛtto 'si, hiṃsāyāṃ vartate bhavān / nâsti ceṣṭā vinā hiṃsāṃ, kiṃ vā tvaṃ manyase, dvija?* – Deussen's translation of 20 c, d: 'All these beings are animated, as you know', fails to appreciate that the *adhvaryu* attributes only to the *yati* the notion of the animation of elements (not: 'beings'); he himself naturally does not share it! In 21a Deussen reads *prāṇâdāne 'nivṛtto 'si* ('and you never stop taking life from them'); but neither the Bombay, nor the Calcutta edition writes the *avagraha* which is otherwise always placed, and the point here is after all that the *adhvaryu* presents the *yati* with the contradiction between his vow of *ahiṃsā* and his actual, unavoidable *hiṃsā*.

to the arguments of the *adhvaryu*, or are simply not intelligible.[106] The *adhvaryu* in his turn replies definitively and very politely that one must only live with good people;[107] cognisant of the view of the *yati*, he is confirmed in his own view even more and commits no sin when he follows the Vedic rule. The narrator of the story then remarks that the *yati* has remained silent on account of the argumentation (*upapattyā*; or 'in an appropriate manner'?) but the *adhvaryu* went on with his sacrifice.

Such a victory of the champion of the bloody sacrifices is, however, an exception; the rule is the triumph of *ahiṃsā* as, for example, in the episode Mbh. XII 246 (Deussen 1922: 473f.) straightforwardly entitled **[37]** 'Reprimand of the sacrifice' (*yajña-nindā*). A pious forest ascetic, who lives strictly according to *ahiṃsā* and makes an offering of only roots and fruits, is led into temptation by a god in that, at his request, another ascetic turns himself into a gazelle and proffers himself for sacrifice. The ascetic refuses but on being allowed to see with divine eyes the *apsaras* and the heavenly palaces to be expected as a reward, softens and wishes to attain heaven through the sacrifice of the gazelle. The gazelle saves him from doing this by turning itself into the god Dharma and explains that this is not the proper manner of sacrifice; but the mere wish to kill has sufficed to deprive the ascetic of his great *tapas*. In other words: killing is not appropriate to sacrifice (27: *tasmād dhiṃsā na yajñiyā*), *ahiṃsā* is total piety; *hiṃsā* in sacrifice is not admissible (*ahiṃsā sakalo dharmo, hiṃsā yajñe 'samāhitā*).

So just as the hero of this story makes his offering with roots and fruits, there are likewise frequent attempts to resolve the conflict between *ahiṃsā* and Vedic sacrifice through the promotion of exclusive vegetabilistic – or spiritual! – offerings. One must then either reinterpret or explain as misunderstood or forged the literal meaning of the Vedic precepts – if one does not dare in fact to discard it openly.[108]

---

106 Even Deussen's alteration of *sad-bhāva in sva-bhāva* in 23 b does not help, and naturally Nīlakaṇṭha's daring explanation of *sva-bhāva as su-abhāva (sutarām a-bhāvaḥ, kāla-traye 'py a-sattvam)* even less so.

107 Vs 25: *sadbhir evêha saṃvāsaḥ kāryaḥ*. Deussen translates: 'Only with the (empirical) real do we have to live together in this world.' To me, the polite commonplace is more probable than the philosophical profundity which does not fit at all in the context.

108 Dayānand Sarasvatī, the founder of the Ārya Samāj and the champion of the 'Return to the Veda', writes in Samullāsa 12 of his chief work Satyârthaprakāś concisely and conclusively: *aur jo māṃs kā khānā likhā hai,*

The second possibility is chosen by the pious tradesman Tulādhāra in his famous instruction of the ascetic Jājali.[109] After he has delivered a long sermon on *ahiṃsā*, in which he condemns agriculture and cattle-breeding, culminating in the statement: 'There is no higher piety than non-violation of living beings,'[110] Jājali raises in Mbh. XII 265, 1–3 the objection that all men, including Tulādhāra, live from agriculture and cattle-breeding and, as without both no offering can be given, he is a nihilist (*nāstika*). Tulādhāra protests his high esteem for sacrifice – but of the 'brahmanic' kind, because the (present-day) brahmins have given up 'their' sacrifice and taken on the *kṣatriya* sacrifice, which was developed by avaricious nihilists in ignorance of the true Veda teaching.[111] **[38]**

The proper sacrifice is made 'with reverence as the sacrifical meal and Veda study as the herbal juices'.[112] According to vs 18, it is an 'offering of truth and self-restraint' (*satya* and *dama*). The offering potion poured into the fire ascends to the sun and comes back from there as rain, from which sustenance and progeny result;[113] in this manner the ancestors attained all their wishes, whereby farming was unnecessary, because 'unploughed, the earth let her fruits ripen; through mere prayers, the plants flourished'.[114] In vs 24 it is said of the pious that they 'walk along the path of the righteous and present the *ahiṃsā* of all living beings as an offering'.[115]

Immediately after the story of Tulādhāra and Jājali follows in Mbh. XII 257 (cr. ed.; Deussen 1922: 436f.) the Vicakhnugītā, the protest of the king Vicakhnu against a cowslaughter on the place of the sacrifice. Here we read the daring words:

> The pious Manu has instructed *ahiṃsā* in all the rituals . . .
> the *ahiṃsā* is to be regarded as the highest of all obligations.

---

vah ved-bhāg rākṣas kā banāyā hai, 'and what is written there about meat-eating, that part of the Veda is made by the devil'.

109 Mbh. XII 254ff., Deussen 1922: 423ff.; Winternitz I 1962: 365ff.

110 Mbh. XII 254, 29: *na bhūtānām ahiṃsāyā jyāyān dharmo 'sti kaścana.*

111 Vs 5f.: *sva-yajñaṃ brāhmaṇā hitvā kṣātraṃ yajñam ihâsthitāḥ // lubdhair vitta-parair, brahman, nāstikaiḥ saṃpravartitam / veda-vādān a-vijñāya satyâbhāsam ivânṛtam.*

112 Vs 8: *namaskāreṇa haviṣā svâdhyāyair auṣadhais tathā.*

113 On these teachings cf. Lüders 1951 ch. IX, on p. 314 our vs 11 is quoted which is almost identical with Manu 3, 76.

114 Vs 12: *a-kṛṣṭa-pacyā pṛthivī, āśīrbhir vīrudho 'bhavan.*

115 *satāṃ vartmânuvartante yajante câvihiṃsayā.* The critical edition reads . . . *yathā-balam a-hiṃsayā*, but the well attested *yajante câvi°* (v.l. *°te tv avi°*, *°ti tv avi°*) appears to me to be preferred.

> Whoever has strengthened his vows through fasting has deviated from the precepts given in the Veda (and says:) the use is an abuse.[116]

The next stanza explicitly turns against only shunning meat not originating from the sacrifice,[117] and vs 9 asserts: '(The enjoyment of) spirits, fish, honey, meat, rum and sesame rice – that has been introduced by unworthy people and not allowed in the Veda.'[118] The key to the understanding of this radicalism is furnished in vs 10: **[39]** brahmins see in all offerings only the one Viṣṇu, to whom only bloodless offerings, above all, milk libations and flowers, are made:[119] We have here already the especially close connection between vegetarianism and Viṣṇuism, which is so notorious and characteristic for modern India.

Viṣṇuist is also, as is narrated in Mbh. XII 324 (Deussen 1922: 764ff.), the story of King Vasu: the very first stanza praises him as a particularly ardent Vaiṣṇava (*bhāgavato 'tyartham*),[120] whereupon Nīlakaṇṭha remarks that the chapter beginning thus illustrates the rejection of the bloody sacrifice by the Vaiṣṇavas.[121] The story is, so to speak, the classical example of the vegetarian reinterpretation of a Vedic word. Gods and *ṛṣi*s (seers) dispute among themselves whether in the precept *ajena yaṣṭavyam* the word *aja* signifies a he-goat, according to the gods, or rather corn, as the *ṛṣi*s maintain.[122] As they cannot agree, they call upon King Vasu, who is acknowledged to be pious and who just came flying near in the

---

116 Vs 5ff.: *sarva-karmasv a-hiṃsāṃ hi dharmâtmā Manur abravīt* ... *a-hiṃsâiva hi sarvebhyo dharmebhyo jyāyasī matā // upoṣya saṃśito bhūtvā hitvā veda-kṛtāḥ śrutīḥ / ācāra ity an-ācāraḥ.*

117 *yadi yajñāṃs ca vṛkṣāṃś ca yūpāṃś côddiśya mānavāḥ / vṛthā-māṃsaṃ na khādanti, nâiṣa dharmaḥ praśasyate.* The reading *vṛthā-māṃsāni* set in the text of the critical edition is at variance with the context. Cf. Mbh. XII 186, 13: *yajuṣā saṃskṛtaṃ māṃsaṃ nivṛtto māṃsa-bhakṣaṇāt / na bhakṣayet* (Deussen 1922: 176: '... should not eat flesh consecrated in sacrifice either').

118 *māṃsaṃ madhu surā matsyā āsavaṃ kṛṣa-raudanam / dhūrtaiḥ pravartitaṃ hy etan, na tad vedeṣu kalpitam.*

119 *Viṣṇum evâbhijānanti sarva-yajñeṣu brāhmaṇāḥ / pāyasaiḥ su-manobhiś ca tasyâpi yajanaṃ smṛtam.*

120 The critical edition reads *yadā bhakto bhagavata āsīd.*

121 *yadā bhāgavato 'tyartham ity-ādir adhyāyo vaiṣṇavānāṃ hiṃsra-yajña-varjanârthaḥ.*

122 The *ṛṣi*s take as a precedent in connection with their firm rejection of every animal-killing that one lives in Kṛtayuga, the golden age, in which

air, to act as an arbitrator. He inquires cautiously which view is supported by either party and then takes the side of the gods. Thereupon the *ṛṣi*s curse him to be swallowed up by the earth, but he is freed later from the curse through incessant devotion to Viṣṇu-Nārāyaṇa. The story is narrated once again in Mbh. XIV 91 but differently: here the *ṛṣi*s protest against an animal sacrifice by Indra, which they characterise as sinful because *hiṃsā* is not *dharma*.[123] They call on Indra to offer three-year-old seeds. He declines and they dispute whether 'movable or immovable' (*jaṅgama* or *sthāvara*, whether animals **[40]** or plants) are to be sacrificed.

Finally with the concurrence of Indra, Vasu is questioned. He gives the unreflected answer that one should offer whatever is available, and disappears into the underworld.[124]

This version, which is not Viṣṇuist and with Indra in the main role gives the impression of being ancient, has forgotten the main point: namely that it is a question of a dispute about the meaning of the word *aja*. Instead of that, it has retained that which substantiates first of all the etymological interpretation of *a-ja* as 'non-germinating (seeds)' and what is missing in the Viṣṇuist setting: the assertion that it is a question of three-year-old seeds which are, therefore, no longer capable of germinating and hence are lifeless.[125] That this is the meaning of the triennial period is confirmed by the Jains, who have seized upon this legend as highly suitable for their ends, have inserted it into their universal history and have expanded it into the 'story of the genesis of the animal sacrifice'.[126] The alterations which

---

no animal is allowed to be slaughtered. Viṣṇu himself proclaims this in Mbh. XII 327, 73 (Deussen 1922: 791): 'The present age, known as the Kṛta, has dawned as the best age; in this age sacrificial animals are not allowed to be killed; and so it is' (*idaṃ kṛtayugaṃ nāma kālaḥ śreṣṭaḥ pravartitaḥ / ahiṃsyā yajña-paśavo yuge 'smin, na tad anyathā*). Already in the next age, the Tretayuga, in which one quarter of the fourfold consummate *dharma* has disappeared, animals are consecrated and killed in sacrifice (not to mention then, what is not expressed, in our Kaliyuga, which has only one quarter of the *dharma*!).

123 Vs 14: *nâyaṃ dharma-kṛto yajño, na hiṃsā dharma ucyate.*

124 Vs 22f.: *yathôpanītair yaṣṭavyam iti provāca pārthivaḥ // evam uktvā sa nṛpatiḥ praviveśa rasātalam.*

125 Agastya also offers triennial seeds in Mbh. XIV 92 when Indra withholds rain from him in connection with a twelve-year sacrifice. The ascetics gathered with him highly extol *ahiṃsā* and pray to him to propagate such *ahiṃsā* in sacrifice (vs 34: *etām ahiṃsāṃ yajñeṣu brūyās tvaṃ satataṃ, prabho*). Why the seeds offered are triennial is not expressed here either.

it sustained in the process need not be investigated here. The disputation on the meaning of the the word *aja* (respectively of the *śruti*: *ajair yaṣṭavyam*) has, however, remained a principal item in all Jain versions, and in Guṇabhadra (67, 330) Nārada expressly explains: *vigatâṅkura-śaktikam/ yava-bījam trivarṣa-stham ajam*, '*aja* is a three-year-old barley-corn deprived of its vitality'.[127]

The fact that the King Vasu, who had been called as an arbitrator, decided in favour of animal sacrifice is confirmed even by the Jains (according to them he passes a wrong verdict against better knowledge and against his vow of truth). This clear role certified by themselves has, however, not prevented the ardent Vaiṣṇavas from maintaining in Mbh. XII 338 – immediately prior to the story of the verdict – that Vasu had, at a horse-sacrifice (!), insisted that no animal be slaughtered **[41]** and that only wild plants were offered – a piety which Viṣṇu rewarded by revealing himself incarnate only to the king.

The material taken from the Mahābhārata could be well-nigh arbitrarily multiplied by resorting to related and later literature, above all the Purāṇas; however, what concerns us here is not so much the completeness of the material (especially since the chronological order would be even more questionable), but rather is the aim of completion and rounding off of the picture obtained from Manu sufficiently reached through the most representative and, in general, almost contemporary source. With this aim, we only briefly turn towards the law-literature after Manu and ascertain that no other work of the second stage, viz. of the metrical Dharmaśāstras has dealt with our theme with such copiousness or offers similar possibilities for contrasting the successively following developmental stages of the textual layers.

The work closest to Manu in time and significance, the Yājñavalkyasmṛti, does indeed present the rules governing permitted and forbidden foods in a comparatively speaking detailed manner – the list of the edible and unedible animals alone spans five *ślokas* –

---

126 See the table of contents of the version in Guṇabhadra's Uttarapurāṇa through von Glasenapp 1926: 343ff. In Jinasena's Harivaṃśapurāṇa, the story stands 17, 38–164. It is also found in the universal history of the Śvetāmbaras, for example Hemacandra, *Triṣaṣṭiśalākāpuruṣacaritra* VII, 2, 362–514.

127 In Jinasena, *Harivaṃśapurāṇa* 17, 69 they are rice grains (*tri-varṣā vrīhayo bījā*). – See also Handiqui 1949: 425 < Yaśastilaka, *Kāvyamālā* II 354, 18ff. (WB).

but there are only three in it compared to thirty stanzas in Manu on 'the consumption of and abstinence from meat' (5, 27–56).[128] Even if one takes into account the fact that there is three times more material on average (in Manu), that is still extraordinarily little. In the reconstruction of the Bṛhaspatismṛti (*GOS* LXXXV) undertaken by K.V. Rangaswami Aiyangar, we likewise find only five pertinent stanzas.[129] There is of course no certainty that we therewith have everything that was in the lost text, but considering the total extent of the quotations gathered together by Aiyangar, five stanzas are in any case very few indeed.

Nārada can have nothing because, as is well-known, he treats law only in the narrow sense. By contrast, we come across two-thirds of the Manu-stanzas in Viṣṇu – undoubtedly cited directly from our Manu text. Of its thirty stanzas (5, 27–56) **[42]** only ten are missing (27–33, 35, 37, 56). It is nevertheless worth noting that the passage 45–55, which is based on uncompromising vegetarianism, is cited in full, whereas it is precisely those which refer to natural law and order of creation (thereby claiming the right of unrestricted meat-eating [28–30]), which belong to the unquoted section vss 27–44. Similarly vs 35, which makes the avoidance of meat-eating commanded by ritual punishable, and vs 56, which, like 28–30, characterizes meat-eating as sinless normal human conduct. In these omissions, the advanced standpoint of the Viṣṇusmṛti is distinctly documented, whether, with J.J. Meyer, one regards the whole as a later work or count our passage to the recognized late additions.

The unmistakable decrease of the discussion on meat and sacrifice in the earlier Smṛtis may be taken as one indication of what is in any case clear: that the problem of the incompatibility of *ahiṃsā* and sacrifice is increasingly declining in practical significance. If it is one of the most well-known features of the development of the old Aryan religion to Hinduism that the sacrifice, the *yajña*, has been replaced

---

128 1, 179 corresponds to Manu 5, 27 and 32; 180 corresponds to 5, 38; 181 corresponds to 5, 53f. In the text Yājñ. is quite independent.

129 Ācārakaṇḍa 81–85 (p. 321f.) 81 d = Manu 5, 50 b; e, f similar to Manu 5, 38 a, b. 82 corresponds to Manu 5, 36. 81 c–f is wrongly arranged: the stanza belongs, as the quotation in Kṛtyakalpataru (III p. 316) proves, between 84 and 85 c–f (84: meat-eating allowed in sickness, *śrāddha* invitation, offering and brahmin feeding; 81 c–f: evil karmic consequences of meat-eating otherwise (*ato 'nyathā*); 85 c–f: whoever even in sickness and despite being urged to eat meat abstains, obtains the reward of a hundred horse sacrifices. 81 a,b and 85 a,b are likewise wrongly arranged; they do not belong here.

by the modern bloodless form of worship, the *pūjā*,[130] it was the growing significance of *ahiṃsā*, above all, which increasingly diminished the (need for) sacrifice. With the inertia of the old beside the new, which is so characteristic of India, sacrifice has survived as a relic within narrow circles. It was never contested in theoretical weight and importance, but in practice is becoming a learned *tour de force*, by virtue of which one occasionally bypasses the actual offences of killing animals and meat consumption by means of substitutes, which on account of the old texts must make the whole sacrificial ritual simply invalid, respectively, ineffective. The report **[43]** of a German indologist (Sontheimer? [WB]) who, two years ago, attended a large sacrificial event in Poona lasting several days was not without a comic touch.

The third stratum of the law literature constitutes, as noted above (p. [21]), the commentaries to the old texts, which are to be considered partly as self-supporting independent law-works only using the shape of commentaries, and the *nibandhas*, compendia which represent essentially more or less comprehensive and systematic compilations of statements of the ancient authors or texts and so can almost take on the character of collections of quotations. Thus the oldest preserved and, at the same time, most extensive and complete *nibandha*, the repeatedly mentioned Kṛtyakalpataru of Lakṣmīdhara written at the beginning of the twelfth century, quotes,

130 It is a particularly striking example of the typically Indian juxtaposition of contrasts which, as we see it, are incompatible, viz. that even in modern Hinduism there are bloody, even very bloody sacrifices. The goat- and buffalo-sacrifices at the Kalighat in Calcutta are particularly well-known; there is evidence of past human sacrifices (*puruṣa-medha*) in Bhavabhūti's *Mālatīmādhava* (act 5 [WB]) which is certainly not a figment of a poet's imagination. On former (and perhaps even today's) human sacrifices in Nepal, and the orgy of blood at the Durgā-festival there see Filchner-Marathe 1953: 132–37 and also the depiction of the Kali sacrifice in Darjeeling in Nebesky-Wojkowitz 1955: 180–84. It needs hardly be emphasized that these bloody sacrifices by no means continue the Vedic, Aryan sacrifice. No one will consider the goddess Kālī-Durgā, to whom they are made, to be an Aryan deity no more than one would derive tantrism from the Aryan religion. – See Mallebrein & von Stietencron 2008: 249 under: sacrifice. There is a trend in Orissa towards raising tribal deities up to the status of a superior, vegetarian god corresponding to recent attempts to abolish animal sacrifices, in which it marks the first step (ibid., p. 106 and Mallebrein 2007). On human sacrifices, see further the references in Tawney-Penzer, X 1928: 181 and Mallebrein and von Stietencron, 2008: 249. (WB).

in its two sections 'Rules pertaining to the eating and avoiding of meat'[131] and 'Rules pertaining to the permitted and forbidden killing of animals',[132] three prose passages and not less than 100 stanzas from as many as 13 authors or works; of the stanzas, 31 come from Manu,[133] 27 from the Mahābhārata, 17 from Yama, 8 from Hārīta and 3 from Yājñavalkya.

Much more modest and much more strongly focused on Manu is a selection of the Smṛticandrikā of Devaṇṇa Bhaṭṭa a little later, which is likewise considered to belong to the most important *nibandhas*.[134] His presentation of the meat problem be briefly sketched as an example of the diverse ways in which commentators and the *nibandha* authors try to harmonize contradictions in the traditional rules which are only intelligible to us through a historical perspective.

Devana Bhaṭṭa begins, as we have just noted (previous note), with the most radical form of the meat-prohibition, Manu 5, 48f. He then interprets the end of vs 49 ('. . . people should renounce every kind of meat') in the way that 'every kind' becomes to mean: 'every kind procured with desire for it (or enjoyment of it)' (*sarvasmād* **[44]** *rāga-prāpta-māṃsa-bhakṣaṇān nivarteta*), but the renunciation does not result out of fear of committing transgression through meat-eating, because Manu 5, 56 indeed says expressly: 'There is no sin in meat-eating.' The conclusion of this stanza

131 *māṃsa-bhakṣaṇa-vartana-vidhi*, *GOS* CXI, p. 311ff.

132 *paśu-hiṃsā-vidhi-pratiṣedhau*, loc. cit., 326ff.

133 Cited are 5, 22f. and the whole of section 5, 26–56, with the exception of 48f. On vs 48 cf. above p. [5]; of it, vs 49 is a repeated emphasis: 'Bearing in mind the origin of meat and the slaughtering and binding of the animals, people should renounce the consumption of every kind of meat' (*samutpattiṃ ca māṃsasya vadha-bandhau ca dehinām / prasamīkṣya nivarteta sarva-māṃsasya bhakṣanāt*). It is difficult to understand why only these two stanzas have been left out. If the reason was that its extremely clear and unequivocal formulation of the requirement of unconditional and unrestricted vegetarianism too clearly contradicted the stanzas which allow or forbid conditional meat-eating, then this contradiction has not in any case disturbed the author of the about to be mentioned Smṛticandrikā, who indeed cites these two stanzas first. – On *vadha* and *bandha* (here with Werba [p.c.] in a ὕστερον πρότερον compound whose remarkable formation is in no dictionary or grammar, though Renou 1930 § 86f. briefly deals with irregular *dvandvas*), see, e.g. Williams 1963: 67 and Bruhn 2007: 46f. and 64 (WB).

134 On this see Winternitz 1920: 502, where Devaṇṇabhaṭṭa's work is thought to have been written about 1200 CE (WB).

emphasizes the general merit of meat-renunciation, but likewise whoever aspires to the reward of such renunciation may partake of meat on four occasions enumerated in Manu 5, 27: sacrifice, feeding brahmins, invitation to *śrāddha*, or risk to one's life.

If the reward for meat-renunciation is not aspired to, then restriction to these four occasions does not hold and likewise Manu 5, 36, according to which one should never (*na kadācana*) eat meat which is 'not consecrated', i.e. not used ritually, applies only to the one aspiring to the reward of renunciation. But just as the general permission to have sexual intercourse pronounced by Manu 5, 56 is of course qualified through special prohibitions on intimacy with the wife of another and with prostitutes, so also is the general permission to eat meat restricted through specific prohibitions on the eating of certain species of animals. Inserted here is now the list of the animals placed in Manu before the section 5, 26–56, cited fully and comprehensively commented upon. After that, it is stated that even with the animals declared to be edible permission has a bearing only on eating but not on killing: *expressis verbis* is taught what we have learnt from the old Buddhists and Jains: 'Mere eating is no sin, but this does not apply when one has killed an animal with the aim of eating it, because one can indeed procure meat without (oneself) killing an animal.'[135] Killing certainly is a sin according to Mann 5, 45 and Yājñ. 1, 180.

There remains then only the fatal stipulation of Mann 5, 51, according to which, just as the sanctioner, the butcher, the killer, the buyer, the seller, the cook and the servant, the eater, too, is considered to be a killer (*ghātaka*). Here the author knows only to avail himself of the not particularly convincing explanation that the designation 'eater' had a bearing only on the one who somehow incited the killer (*hantṝṇāṃ kathaṃcid preraka-bhūtasya*), but not on one completely uninvolved (*udāsīna*), who does not bring about the killing in any manner. We could also formulate, as we have already done above: the eater must neither directly nor indirectly be responsible for the killing.

Regarding variation in particular details, above all, in the arrangement of the subject-matter and **[45]** the logical linking together, most of the authors proceed, on the whole, alike. Besides,

---

135 *bhakṣaṇīyeṣu bhakṣaṇa-mātreṇa pratyavāyo, nâstîti gamyate, na tu bhakṣaṇāya prāṇi-vadhe̦ kṛte 'pīti, prāṇi-vadham a-kṛtvā māṃsârjana-saṃbhavāt, 'na hiṃsyāt sarva-bhūtāni' iti hiṃsā-pratiṣedhāc ca.*

it would indeed be sufficient for them and for the reader, to appeal to Manu rule 2, 14, according to which conflicting Vedic precepts are alternatively both valid;[136] or one assumes that the last opinion expressed is valid as *siddhânta*, the preceding contradictory one, a *pūrva-pakṣa*. However, it does occur that one unequivocal rule is quite inconsistent with the view of the time: this is true, for example, of the command to slaughter a large cow or a large goat for the guest. Here Vijñānêśvara, in his famous commentary to Yājñavalkya, the Mitâkṣarā, makes good use of the rather vague expression of his basic text: he explains the words *mahôkṣaṃ vā mahâjaṃ vā śrotriyôpakalpayet* (above p. [18] note 49) by saying that with *upakalpayet* ('he should prepare' or 'he should give to a person a person's share') is meant here: one should show an ox or a goat to a guest as meant for him symbolically but not give it to him, or slaughter it in reality, because one could not afford an ox for every single *śrotriya* and, moreover, the rule holds good that one should not do anything which does not lead to heaven and is a vexation to men, even when it is right.[137]

The author of the Kṛtyakalpataru solves the difficulty differently. He concedes that the text of Yājñavalkya demands the killing of a cow but establishes that this is no longer appropriate in the Kaliyuga and applies only to another age.[138] He thus arranges the old rule under the not insubstantial number of cases of the Kali-varjyas,[139] the commands and prohibitions which were valid in the olden times but are no longer appropriate in our iron age: a doctrine of the Smṛtis which with its noteworthy acknowledgement of a change which occurred in customs and opinions can be regarded as a modest attempt to put it into historical perspective.

It has been extraordinarily difficult to obtain a picture of the actual spread of vegetarianism up to the present day. No statistics document it; **[46]** literary testimonies which of course could be collected in large numbers, are not necessarily a reliable reflection

---

136 *śruti-dvaidhaṃ tu yatra syāt, tatra dharmāv ubhau smṛtau / ubhāv api hi tau dharmau samyag uktau manīṣibhiḥ.*

137 *mahāntam ukṣāṇam dhaureyaṃ mahâjaṃ vā śrotriyāyôkta-lakṣaṇāyôpakalpayet, 'bhavad-artham ayam asmābhiḥ parikalpita' iti tat-prīty-arthaṃ, na tu dānâya vyāpādanâya vā, yathā 'sarvam etad bhavadīyam' iti prati-śrotriyam ukṣâsaṃbhavāt, 'a-svargyaṃ loka-vidviṣṭaṃ dharmyam apy ācaren na tu' iti niṣedhāc ca.*

138 III 190: *atra yady api gṛhâgata-śrotriya-tṛpty-arthaṃ go-vadhaḥ kartavya iti pratīyate, tathâpi kaliyuge nâyaṃ dharmaḥ, kiṃtu yugântare.*

139 Cf. perhaps Kane 1977 (VI) Index see under Kali Age.

of actual practice, particularly because they predominantly originate from brahmins: but it is not doubtful that vegetarianism is first of all and preeminently a brahmanic custom.[140] The relativist ethics of Hinduism allots each caste its proper codex of obligations, so that what is prohibited for one can be permitted to another; thereby the ritual and customary demands are always the highest for the brahmins. Leaving aside the pariahs, there are many lower castes which are, therefore, not vegetarian; but even the warring nobility is by and large absolved from *ahiṃsā* – not only because, as we saw above (p. [32]), it was not inclined to renounce hunting, but also because its typical caste duty is bloody battle.

As a chiefly brahmanic custom, vegetarianism had a strong tendency to ever increasing expansion because social distinction clings to all brahmanic customs and, therefore, adoption of brahmanic regulations or at least attempts to approximate them promises an improvement of the social classification of a caste; it is well-known how this tendency has created a hindrance to social reform in issues such as child-marriage (Bruhn 2008: 11; 102) or the prohibition on widows remarrying (Bruhn 2008: 101f. [WB]).

A modern Indian expert, P.V. Kane,[141] comments on the modern state of affairs as follows: 'Gradually large sections of the population of India gave up flesh-eating and even those who did not regard it as forbidden to them rarely partook of it, or did so in an apologetic way. The spread of Vaiṣṇavism tended to wean people away from flesh as required by the Bhāgavatapurāṇa (VII 15, 7–8)[142] **[47]** which

---

140 Yet, the assertion of Patil (1946: 214): 'Megasthenes and Strabo state that the caste of philosophers abstained from animal food' is quite wrong because the renunciation of meat-eating and sexual intercourse recorded by the brahmins (Breloer-Böhmer 1939: 28; McCrindle 1926: 99) ensued only during their state as a religious student, of *brahmacarya*; a few lines further on it is added then that when the brahmins commence worldly life after 37 years, they eat meat with the exception of the meat of animals used for work (which may have excluded cattle). Megasthenes thus explicitly testifies the converse of what Patil ascribes to him (see also Haussleiter 1935: 46; ibid., p. 44 and 53 in which all the ancient information on Indian vegetarianism is collected).

141 Kane II/2: 780. Kane's very detailed description of the meat-eating problem is an exceedingly commendable collection of matter, but he does not succeed in sorting out historically the conflicting statements in the texts.

142 *na dadyād āmiṣaṃ śrāddhe na câdyād dharma-tattva-vit / muny-annaiḥ syāt parā prītis tathā na paśu-hiṃsayā // etādṛśaḥ paro dharmo nṛṇāṃ sad-dharmam icchatām.*

is to the Vaiṣṇavas what the Bible is to the Christians. In medieval and modern times all *brāhmaṇas* avoid flesh (except some *brāhmaṇas* in northern and eastern India who hold that fish may be eaten); so also do many *vaiśyas*, particularly those who are Vaiṣṇavas, and even among *śūdras* there are many who do not touch flesh and regard abstention from flesh as meritorious. From ancient times the *kṣatriyas* have been meat-eaters.'[143]

What we have learnt about the significance of sacrifice for the evolution of *ahiṃsā* and vegetarianism enables us now to comprehend still more precisely the role of the reform religions of Buddhism and Jainism within this central Indian movement. The essential distinction between them and their Brahmanic adversaries is that, with them, thanks to their heterodoxy, the new ideal did not clash with the heavy impediment of the tradition as cult of sacrifice and further animal-killing customs. One of their most essential motivations was indeed resistance against and attack on the whole sacrifice system which had degenerated into an over-elaborate ritual science and the arrogance of its brahmanic supporters, whereby – as perhaps the above-discussed Vasu story (p. [39]) shows – *ahiṃsā* could indeed afterwards become the chief point of view, although to begin with this was not by any means apparent.

This is illustrated by two precious creations of old ascetic poetry which are preserved for us in one of the oldest texts of the Jain canon, the Uttarajjhāyā.[144] Both describe the appearance of a Jain monk at a place of sacrifice and his argument with the brahmanic sacrificers. In both, the Jain monk does not come in order to protest against the bloody sacrifice; on his normal begging-tour he simply calls and requests a share of the sacrificial repast, which in both cases is denied to him as a non-brahmin. In the ensuing verbal skirmish, the Jain instructs the sacrificers in phrases, many of which can be found just so in Buddhism, on the perversity of their doings, on the true brahminhood and the true and proper sacrifice: **[48]** One becomes and is a brahmin not through birth but through right conduct; the true brahmin is the Jain monk, the proper sacrifice is his ascetic way

143 Bühler states in his Report of 1877: 23 that the Kashmir brahmins collectively eat not only fish but also lamb and goat's meat.

144 Chap. 12: Hariesijjaṃ, and 25: Jannaijjaṃ, translation by Jacobi in *SBE* XLV. In our context it is irrelevant that Chap. 12 has a parallel in a Jātaka (treated by Charpentier 1908: 171ff. and in the commentary to his textual edition); here only the Jinistic frame of the narration matters. – For another parallel see Hemacandra, Pariśiṣṭaparvan 5, 9f. (WB).

of life. To this naturally belongs also the *ahiṃsā*, but the polemic against brahmanic sacrifice is not at all concentrated on *ahiṃsā*. It appears in a sequence with all the other requirements of ascetic life and most of all in its characteristic extension or generalization of non-violence to all the elements (cf. above p. [14f.]) that is, without any special reference to the sacrificial victim.

Therefore, in Uttar. 12, 38f. it is said:

> Why do you brahmins kindle fire[145] and seek external cleansing with water? The external purity which you seek is not looked upon by the wise as a good sacrifice! *Kuśa*-gras, sacrificial pole, straw, wood, fire, touching water morning and evening (and thereby) injuring the animated elements[146] – you fools commit ever more transgressions.[147]

In the next stanza, to the question addressed to him, how then one should sacrifice properly, the Jain then answers in vs 41: 'Not violating (*a-samārabhantā!*) the six classes of souls,[148] abstaining from falsehood, (not taking) that what is not given, property, women, pride, deceit – renouncing these, men under self-restraint are wandering.'[149]

Except for the passages reproduced here, there is nowhere in the entire chapter any reference to *ahiṃsā*. In the 45 stanzas of chapter 25, it appears likewise only twice. In the section comprising 14 stanzas on everything that constitutes the true brahmin, it says in vs 23: 'Whoever is fully cognizant of all moving as well as the immobile beings; whoever does no injury to them in the three-fold

---

145 An equally good or better translation could be: 'violating the fire'. In any case, the handling of fire here is signified as *hiṃsā*, cf. above p. [15].

146 Jacobi translates: 'living beings' which may likewise be possible, but it appears clear to me that the Jain is sermonizing on non-violence to all the elements.

147 *kiṃ māhaṇā joisaṃ, ārabhantā udaeṇa sohiṃ bahiyā vimaggaha? / jaṃ maggahā bāhiriyaṃ visohiṃ, na taṃ suiṭṭhaṃ kusalā vayanti // kusaṃ ca jūvaṃ taṇa-kaṭṭham aggiṃ sāyaṃ ca pāyaṃ udagaṃ phusantā / pāṇāi bhūyāi viheḍayantā bhujjo vi mandā pagareha pāvaṃ.*

148 These are, as the fourth chapter of the Dasaveyāliya (Chajjīvaṇiyā) named after them ennumerates, those embodied in the four elements earth, water, fire and air just as the souls of plants and of moving beings.

149 Utt 12, 41: *chajjīva-kāe a-samārabhantā mosaṃ a-dattaṃ ca a-sevamāṇā / pariggahaṃ itthio māṇa-māyaṃ eyaṃ parinnāya caranti dantā.*

manner (in thought, word and deed), him we call a brahmin,'[150] and in vs 30: 'The tying of animals (to the sacrificial pole), all the Vedas and **[49]** performing sacrifices do not protect the wicked from the karma of sinful deeds,[151] for the karmas are powerful.'[152] Even in this unique direct mention of animal sacrifice this stands only as one piece of a more comprehensive whole.

It can only be concluded from this that for the Jains, opposition to brahmanic sacrifice was, at least to begin with, only a part of the overall battle against brahmanic religion and brahmanic arrogance, in the course of which the main accent was by no means on *ahiṃsā*, and animal sacrifice as such was scarcely stressed. When then, later, a sharp attack especially on animal-sacrifice ensues, it occurs through the adoption of the brahmanic story of King Vasu, so that here too, the Jains only follow the example given by the brahmins themselves. This can indeed only signify that Jainism – and the same holds true a fortiori of Buddhism – was not the actual source of *ahiṃsā*, which, as often assumed, had spread from the reform religions to the brahmanic religion. Rather it is the case that Buddhism and Jainism are only a part of a common Indian spiritual movement (*Geistesbewegung*), to which they had a particularly favourable predisposition and which, therefore, caught on with them and was pursued with extraordinary zeal.

This should be taken into consideration in the interpretation and evaluation of the justifiably most famous and frequently cited testimonies for ancient Indian vegetarianism in the inscriptions of the Emperor Aśoka, the particular value of which lies in the fact that we finally have here, once and for all, quite a strong historical foothold. While we can only assign a fundamentally important work such as Manu's rather vaguely to the period between the second century BCE and the second century CE (and here we need to orient ourselves to the upper rather than the lower limit), Aśoka can be clearly dated to the middle of the third century BCE – in some instances, to the very year. The inscriptions which the emperor had put on rocks and columns according to the Achaemenid prototype are, as is well-known, chiefly literally moral sermons to his people. Already in the first of the fourteen great Rock Edicts, we read the

150 *tasa-pāṇe viyāṇettā saṃgaheṇa ya thāvare / jo na hiṃsai ti-viheṇa, taṃ vayaṃ būma māhaṇaṃ.*

151 I have corrected *-kammuṇā* to *-kammuṇo*.

152 *pasu-bandhā savva-veyā ya jaṭṭhaṃ ca pāva-kammuṇo / na taṃ tāyanti dussīlaṃ, kammāṇi balavanti hi.*

fundamental sentence: 'There should not be any killing of a living being here for sacrifice.'[153] A little later are seen the often quoted sentences:

> Formerly many hundreds of thousands of living beings were being killed to make curry in the kitchen of the god-beloved king Piyadassi; **[50]** now, after the decree of this religious edict not more than three living beings were killed, two peacocks and one gazelle, but later even these three living beings will not be killed any more.[154]

More than once non-violence to living beings[155] appears in a list of virtues recommended to the people and, in the eighth Rock Edict, the emperor contrasts his pilgrimage to the abode of Buddha's enlightenment to the hunting expeditions of earlier rulers. The inscription in the Greek language, found in Afghanistan in 1958, even asserts that hunting and fishing were discontinued in the realm of Aśoka and, without further ado, makes him a vegetarian[156] using the phrase ἀπέχεται τῶν ἐμψύχων common in the Greek discussion about vegetarianism. Here at least the assertion about hunting and fishing should be taken no more literally than the 'many hundreds of thousands' of animals slaughtered daily in the imperial kitchens. The passage of the fourth Rock Edict, where the emperor boasts that due to his moral teaching the non-killing and non-violation of living beings (mentioned first in a list of virtues) had increased to such an extent as had not been the case for many hundreds of years. That he would support a further increase and hoped that his descendants would act similarly, is quite an impressive proof of historical development.[157]

---

153 *hida no kiṃci jīvaṃ ālabhitu pajohitaviye.*

154 *puluvaṃ mahānasasi devânaṃpiyasa Piyadasine lājine anudivasaṃ bahūni pāna-sata-sahasāni ālabhiyisu sūpaṭhāye. se aja adā iyaṃ dhamma-lipī likhitā tiṃni yeva pānāni ālabhiyaṃti, duve majūlā eke mige, se pi cu mige no dhuvaṃ; etāni pi cu tiṃni pānāni pachā no ālabhiyisaṃti.*

155 Rock Edict. III *jīvesu anālaṃbhe sādhu (Kālsi: pānānaṃ anālaṃbhe sādhu)*; IX *pānesu (pānānaṃ) saṃyame*; XI *pānānaṃ anālambhe.*

156 Journal Asiatique 1958: 3.

157 *ādise bahūhi vasa-satehi no hūta-puluve, tādise aja vaḍhite devânaṃpiyasa Piyadasine lājine dhaṃmânusathiyā an-ālaṃbhe pānānaṃ avihisā bhūtānam nātisu saṃpaṭipati samana-bābhanesu saṃpaṭipati māti-pitu-susūsā. esa aṃne ca bahuvidhe dhaṃma-calane vaḍhite, vaḍhayisati ceva devânaṃpiye Piyadasi lājā dhaṃma-calanaṃ imaṃ ...*

The fifth Pillar Edict is nearly entirely dedicated to the protection of animals. It begins with a long list of animals which the king prohibits from killing, followed by supplementary regulations regarding days on which there is not to be any slaughtering or castration, etc.; the end of the edict is a short sentence reporting the decree of twenty-five amnesties in twenty-six years of office. In the animal list, we find a series of old acquaintances of inedible animals from the Smṛti-lists. That Aśoka's list historically belongs together with these lists of the law-books is shown by, among other things, the regulation that also not be killed are chiefly 'all four-footed **[51]** animals which are not working animals a n d a r e n o t e a t e n'[158] – also in this Edict (first issued towards the conclusion of the reign) the relishing of other animals is presumed to be normal and not prohibited or even disapproved of.

Further, Hultzsch (Inscriptions of Aśoka p. 218 n.8) has detected in the Kauṭilīya Arthaśāstra an exact parallel to some regulations on forbidden slaughter days, etc. The decree of these edicts thus shows Aśoka as only a normal Hindu sovereign; it has nothing to do with his Buddhism. That he – quite naturally – interprets his animal protection regulations, regardless of their traditional pre-vegetarian character, in the light of the new *ahiṃsā* thinking so strongly dominating him, is shown in a passage at the conclusion of the seventh ('separate') Pillar Edict only available in Delhi Topra:

> This increase of the piety of the people, I have brought about in a two-fold manner: through religious prescription and through (friendly) exhortations. Of these (two), however, the religious prescription is unimportant; through (friendly) exhortation much more can be attained. It was a religious prescription, for example, that I decreed: 'such and such (animal) species are not to be killed'. There are, however, many more religious prescriptions, which I have ordered. However, through (friendly) exhortations, a higher level of the growth of people's piety came to be reached with the objective of non-injury to beings and non-killing of animals.[159]

---

158 *save catupade ye paṭibhogaṃ no eti na ca khādiyati.*

159 *munisānaṃ cu yā iyaṃ dhaṃma-vaḍhi vaḍhitā duvehi yeva ākālehi: dhaṃma-niyamena ca nijhatiyā ca. tata cu lahu se dhaṃma-niyame, nijhatiyā va bhuye. dhaṃma-niyame cu kho esa ye me iyaṃ kaṭe: imāni ca imāni jātāni avadhiyāni. aṃnāni pi cu bahukāni dhaṃma-niyamāni yāni me kaṭāni. nijhatiyā va cu bhuye munisānaṃ dhaṃma-vaḍhi vaḍhitā avihiṃsāye bhūtānaṃ.*

To what extent are the sayings cited above an outpouring of Aśoka's Buddhism?

In his inscriptions the emperor attests more than once that he was a pious Buddhist; in the Small Rock Edict, he even relates his conversion and his initially very modest but, later, growing religious zeal. Apart from these personal avowals, however, in all the edicts intended for the people (as distinct from those directed to the Buddhist community) anything specifically Buddhist is missing; neither is the name of the Buddha found nor does a single one of the essentially Buddhist terms and items of doctrine appear. One has tried to explain this striking contrast with the doctrine of morals and customs preached here as being a kind of simplified **[52]** layman's Buddhism or Buddhism *in statu nascendi*;[160] yet it appears to me quite certain that the removal of anything specifically Buddhist is a state-political act of the characteristic Indian religious tolerance, which the emperor announces in the famous twelfth Rock Edict in classical phrases. What he preaches to the entire population should be likewise acceptable to the followers of all religions (and actually is largely the people's normal popular religion of the time, as is reflected in the pre-Buddhist *gāthā*s of the Jātakas or of the Dhammapada). Thereby the possibility of considering the *ahiṃsā* of the edicts as specifically Buddhist – as is often the case – is ruled out.

At only one place does the emperor reveal himself as a Buddhist: scarcely any Hindu monarch of his time would have written: 'No animal should be killed as a sacrifice here.' This sentence should by no means simply be seen as a general prohibition on sacrifice. If the emperor had wished to issue such a decree – which must be doubted in view of his former religious policy – he would probably have expressed himself much more decidedly. On the one hand, Hultzsch (1925: 2, note 3) wants to understand the use of 'here', with which the edict begins, as 'in my territory' and refers for that to two places of the Rock Edict 13 and one in Rūpnāth. The last is very doubtful:

160 See Hultzsch 1925: XLIXf., LIII. Compared to this, Lamotte 1958: 255 is right; cf. the present author, 1960: 66. In an essentially certainly pertinent manner K.V. Rangaswami's excellent introduction to the Edicts of Aśoka, Adyar Library 1951 (p. XIX) expounds the non-Buddhist, 'brahmanic' character of Aśoka's *dharma*: 'the background of life and belief in Aśoka's time furnished by Dharmaśāstras has not received adequate attention.'

the 'here' is probably a simple mistake.[161] In RE 13 (Q) 'here' stands in contrast to 'in the frontier regions', and in the next sentence (R) the 'here' is complemented by the statement 'in the king's empire'; this expression stands in contrast to the foreign kingdoms mentioned immediately before.

When, on the other hand, one sees how RE 2 begins with the words 'Throughout in the empire of the king' (*savata vijitasi devânaṃ-piyasa Piyadasine lājine*) and how, also in RE 3, the emperor defines the domain of his measures by 'throughout my empire' (*savata vijitasi mama*), the plain 'here', directly in the beginning of the first **[53]** of the fourteen edicts and for a well-nigh unheard-of measure like a general prohibition on sacrifice sounds much too weak: one rather has the impression that the sovereign is announcing a good example which he personally sets in his immediate circle.

This exhortation of *hida* is confirmed by RE 5 (M), where the eastern (and northwestern) text speaks of *hida ca bāhilesu ca nagalesu* 'here and in the outward cities', while Girnar certainly interprets the emperor's intention correctly by substituting *hida* with *Pāṭalipute*. The interpretation of *hida* of RE 1 (B), too, in the sense of 'here in Pāṭaliputra at the emperor's court' (which Rangaswami Aiyangar also advocates, loc. cit., p. XXI) is thus further supported in that the entire greater second part of the edict reports only one further good example at the imperial court, namely, the reduction of the daily slaughtering in the palace kitchen. For all that, it is nevertheless noteworthy that, even in the measures dealt with in this edict, a reference to the Buddha and his Doctrine, as could be commonly expected, is missing.

So we may well say in conclusion that even Aśoka's *ahiṃsā* and vegetarianism are not of Buddhist origin, but are part of the common Indian religious evolution, although they have been favoured and strengthened through his Buddhism.

Now if the magical awe of extinguishing life was alien to the Indo-Aryans, and we cannot even regard the reform-religions as its source – from where does *ahiṃsā* really come? From where does it begin

161 Hultzsch (1925: 167 n. 9) says that the *hadha* of the text is in any case incorrect in this form: 'Bühler and Senart corrrect *hidha*. Instead of it, the context seems to require *yata* (= Skt. *yatra*); but this change would be so violent that it cannot be seriously entertained.' The context appears to me to require so imperatively a relative 'where' that the hypothesis of a mistake by the stone-mason or scribe cannot simply be ruled out.

the gradual but unceasing triumphal procession which makes it one of the dominant hallmarks of Indian culture?[162]

There remains hardly any answer but the one that belongs to those pre-Aryan, or so to speak 'arch-Indian' elements which were first suppressed through the Aryan conquest and for a long time remained buried, but which then gradually resurface and in their increasing persistance ultimately causing the transformation of the Aryan to the 'Hindu'. Ever since we have encountered in the pre-Aryan Indus culture undoubted precursors of typical un-Aryan traits of Hinduism – as, for example, an earlier form of Śiva; the veneration of the phallus, the Hinduist *linga*, abhorred by the Aryans, or the sanctity of the Pipal tree, worshipped to this day, under which, according to the legend, the Buddha reached enlightenment – ever since then the assumption of the origin from a pre-Aryan source can no longer be viewed merely as the convenient assignment to an unknown quantity.

I am convinced that this assumption also turns out to be true for the belief in metempsychosis, for example, and for the **[54]** ritual formation of the caste system (as distinguished from the Aryan three- or four-tiered order of estates). Among these non- or pre-Aryan, but all the more genuine, elements of Hinduism we must, in my opinion, also class the *ahiṃsā*, the magical life-taboo; – irrespective of the fact that, as pointed out above (p. [42] note), we are compelled to ascribe the same pre-Aryan origin to the direct opposite of *ahiṃsā*, viz. the bloody Kālī sacrifices. The assumption that both manifestations have their roots in a pre-Aryan source (*Urgrund*) is in fact not stranger than their undeniable juxtaposition in modern Hinduism, which defies all consistency and logic.

Finally, also the particular cattle-taboo that cannot be explained through *ahiṃsā* alone is – at least partly – attributable to a pre-Aryan origin. Here, though, things are even more complicated, and the present investigation can even less claim to treat the subject conclusively than in the case of the common *ahiṃsā*.[163]

---

162 See, e.g. Mallebrein and von Stietencron 2008: 107 (WB).

163 However, in his note on p. [69] Alsdorf withdraws from this conclusion because of the find of cattle bones in Mohenjo-Daro, whereas Chapple 1993: 5 opines this must not mean that all inhabitants ate meat. For him a thematic continuity stretching from the Indus Valley into classical and

Mahātmā Gandhi, as a prominent representative of modern Hinduist sentiments may be asked to speak first:[164]

> The real essence of Hinduism consists in the protection of the cow. The protection of the cow is for me one of the most wonderful manifestations in the evolution of mankind. It leads mankind beyond the limits of its own species. The cow signifies to me the entire sub-human world. Through the cow mankind is led to acknowledge his one-ness and equality with all living existence. Why exactly the cow was chosen for veneration is absolutely clear to me. The cow has always been the best companion of man in India. She was the dispenser of all wealth. Not only does she give milk but also made possible agriculture. The cow is a poem of pity. One sees compassion in these gentle animals. She is the mother of millions of Indians. Protection of the cow signifies protection of all the dumb creatures of God. Certainly already our most ancient prophets venerated the cow in this sense. The call of the deeper layers of our being is all the more compelling as it remains wordless. The protection of the cow signifies the gift of Hinduism to the world, and Hinduism will last as long as there are Hindus who protect the cow.

With most respectful appreciation of the intensity and ethical height of the **[55]** religious sentiments expressed here, the western

---

modern Jainism seems evident (p. 9). – Eliade 1954: 351ff. had given similar at first sight attractive views of the connections between the Indus civilisation and Hinduism which were then criticised by Gonda 1965: 20. Doniger O'Flaherty 1980: 244f. criticizing the Indus Valley Civilisation theory asks: 'Why does it seem more likely that a new idea came into India from another culture than that it developed in the head of some Indian raised within the Vedic tradition? More specifically, what is the basis for the hypothesis that the cow (as opposed to the bull) or cattle (as opposed to horses) were venerated in the Indus Valley?' and her reply is that there are neither cows on the Indus seals nor were there horses in the Indus Valley. 'For the development of the cow imagery, we must turn to later Hinduism' (p. 246). – Seyffort Ruegg 1980: 236 thinks it improbable that vegetarianism in Buddhism, at least in the practice of very many Mahāyānists, derives from a primitive pre-Aryan source, but rather in close connection with a specific religious and philosophical teaching: the *tathāgatagarbha* doctrine. Finally, Houben 1999: 124 note 35 thinks Alsdorf's hypothesis on the source of *ahiṃsā* and vegetarianism is not quite convincing and seems to prefer a pan-Indian spiritual movement as expressed earlier by Alsdorf, p. [49] (WB).

164 Cited from Glasenapp 1943: 26.

scholar is nevertheless required to state that, in his critical view, Gandhi's explanation of the unique place of the cow in Hinduism remains quite inadequate; he must first of all contradict the belief that 'already the most ancient prophets had venerated the cow in this sense' and he can only agree with von Glasenapp when he concludes his commentary on Gandhi's observations with the sentence: 'There is no doubt that cow-worship in India can be traced back to primitive perceptions but it is difficult to establish its origin; in older Vedic times, in any case, it does not appear to have existed.' The rules about the slaughter of an ox for the guest and the latter's designation as *go-ghna* 'cow-killer' has proved to us, just as King Rantideva's mass sacrifices of cattle have (without Kālidāsa's expressing any surprise or poetically utilized disapproval) that a much more definite judgement can be passed on the conditions of the older times. Further evidence of cattle sacrifice and consumption of beef even in the late and post-Vedic period is not missing.[165]

Schlerath (1960: 133) concludes that cattle sacrifice is well attested as a living custom to the Ṛgveda. In his description of the Brāhmaṇa period,[166] Rau discusses the office at court of the *go-vikartá* 'cow-carver', whose 'position proves that his office was not disreputable in ancient times. Beef was regarded as a prized food during the Brāhmaṇa period'.

Often cited but always misunderstood is the passage ŚatBr. 3, 1, 2, 21. On it, Weber (1885: 281) says:

> Revered Yājñavalkya, the celebrated prophet of the *śuklāni yajūṃṣi*, roundly declared he would not want to miss the enjoyment (of the meat) of cow and ox (*dhenv-anaḍuhayoḥ*) 'if it only is fat': *aśnāmy evâham aṃsalaṃ ced bhavati*.[167]

Oldenberg says (1919: 209 note):

> Here I would like to mention incidentally occurring typical expressions **[56]** which, in a tone with a certain freedom

165 Summaries by Weber 1885: 280f. and Hultzsch 1925: 127 n. 8. Particularly copious (also extra-Indian) material on the entire cow-problem is offered by Crooke 1912.

166 Rau 1957: 111.

167 Weber's subsequent assertion needs no longer be refuted: 'Only Buddhism has so precisely accomplished the inviolability of the cow as it specifically set a purpose for animal-sacrifice through its *ahiṃsā*-doctrine.'

> from prejudice, make any ritual limitation out to be superfluous. After it has been said that one should not eat beef: Yājñavalkya, however, said: as for me, I eat it if only it is in order.

Jacobi writes in the *Encyclopaedia of Religion and Ethics* s. v. Cow (Hindu): 'The Śatapatha Brāhmaṇa, when prohibiting the eating of the flesh of the cow (III 1, 2, 21), adds the interesting statement: "Yājñavalkya said: 'I, for one, eat it, provided that it is tender.' Hultzsch, *loc. cit.*, merely states: 'According to the Śatapatha Brāhmana (3, 1, 2, 21) Yājñavalkya was fond of tender beef.'"' Similarly A.B. Keith in the *Cambridge History of India* (1922) I 137:

> But it was still the custom to slay a great ox or goat for the entertainment of a guest, and the great sage Yājñavalkya ate meat of milch cows and oxen, provided that the flesh was *aṃsala,* a word of doubtful import, rendered either 'firm' or 'tender' by various authorities.[168]

From the wider context of the text, it is quite clear that the prohibition of eating beef is only one of the restricting observances of the *dīkṣā*, the sacrificial consecration. Yājñavalkya, therefore, does not bypass a general food regulation, by acting as a freethinker but, on the contrary, the imposition of the restriction to the sacrificial consecration proves that, outside of it, consumption of beef was common and normal.[169]

---

168 See Mayrhofer 1992: 38 (WB).

169 Rau (1957: 64) notes of the Brāhmaṇas generally: 'The passages where food prohibitions and instructions about mixing with impure people are given, hold true only for the priesthood or while sacrifices are being made; it is here originally a matter of ritual observances of a limited duration, as I hope to prove elsewhere.' – For the Śat.Br. passage discussed above it must be added that all the various translations of *aṃsala* (from which Keith distances himself with good reason) turn out to be simple. The meaning of the word is unknown; it appears to me extremely unlikely that it would mean 'tender', 'juicy', 'good', 'fat' or something similar; it is more likely that it might signify a ritually relevant feature which, according to Yājñavalkya, makes the beef unobjectionable even during the *dīkṣā*; thereby Weber's mocking, as well as Oldenberg's 'freedom from prejudice', would become superfluous. – Thus for Alsdorf a corruption (after *aham* haplography) of *māṃsala* seems excluded (the vertical line of the *ā* is easily omitted in the Devanāgarī script. Is it a synonym of *medhya* 'destined for sacrifice' (p. [60])? [WB]).

In the ritual of the Gṛhyasūtras, cattle sacrifices play an important role. As to this Hillebrandt (1903: 73) remarks:

> Āpastamba 3, 9 mentions as occasions for the sacrifice of a cow 'a guest, the fathers, weddings, . . . Accordingly we find cattle sacrifices at the *argha*-festival (P. 1, 3, 26, etc.), at the second *aṣṭakā* (P. 3, 3, 8, etc.), at weddings and at the sacrifice of a so-called "cow on the spit".'[170]

We have already seen that the cattle sacrifice for the guest was still adhered to in the entire law-literature as it also was in the metrical Smṛtis, **[57]** but in it even the use of beef at the sacrifices for the dead can still be proven.

In a number of legal texts, we find a long list of the foods to be offered to the fathers with instructions about how long each of these foods can satisfy the fathers. Manu 3, 266–273 contains this odd menu card for the fathers. It begins with seeds, roots and fruits satisfying only for one month. There follows fish meat which satisfies for two months, and then a list of eleven kinds of meat by which the duration of satisfaction increases from three to eleven months: '. . . boar and buffalo meat satisfy them for ten months, but that of hares and tortoises for eleven months.'[171] Then vs 271 continues:

> One year *gavyena payasā pāyasena vā*; through the flesh of an old he-goat a twelve-years' satisfaction takes place. (The vegetable) Kālaśāka, (the fish) *mahā-śalka*, rhinoceros' and red goat's meat as well as honey satisfy indefinitely, and (likewise) all foods for ascetics.[172]

Bühler translates the words *gavyena payasā pāyasena vā* as 'with cow-milk and milk-rice'. However, Medhātithi's commentary, which states

170 For more on this so-called *śūla-gava* see Hillebrandt 1897: 83 (and Gonda 1980: 435ff. [with further literature in note 64], where the 'spit-ox sacrifice' is explained as 'a special animal sacrifice in honour of Rudra' (WB).

171 *daśa māsāṃs tu tṛpyanti varāha-mahiṣâmiṣaiḥ / śaśa-kūrmayor māṃsena māsān ekādaśâiva tu.*

172 *saṃvatsaraṃ tu gavyena payasā pāyasena vā / vārdhrīṇasasya māṃsena tṛptir dvādaśa-vārṣikī // kālaśākaṃ mahāśalkaḥ khaḍga-lohâmiṣaṃ madhu / ānantyāyâiva, kalpante muny-annāni ca sarvaśaḥ.*

first that *gavyena* should be connected with *payasā*, not with the *māṃsena* of the preceding line, afterwards quotes the different opinion of others who take up this rejected connection and in whose opinion one should interpret: 'Through beef or milk and milk-rice.'[173]

As a matter of fact it would be more than curious if, in the midst of this impressively long meat-list, in the case of the cow, suddenly only the milk and not the flesh would be mentioned, and we would probably even then prefer the view of the 'others' if it were not be confirmed by the Āpastamba-Dharmasūtra. For there (2, 16, 26–28) we read: *saṃvatsaraṃ gavyena prītiḥ, bhūyāṃsam ato māhiṣeṇa, etena grāmyâraṇyānāṃ paśūnāṃ māṃsaṃ medhyaṃ vyākhyātam*. Bühler translates:

> Beef satisfies (the fathers) for a year, buffalo's (meat) for a longer (time) than that. By this (permission of the use of buffalo's meat) it has been declared that the meat of (other) tame and wild animals is fit to be offered.

With this rendering of *gavya* as 'beef', he finds himself in agreement with the **[58]** commentary which explains on vs 26 (*saṃvatsaraṃ gavyena prītiḥ*) that since in the following the word 'meat' is used, here too the issue is about meat (*uttaratra māṃsa-grahaṇād ihâpi māṃsasyâiva grahaṇam*).

On examining the other legal treatises, we find in Baudhāyana no menu card for the fathers at all; in Vasiṣṭha, only one stanza,[174] in which nevertheless milk and milk-rice (*payas* and *pāyasa*) maintain a place of their own beside vegetables and meat, and that without *gavya*. When, in the face of Baudhāyana's complete silence and the scantiest treatment in Vas. and Āp., Gautama (15, 15) offers an although summarising nevertheless considerably more detailed list which, with regard to *gavya, payas* and *pāyasa*,[175] seems to agree with Manu, this may perhaps be appreciated, as in terms

---

173 *śrutânumatayoḥ śruta-sambandhasya balīyastvād gavyena payasêti sambandhaḥ, na māṃsena prākaraṇikena. anye tu ca-śabdaṃ samuccayârthaṃ paṭhi-tvā vyākhyānayanti: māṃsena gavyena payasā pāyasena vā.*

174 Vas. 11, 40: *madhu-māṃsaiś ca śākaiś ca payasā pāyasena ca / eṣa no dāsyati śrāddhaṃ varṣāsu ca maghāsu ca.*

175 I conclude this from Bühlers translation: 'The fathers are satisfied . . . , for twelve years by cow's milk and messes made of milk.' In the text edition of L. Srinivasacharya, Mysore, 1917, the only one available to me, the *Sūtra* containing the menu card for the fathers is entirely missing.

of Meyer (1927: VI), as an indication of Gautama's not belonging to the ancient authors, but 'at the end of our Smṛti-series' (Differently Thieme 1971: 442 [WB]). With the remaining authors, the lists partly differ widely with regard to the kind and sequence of the animals ennumerated as well as to the specified periods of satisfaction, without showing a simple way to sort out this jumble or explain it meaningfully.

As to beef, milk and milk-rice, Viṣṇu (80, 12) has the formulation *saṃvatsaraṃ gavyena payasā tad-vikārair vā,*[176] and quite similarly Kātyāyana cited in the Kṛtyakalpataru IV p. 43 expresses himself; but his wording: ... *nava meṣa-māṃsena, daśa māhiṣeṇa, ekādaśa pārṣatena, saṃvatsaraṃ gavyena pāyasena payasā vā* scarcely admits of a different interpretation than: '... by beef or through milk-rice and milk.' This is confirmed by him prescribing, as a preliminary, that the meat of he-goats, oxen and rams should only be used when it stems from sacrified animals, while for other kinds of meat this restriction does not apply.[177] Completely unequivocal is finally the Paiṭhīnasi also cited in the Kṛtyakalpataru (VI 44) **[59]** who, in several instances before, has *pāyasena* altogether separate from *gavyena*. In his text: ... *ājena māṃsena pañca, pāyasena ṣaṇ māsān, śākunena sapta māsān, aṣṭau māsān aiṇeyena, nava māsān gavyena, ekādaśa māsān māhiṣeṇa,* one can translate *gavyena* only by 'beef'.

In recapitulation, we may state that beef originally belongs to the most favoured kinds of meat prescribed for the *śrāddha*-meal (and thus consumed by the brahmins invited to this meal). Several legal texts still convey this quite unequivocally; others completely omit beef; still others (just as Manu) apparently use the ambiguity of the expression *gavya* 'bovine' in order to avoid a clear declaration that possibly had become offensive then. Thus it is also significant that the older Manu commentary by Medhātithi, which today is recognised by us as the best one, still transmits the correct interpretation of *gavyena* alongside the wrong one, while Kullūka, who in India later came to the fore, only presents the incorrect one prevalent today.

---

176 Shortly before in the enumeration, Viṣṇu (80, 9) mentions the Gayal (domesticated ox), and Jolly translates *gāvayena* by 'beef'. This, however, is not exact because, as we know from the well-known typical example of the logicians for the analogism, the *gavaya* is only *go-sadṛśa*, 'cow-like'.

177 *chāgôsra-meṣā ālabdhāḥ, śeṣāni kṛtvā labdhvā vā svayaṃ mṛtānāṃ vâhṛtya pacet.* The author of the Kṛtyakalpataru subsequently explains *usra* by *anaḍvān*.

To the positive testimonies for cattle-sacrifice and beef-consumption enumerated so far, we may add a not unimportant negative one for cow-protection and veneration. When, as we noted above on p. [50], Aśoka proclaims an animal-protection edict, we should expect the cow at the top of the list of animals not to be killed. This is not only not the case; indeed the list actually includes the *ṣaṇḍaka*, the released bull that is, and when the prohibition to kill this sacred object of a pious donation emerges as all too intelligible and in fact self-evident, it follows from the particularization of the prohibition that, for cattle other than the released bulls, a prohibition to kill did not exist in the middle of the third century BCE and was not proclaimed by the pious emperor.

In accordance with this, the cow is completely missing in Manu, Yājñavalkya and Viṣṇu from the list of the animals not to be eaten (above on p. [17]), and even in Baudhāyana can at best be understood as included in the prohibition on eating any domesticated animal except goats and sheep. In Meyer's (1927: 46) opinion, Manu, Yājñ. and Viṣṇu considered it 'certainly not worthwhile, even so much as to mention that the cow is not to be eaten'. That is even less credible when in the oldest Dharmasūtras we find an explicit, although, as we shall see, restricted permit on eating cows and oxen. Vas. 14, 45f. reads: *dhenv-anaḍuhāv a-panna-dantāś ca. bhakṣyau tu dhenv-anaḍuhau medhyau* **[60]** *vājasaneyake vijñāyate.* Bühler translates this as: 'Not milch-cows, draught-oxen, and animals whose milk teeth have not dropped out. It is declared in the Vājasaneyaka that (the flesh of) milch-cows and oxen is fit for offerings.' Bühler has, no doubt inadvertently, left untranslated the word *bhakṣyau* in the text. Except for this, Meyer (1927: 46) objects to the translation of *medhya* with 'fit for offerings'; it would be much more likely to mean: 'magical-ritually pure'. Accordingly he translates: 'However, in the Vājasaneyaka(-brāhmaṇa) the statement from the Scriptures is found that milch-cow and draught-oxen are kosher animals and thus edible.'

Now this Sūtra 46 of Vas. evidently corresponds exactly with the two *sūtras* Āp. 1, 17, 30f.: *dhenv-anaḍuhor bhakṣyam. medhyam ānaḍuham iti Vājasaneyakam*, '(meat of) cow and ox is edible. According to the Vājasaneyaka, ox-meat suitable for sacrifice (is edible).' Here what Vas. has comprised into one *sūtra* is simply spread over two. In view of the evident parallelism, there can be no question of correcting, as done by Meyer, Āpastamba's *bhakṣyam* to its opposite *a-bhakṣyam*. Meyer substantiates his correction with the fact that in Āp. there is evidently the same contrast between the author's own doctrine and that of the former (of Vāj.) as that with Vas. Now in fact in Vas. 14, 45 the consumption of beef and ox-meat is generally prohibited, but in 46 an apparently opposite doctrine of Vāj. is quoted. However, we have exactly the same contrast also according to the uncorrected text of Āp., where *sūtra* 29 enumerates the cow as the last of a series of inedible animals,[178] followed by the two *sūtras* 30f. just discussed with Vāj.'s doctrine.

I believe that everything will become clear when we understand the word *medhya* correctly in a very succinct sense in that we recall Kātyāyana's rule reproduced above (p. [58]), viz. that beef should be eaten at the Śrāddha only when it originates from sacrified animals: *medhya* is in the Vāj. quotation, which is common to Āp. and Vas., not simply 'suitable for sacrifice', but 'destined for sacrifice', consecrated for sacrifice or, more freely expressed, 'originating from a sacrificial animal'.

Accordingly I render Vas. 14, 45f.: 'cow and ox as well as animals whose milk-teeth have not yet fallen out (are prohibited), but according to Vājasaneyaka's doctrine cow and ox are edible, when it concerns sacrificial animals.' Consequently, the concurrent doctrine of Āp., Vas. and Kāty. is that beef should only be eaten if it originates from a sacrificial animal. This rule will naturally become superfluous as soon as the claim is raised that only sacrificed or consecrated meat should be eaten. Earlier we **[61]** noted that this claim is characteristic for the second layer of the legal literature, the metrical Smṛtis, yet is still alien to the first layer, the Dharmasūtras. We see this again confirmed now by the fact that our ancient authors mention a special rule on beef ascribed by themselves to an ancient Vedic authority, which becomes superfluous through the later general limitation of meat consumption to sacrificial meat, and hence can also be omitted by later authors such as Manu and Yājñ.[179]

178 *eka-khurôṣṭra-gavaya-grāma-sūkara-śarabha-gavām.*

179 If the interpretation presented here is correct, then at least in this respect it is clearly proven that Gautama is our latest Smṛti for he teaches in 17, 30: *dhenv-anaḍuhau ca,* and 31: *a-panna-dad-avasanna-vṛthā-māṃsāni,* (Bühler:) '(Nor) milk-cows and draught-oxen. Nor the flesh of animals whose milk-teeth have not fallen out, which are diseased, nor the meat of those (which have been killed) for no (sacred) purpose.' Therefore, the prohibition on cow and ox is not followed here by permission to use the beef of sacrificial animals, thus limiting the prohibition but, on the contrary, by the general prohibition characteristic for the later Smṛtis regarding non-ritual meat (*vṛthā-māṃsa*).

For the purpose of our investigation it follows that, at least in the theory of certain ritual directions, the cow already had a certain special position in the late-Vedic period, in as much as its killing and its consumption are only allowed at a sacrifice at which, however, they remain common and permitted. This does, on the one hand, accord with what we shall have yet to say on the position of the cow in the Veda and has, on the other hand, evidently still nothing to do with *ahiṃsā* and the cow-taboo in the modern sense.

The Gahapatijātaka (199) shows, for example, that the rule to consume only the beef of sacrificial animals was, however, by no means generally followed in that at a famine the inhabitants of a village let the patil give them an old cow, the meat of which (vs 2: *maṃsaṃ jaraggavaṃ*) they eat and promise to pay back in rice two months after the new harvest. The account of the consumption of the old cow is all the more credible as this feature is only of secondary significance for the story, which is actually a story of adultery. It is of particular interest, however, as a striking refutation of the rationalist explanation or justification of the sanctification of the cow which reads into it the judicious protection of the indispensable working helper and milk-supplier before its destruction in times of hunger.

A testimony to beef consumption which again admittedly cannot be accurately dated, but in any case is comparably late, is the most well-known medical text-book, the Suśruta-Saṃhitā. At this point, it goes without saying **[62]** that physicians are basically characterized by a remarkable unscrupulousness with regard to meat eating. In the important chapter on foodstuffs and their medical qualities and therapeutic value, meat plays a significant role; and a formal cook-book of meat dishes and broths, presented to us on that occasion, stresses that it is not a matter of grey scientific theory. Physicians, however, do not make any distinction at all between kosher and non-kosher animals: among the numerous animals they divide into a number of classes according to various principles and of which they specify the qualities of their meat, those permitted and those prohibited by the Dharma works stand indiscriminately side by side and mixed up.

With Suśruta (*Sūtrasthāna*, Chap. 46) the cow – after the horse and the mule, but before ass, camel, goat, sheep and fat-tailed sheep – belongs to the 'village animals' (*grāmya*), and in vs 89 it is said: 'Beef is a good remedy for asthma, cough, catarrh, chronic fever, exhaustion and for quick digestion; it is purifying (*pavitra*) and alleviates wind.'[180] Moreover, Suśruta (*Śarīrasthāna* 3) deals with pregnancy whims. First he explains the well-known doctrine according to which, in order to avoid disadvantageous consequences for the child, such cravings must be fulfilled; then for a series of cravings he lists what from them can be concluded for the nature of the expected child. In vs 25 he says: '(With a longing) to eat a monitor lizard's meat (she gives birth to) a sleepy and stubborn (*dhāraṇâtmaka*) son, (with a longing) for beef, by contrast, a strong one and one forbearing all hardships.'[181] Now pregnancy whims, particularly also for impossible or offensive and forbidden things (for example, blood or human flesh), are certainly favourite fairy-tale motives; but when a medical textbook enumerates cravings which, according to its instructions, must be complied with, the objects of these cravings can only be 'possible' and 'proper', and if in this context beef is actually connected with an extremely favourable prognosis for the child, we can only deduce from this, just as from the treatment of beef in the chapter on foodstuffs, **[63]** that for Suśruta beef is not only an inoffensive but even an esteemed food.

In its original form Suśruta's textbook belongs 'at the latest to the first century of our era'; but the text we have now has been completed and revised, and that either in the sixth or the tenth century.[182] What we read in it can still be much older than 'Suśruta', but on the other hand the revisor (*pratisaṃskartṛ*) in the sixth or tenth century has still kept it. We can, therefore, formulate accordingly: in the special tradition of physicians, beef is an esteemed food, and a craving for it during pregnancy – which can and must be fulfilled – is a good omen; an important doctor of at least the sixth, perhaps even of the tenth century CE, did not see any occasion to suppress the passages teaching this.

Accordingly we have ample evidence of cow slaughter – even non-sacral – and beef consumption in Indian antiquity and right up to the Middle Ages. Moreover, how significant a role is played by the cow already in the oldest period of the Vedic religion is so well-

---

180 *śvāsa-kāsa-pratiśyāya-viṣama-jvara-nāśanam / śramâtyagni-hitaṃ gavyaṃ pavitram anilâpaham*. Bhishagratna's translation (1907: I 487) runs: 'Beef is holy and refrigerant, proves curative in dyspnoea, catarrh, cough, chronic fever and in cases of a morbid craving for food (*atyagni*), and destroys the deranged *vāyu*.' – See also Jha 2004: 99 where *pavitra* is rendered by 'holy' (WB).

181 *godhā-māṃsâśane putraṃ su-ṣupsaṃ dhāraṇâtmakam / gavāṃ māṃse tu balinaṃ sarva-kleśa-sahaṃ tathā* (sc. *prasūyate*).

182 See Renou-Filliozat II 1953 § 1635.

known that there is no need for a closer explanation; it was after all the most important possession of the Aryan, just as that of the Italic peoples, with whom *pecunia*, derived from *pecus* 'livestock',[183] became the term for money; *gaviṣṭi*, 'search for cows, need of cows' are familiar Ṛgvedic terms for the campaign or raid.[184] Thus the whole Ṛgveda is full of heavenly bulls and cows, of cow and milk symbolism, wherein poetic metaphor and mythological speculation reciprocally fructify and often blend inextricably. With the Iranian cousins things are, as is well-known, similar, although the Iranists' dispute about the significance of the cow, and its protection under Zarathuštra makes it difficult for the Indologist to refer to the circumstances there comparatively. Nevertheless there is one feature in particular which appears to me as clear as it is characteristic.

In the classical Hindu ritual, as it holds good still today, the five products of the cow, the *pañcagavya*, to which urine and dung belong along with milk, sour milk and butter, are important purificatory and cleansing agents. The prescriptions of the law texts concerning the utilization of the first two, which are to be consumed for atonement too, have often excited the scorn and disgust of modern Europeans. It is less known that even with the Indian Zoroastrians, the Parsis, **[64]** cow urine actually plays an exceptional role. It is precisely the member of this small religious community, which is considered particularly progressive and open to modernity, who are, for example, still essentially bound to washing hands, feet and face with cow's urine as the first thing after getting up in the morning.[185]

---

183 *Pecus* ~ Sa. *paśu* 'cattle, domestic animal' (MW) is, however, a general term, not 'cow' (WB).

184 Cf. Jha 2004: 38 (WB).

185 In his book *Zoroastrian Theology from the earliest times to the present day*, Dhalla, 'High priest of the Parsis of North-western India', writes (1914: 309): 'Bull's urine, or golden water, as it is now called, has been an indispensable article in the purificatory rites and ceremonial ablutions among the Zoroastrians from the earliest times . . . A most extravagant sanctity came to be attached to the drinking of it. Elaborate rituals are now performed over the liquid, and the drinking of this consecrated fluid forms an indissoluble part of certain Zoroastrian ceremonials . . . this sanctified liquid is the very life of religion.' (p. 350) 'The very first thing that a Parsi is expected to do immediately after leaving his bed is to take a handful of bull's, or cow's or she-goat's urine and, upon reciting a spell composed in Pazand, to rub it over his face, hand and feet. The reformer declared that the filthy practice was highly objectionable, and should be done away with. This shocked the sentiment of righteousness in the orthodox believer. He retorted that the liquid had great purifying

As the rules on cow's urine, the *gaomez*, already appear in the Awesta, the conclusion is inevitable that in ancient Aryan time, before the Aryan immigration to India that is, the Aryans used the urine of the cow for ritual purification. With the Aryans, therefore, the cow was sacred – if one does not want to understand that word incorrectly – which, however, did not stand in the way of its slaughter and consumption: it is not particularly remarkable that a sacred animal is actually favoured for sacrifice, but it is crucial that 'cow protection' in the modern Hindu sense, which is characterized by a taboo on slaughter and a prohibition on consumption, is not yet the point.

Or can after all perhaps a first sign of protest against cow slaughter be found, does one root of the *ahiṃsā* extend into the Ṛgveda?

Wilhelm Schulze (1933: 207) wrote:

> Early on the protection of the obligation to humanity at least started to be extended early onto the animals. Even beginnings of a development which has been stringently brought to a conclusion in the Indian religions as *ahiṃsā*, are to be found already in ancient Hellas ... They will have continued the certainly age-old prohibition to sacrifice the workmate of man, the plough-bullock, **[65]** which, handed down in connection with the previously discussed burial obligation, certainly finds its proper place also in the ἀραὶ βουζύγειοι, and to which one must connect the fact that in Ṛg- and Atharvaveda *aghnya* (literally 'what should not be killed') confronts us as a familiar kenning of the cow, which was destined to become a sacred animal to the Indians.

Referring to this, B. Schlerath recently used the word *aghnya* as the main argument for the thesis 'that there must have been an opposition (to the cow sacrifice) in the Ṛgveda'.[186] He points out that

qualities, and its use should be continued ... Tracts and pamphlets were issued on both sides, and a heated controversy ensued in the Parsi press. The reformer today has given up the practice altogether, but the orthodox continues still most scrupulously to use it every morning.'

186 Schlerath 1960: 133. In any case it appears to me misleading to conclude from Atharvaveda 12, 4 and 5 'which threaten the violator of the brahmins' cow with punishment', 'that the rejection of slaughtering and the particular tending of dairy-farming belonged to the priestly circles'.

aghnya is an inherited word, because it agrees with the ancient Iranian *agənyā* 'cow' in Yašt 38, 5. It is not clearly expressed why the cow should not be killed, but most of the verses in which it is named *aghnyā* speak of her as a producer of milk. After examining some references, he is finally of the opinion that:

> When we compare the Rigvedic proofs with the Iranian ones, it follows that, as early as the Aryan period, besides the sacrifice of cattle and soma, probably favoured by the martial class to which the war god Indra was invited as a guest, and the culmination of which was the roasting and pressing, existed a butter libation and perhaps even an independent soma sacrifice, in the context of which the cow was seen as inviolable, '*aghnya*'. Here seem to lie the common roots of later Indian vegetarianism as well as of the Zoroastrian damnation of false priests and their practices.

To begin with, general *ahiṃsā*-vegetarianism and cow taboo are thrown together here in an inadmissible manner, but we have no basis or indication for vegetarianism to have originated from cow-veneration or started from abstinence from beef. Moreover, the attempt to parallel the rejection of traditional religion – particularly of the bloody cow sacrifice, by the solitary personality of a towering religious reformer, Zarathuštra – with the Hindu **[66]** 'protection of the cow', which arose and prevailed gradually throughout centuries and was not clearly ascertainable at the beginning as well as in its various stages, seems very doubtful. Apart from this, Schlerath's explanation of the term *aghnya* as 'cow' would require for its proof a fundamental investigation of all references, especially of the three ṛgvedic ones not mentioned at all by him, where the word is masculine, or the four AV. passages where a s a c r i f i c i a l cow is spoken to as *aghnye*.[187] Because such an investigation, which is being prepared elsewhere,[188] must not be anticipated here, the following observations can only be of a provisional nature.

In both AV. hymns the point is only to protect the cow entitled or belonging to the brahmin from any encroachment on the part of the Rājanya: only he should not violate or consume it, since he would, thereby, damage the property of the brahmin.

187 ṚV 10, 9, 3. 11. 24; 10, 10, 1.

188 I thank H.P. Schmidt for oral and epistolary suggestions and comments on which the following is partly based.

Repeated attempts to attribute to the word *aghnya* another meaning or etymology than just 'not to be killed'[189] show that, in view of the bovine sacrifices and other attestations of cow slaughter in Indian antiquity, this Vedic term for 'cow' is a crux. Thus Weber (1885: 306f.) writes:

> I do not like to explain, either with the scholia and Lassen 1867 I 792, . . . *aghnyā* 'cow', feminine of *aghnya* 'bull' . . . to mean 'not to be killed' or, with PW, 'not or, accurately, difficult to conquer, to cope with,' and would prefer to derive it from *ahanya* 'in broad daylight', cf. *ahan ahanā* 'day', and that with the same meaning: bright coloured, as *usra, usrā, usriya, usriyā* 'bull, cow; ray, light of day, brightness' belong to √ *vas* 'to be bright', cf. also conversely *gaura* 'bright coloured' < *go*.

Roth's quite implausible explanation of *a-ghnya* as 'difficult to conquer, to cope with' is already dropped in the small PW, where only 'm. bull, f. cow' appears as meaning; Grassmann says: 'm., the bull, as a rule f., the cow, as the one which is not to be hurt (*han*).' Weber's own explanation, as far as I can see, has found approval nowhere. In Mayrhofer's etymological dictionary it is not even mentioned; there, after equating it with 'Avestan *agənyā* milk cow', it is only stated that: 'The interpretation "the one not to be killed" (: *a-*[1], *hánti*) is made very plausible by Schulze 1933: 207.' Finally Bartholomae states in the *Altiranisches Wörterbuch*, col. 49 for *agənyā* 'milk cow', but advances no opinion, either here or in *Arische Forschungen* 3, 39, on the etymology.

Recently, however, Bailey has advanced quite a different etymology:[190]

> For this word *agənyā-* the etymological **[67]** connexion seems obviously to lie in the verb *gan-* 'abound, be exuberant', the Indo-European *g*^{u}*hen-* 'swell, overflow; fulness, well-being', leading to 'full of liquid' on the physical side and 'wanton' on the animal. This verbal base is frequent in Greek θεν-, φον-, φαν- as in εὐθένεια 'fulness, flourishing

---

189 Thus it was – self-evidently – understood later as Mbh.12, 263, 47: *aghnyā iti gavāṃ nāma, ka etā hantum arhati? / mahac cakārâkuśalaṃ vṛṣaṃ gāṃ vâlabhet tu yaḥ* may show.

190 Bailey 1957: 40–49. – Now see Mayrhofer 1992: I 46f. (WB).

> state', εὐθενής 'prosperous'. For φον- and φαν- are quoted πολυφόντης and φανᾶν θέλειν. It is found in Baltic and Slavonic: Lit. *ganà* 'enough', *ganěti* 'to suffice', Slav. *goněti* 'to suffice'.

Bailey further connects *agənyā/aghnya* with Skt. *ghaná, ahanyá, ahaná* and *āhanás*.

This new etymology would certainly remove all the difficulties with regard to the meaning; it is questionable, however, because of the initial *a*-. In it, Bailey is obliged to see a 'preverb *a*- "to"' which would go back to Indo-Eur. *o*- and would occur in ὀκέλλω, ὀφέλλω and in Vedic *abhvan*. This meagre material, even with Bailey's further examples from Ossetic and Armenian, hardly suffices for a convincing interpretation of the *a*- as against the prevailing one of an *a- privativum*.[191]

There are, however, two possibilities to keep the prevailing explanation of *aghnya* without resort to Schlerath's theory of the Ṛgvedic opposition to animal sacrifice, both of which H.P. Schmidt referred me to.

aghnya 'not to be killed' might not signify 'what may not be killed' but rather 'what is impossible to kill'. We have seen before that, according to a Ṛgvedic interpretation and one still represented in the Dharmaśāstras, killing in a sacrifice is not killing, and one assured the sacrificial horse that it would go to the gods without having to die or coming to grief. The kenning *a-ghnya* could thus indicate the cow as the privileged sacrificial animal, the sacrificial animal κατ᾽ ἐξοχήν. Schmidt, however, has himself given up on this explanation (in a letter) because, as more precise examination would show, in the Ṛgveda the word would have nothing to do with the sacrificial animal. He believes now that only certain cattle might have been considered as *a-ghnya* 'not to be killed', viz., the breeding bulls, the mother-cows and the milch cows.

Without wishing to anticipate a further discussion of the question, for the present I can only go so far as to say that, to me, the explanation of the euphemistic kenning for the sacrificial animal continues to be the more plausible. The designation of the sacrificial animal as 'what is not killed' corresponds well to the otherwise meticulous avoidance of the word 'to kill' in connection with animal

191 Mayrhofer 1992: 94 *ábhava*- n. *'Unding, Unwesen ...'* (absurdity, sinister doings, terrible state of affairs) (WB).

sacrifice: sacrificing an animal is called, as is well-known, *ā-labh* 'to seize, to lay hold of', and the real killing which the priests not directly executing it are not allowed to observe,[192] **[68]** is described as 'put to rest' (*śamayati*).

On the one hand, the fact that *aghnya* in the Veda 'has nothing to do with the sacrificial animal' can simply be explained thus that the ancient kenning (which is attested only once: Avestan *agənyā*) had long ago become a simple designation for cow when its literal sense was no longer felt, which is quite rare already in the Veda; Schmidt himself notes that it had become obsolete in the Brāhmaṇas. On the other hand, the assumption that the breeding or gregarious bull, the mother-cow and the milch-cow would have been designated as excepted from sacrifice, appears doubtful, because it presupposes that one had systematically kept back the most valuable animals from the gods, whereas the contrary is not only to be expected but, occasionally, expressly demanded by the texts. A judgement is possible, as noted before, if at all, then only after a detailed examination of all the references; but either of the explanations and even Bailey's new etymology appear to me preferable to Schlerath's theory, which is far too incompatible with the other testimonies of the Vedic and post-Vedic literature.

Now if it is the case that in Vedic, indeed even in pre-Vedic times, cattle played an extraordinary role in mythology and ritual, and then later the newly emerging *ahiṃsā* ideal amalgamated itself with its 'sanctity', this could have had one result which would explain the unique position of the cow and the taboos concerning it in Hinduism. Indeed for instance even Jacobi, in his contribution 'Cow (Hindu)' in the *Encyclopaedia of Relegion and Ethics*, saw no problem in tracing the sacredness of the cow in Hinduism historically from Aryan ideas and customs.[193] If I, nevertheless, prefer to acknowledge, apart from this Aryan, also a significant non-Aryan, i.e. autochthone-Indian component, I am led not only by the analogy of the typically non-Aryan features of Hinduism, listed above in the discussion of the origin of *ahiṃsā*, features to which one should like to add even the ever so unique position of the cow; there is perhaps

192 Schwab 1886: 106.

193 In Crooke's essay (1912, mentioned above p. [55]) the conclusive point of the transition from Aryan 'cow-veneration' with sacrifice and meat consumption to Hinduist killing and meat-taboo is not explained convincingly.

even a direct indication that is certainly not strictly speaking proof, yet should by no means be overlooked.

As is well-known, most of the hundreds of seals of the Indus culture, whose representations are nearly the only source of our modest knowledge of its religion, bear **[69]** the picture of an animal, and the overwhelming majority of the animal seals depicts a slightly mythical animal, ordinarily designated as a unicorn which, however, is unmistakably based on an essentially bovine animal. Moreover, apart from these, ordinary cows, zebus and others without a hump are found. From that we may in any case and at least conclude that even in the pre-Aryan (or in one pre-Aryan) Indian religion, which by the way showed typically un-Aryan features of later Hinduism, the cow played an important role. This assumption is corroborated by some rare seals from which we can deduce that people at the Indus conducted the same cultural bull games as at the court of Minos in Crete.[194]

An answer to the question of the origin of vegetarianism and cow-veneration in Hinduism, which, without concrete proof, refers to a past our sources may never be capable of elucidating, may seem rather unsatisfactory. Yet, if it at least shows us the limits of our knowledge more precisely and blocks off superficial rationalist answers, something may nevertheless have been already gained. For the Indologist, it is indeed not a new experience that the pursuit of pressing problems in the present leads him back into the dim and distant past.

---

194 Cf. Fabri 1934/5: 93–101. Admittedly, the bull-leapings or -sacrifices at the Indus, too, seem to have been connected with k i l l i n g the animal; thus it is doubtful whether they can be used for our argument. In the same way bone finds may prove that the Indus valley people also ate beef (Marshall I 1931: 27; Mackay 1938: 139).

BIBLIOGRAPHY

1932 **Abbott**, John, *The Keys of Power*. London: Methuen (repr. Seacaucus, 1974).

1984 ——, *Indian Ritual and Belief*. Delhi: Motilal Banarsidass.

1951 **Aiyangar**, see **Rangaswami**.

1953 **Allen**, William S., *Phonetics in Ancient India. A Guide to the Appreciation of the Earliest Phoneticians*. London: OUP.

1955 **Alsdorf**, Ludwig, *Vorderindien. Bharat, Pakistan, Ceylon*. Eine Landes- und Kulturkunde. Braunschweig, etc.: Georg Westermann.

1960 ——, Zu den Aśoka-Inschriften. In: **Waldschmidt** 1960: 58–66.

1997 **Amar** (muni) and Shrichand Surānā **Saras** (eds). *Illustrated Dashavaikalik Sutra*. Delhi: Padma Prakashan.

1957 **Bailey**, Harold W., *Dvārā Matīnām*. In: *BSOAS* **20**: 41–59.

1980 **Balasooriya**, Somaratna et al. (eds), *Buddhist Studies in Honour of Walpola Rahula*. London: Gordon Fraser; Śrī Lanka: Vimamsa.

1984 **Balbir**, Nalini, Normalizing trends in Jaina narrative literature. In: *Indologica Taurinensia* **12**: 25–38.

2009 ——, Layman's Atonements: The Sāvayapacchitta and the Shrāddhajitakalpa. Paper read at the 11th Jaina Workshop at SOAS 12–13 March.

1887 **Bartholomae**, Christian, *Arische Forschungen* 3. Halle: Niemeyer.

1904 ——, *Altiranisches Wörterbuch*. Straßburg: Karl J. Trübner (repr. Berlin: De Gruyter, 1979).

2009 **Bhaṭṭ**, Bansidhar, Is Pārśva the twenty-third Jina a legendary figure? A critical survey of early Jaina sources. In: *Jaina Studies* **4**: 6.

1907 **Bhishagratna**, Kunjalal, *The Sushruta Samhita*. English Translation I–III. Calcutta (2nd edn. Varanasi: Chowkhamba Sanskrit Series 30, 1963).

1976 **Biardeau**, Madeleine and **Malamoud**, Charles, *Le sacrifice dans l'Inde ancienne*. Paris: Presses Universitaires de France (Bibliothèque de l'Ecole des Hautes Etudes. Section des Sciences Religieuses, Volume LXXIX). [To these authors the present study was apparently unknown (WB)].

2007 **Bilimoria**, Purushottama et al. (eds), *Indian Ethics. Classical Traditions and Contemporary Challenges Vol. I*. Aldershot: Ashgate.

1999 **Bodewitz**, Henk W., Hindu ahiṃsā and its roots. In: **Houben** 1999: 17–44.

1993 **Bollée**, Willem, Le Végétarisme défendu par Haribhadrasūri contre un bouddhiste et un brahmane. In: **Wagle** and **Watanabe** 1993: 22–28.

2006 ——, *Gone to the Dogs in Ancient India*. (Bayerische Akademie der Wissenschaften. Philosophisch-Historische Klasse Sitzungsberichte Jahrgang 2006, Heft 2). München: Verlag der Bayerischen Akademie der Wissenschaften.

2008 ——, Glossary to Robert Williams, *Jaina Yoga*. In: *IJJS* **4(3)**: 1–53.

2008a ——, *Pārśvacaritram. The Life of Pārśva*. Mumbai: Hindi Granth Karyalay.

1939 **Breloer**, Bernhard, *Fontes historiae religionum indicarum*. Bonn: Röhrscheid.

2007 **Bruhn**, Klaus, Die *ahiṃsā* in der Ethik des Jaina-Autors Amṛtacandra. In: *BIS* **18**: 1–78.

2008 ——, *The Predicament of Women in Ancient India*. Berlin: Herenow4u.

1879 **Bühler**, Georg, *Sacred Laws of the Āryas*. Oxford: Clarendon Press (Sacred Books of the East 2 and 14).

1886 ——, *The Laws of Manu*. Oxford: Clarendon Press (Sacred Books of the East 25).

2007 **Caillat**, Colette, *Ahiṃsā – cur et quomodo?* Eine vierfache Antwort in einem alten Jaina-Text. In: *BIS* **17**: 79–100.

1991 **Carrithers**, Michael and Caroline **Humphrey** (eds), *The Assembly of Listeners: Jains: in Society*. Cambridge: Cambridge University Press.

1993 **Chapple**, Christopher K., *Nonviolence to Animals, Earth, and Self in Asian Traditions*. New York: State University Press.

1908 **Charpentier**, Jarl, Studien über die indische Erzählungsliteratur 2. In: *ZDMG* **63**: 171–188.

1922 ——, *The Uttarajjhayanasūtra*. Uppsala (repr. Delhi, 1980).

1991 **Cottam Ellis**, Christine, The Jain merchant castes of Rajasthan: some aspects of the management of social identity in a market town. In: **Carrithers**/Humphrey 1991: 75–109.

1912 **Crooke**, William, The Veneration of the Cow in India. In: *Folklore* **23**: 275–306.

1990 **Dandekar**, Ramchandra Narāyaṇ, *The Mahābhārata Revisited*. New Delhi: Sahitya Akademi.

1997 *Daśavaikālikasūtra* ed. by Amar Muni. (Hindi: Sricand Surana 'Saras', English: Surendra Bothra). Delhi: Padma Prakashan.

1933 ——, see **Patwardhan**.

1962 **De**, Sushil K. et al., *Cultural Heritage of India* II. Calcutta: The Ramakrishna Mission Institute of Culture.

2007 **Deleu**, Josef, Die Schonung der Lebewesen in der Viyāhapannatti. In: *Berliner Indologische Studien* **18**: 101–110.

1956 **Deo**, Shantaram Bh., *History of Jain Monachism. From Inscriptions and Literature*. Poona: Deccan College Postgraduate and Research Institute.

1922 **Deussen**, Paul, *Vier philosophische Texte des Mahābhāratam*. Leipzig: F.A. Brockhaus.

1914 **Dhalla**, Maneckji N., *Zoroastrian Theology from the Earliest Times to the Present Day*. New York: AMS Press.

2009a **do**, Altitudes indiennes via-à-vis de l'animal domestique. In: **Balbir** and **Pinault** 2009b: 811–58.

2009b **do** et Georges **Pinault**, *Penser, dire et representer l'animal dans le monde indien*. Paris: Librairie Honoré Champion.

1922 **Dodwell**, Henry; **Rapson**, Edward, et al., *The Cambridge History of India* I. Cambridge: Cambridge University Press.

1991 **Doniger**, Wendy and Brian K. **Smith** (trans), *The Laws of Manu*. Harmondsworth: Penguin.

1976 **Doniger O'Flaherty**, Wendy, *The Origins of Evil in Hindu Mythology*. Berkeley, Los Angeles, London: University of California Press.

1980 ——, *Women, Androgynes, and Other Mythical Beasts*. Chicago and London: University of Chicago Press.

1985 **Dundas**, Paul, Food and freedom: The Jaina sectarian debate on the nature of the Kevalin. In: *Religion* **15**: 161–98.

1997 ——, *The Meat at the Wedding Feasts: Kṛṣṇa, Vegetarianism and a Jain Dispute*. The 1997 Roop Lal Jain Lecture. University of Toronto.

2002 ——, *The Jains*. Second Revised Edition. London: Routledge.

1882–1900 **Eggeling**, Julius, *The Śatapatha-Brāhmaṇa* I–V. Oxford: Clarendon Press (Sacred Books of the East 12, 26, 41, 43 and 44). Repr. Delhi: Motilal Banarsidass, 1963.

1954 **Eliade**, Mircea, *Le Yoga*. Paris: Payot.

1991 **Ellis**, see **Cottam Ellis**.

1934–5 **Fabri**, Charles L., The Cretan bull-grappling sports and the bull-sacrifice in the Indus Valley civilisation. In: *Annual Report Archeological Survey of India 1934–5*: 93–101.

1953 **Filchner**, Wilhelm und **Marathe**, D. Shrīdhar, *Hindustan im Festgewand*. Celle: Verlagsbuchhandel Joseph Giesel.

1913 **Franke**, R. Otto, *Dīghanikāya*. Das Buch der langen Texte des Buddhistischen Kanons. Göttingen: Vandenhoeck & Ruprecht; Leipzig: J.C. Hinrich'sche Buchhandlung.

1927–9 **Gandhi**, Mohandas K., *An Autobiography or My Experiments with Truth* I–II. Translated from the Original Gujarati by Mahadev Desai. Ahmedabad: Navajivan (2nd Edn. Repr. 1963).

1960 ——, *Mahatma Gandhis Autobiographie*. Die Geschichte meiner Experimente mit der Wahrheit. Freiburg: Verlag Karl Alber.

1917 **Gautama**, *Dharmasūtra*, ed. by L. Shrinivasacharya. Mysore (Government Oriental Library Series Bibliotheca Sanscritica 50).

1966 ——, *Dharma-sūtra* with the Mitākṣara Sanskrit Commentary of Haradatta, ed by Umeśacandra Pāndeya. Varanasi: Chowkhamba Sanskrit Series.

1926 **Glasenapp**, Helmuth von, Das Triṣaṣṭilakṣaṇamahāpurāṇa der Digambaras. In: **Kirfel** 1926: 331–345.

1943 ——, *Die Religionen Indiens*. Stuttgart: Kröner.

1965 **Gonda**, Jan, *Change and Continuity in Indian Religion*. London, The Hague, Paris: Mouton.

1980 ——, *Vedic Ritual. The Non-solemn Rites*. Leiden-Köln: E.J. Brill.

1960 **Hagen**, Toni, *Nepal Königreich am Himalaya*. Bern.

1949 **Handiqui**, Krishna K., *Yaśastilaka and Indian Culture*. (Jīvarāja Jaina Granthamālā 2). Sholapur: Jaina Saṁskṛti Saṁrakshaka Sangha.

1935 **Haussleiter**, Johannes, *Der Vegetarismus in der Antike*. Berlin: Töpelmann.

1984 **Heesterman**, Jan C., Non-Violence and Sacrifice. In: *Indologica Taurinensia* **XII**: 119–127.

1897 **Hillebrandt**, Alfred, *Ritual-Litteratur Vedische Opfer und Zauber*. Strassburg: Karl J. Trübner (Grundriss der Indo-Arischen Philologie und Altertumskunde III, 2).

2001 **Hiltebeitel**, Alf, *Rethinking the Mahābhārata: A Reader's Guide to the Education of the Dharma King*. Chicago and London: Chicago University Press.

1977 **Hirachand**, Lalchand, *Bibliography of the Works of Dr A.N. Upadhye*. Sholapur: Jaina Samskrti Samrakshaka Sangha.

1951 **Hoens**, Dirk, *Śānti*. A Contribution to ancient Indian religious Terminology. 1. *Śānti in the Saṃhitās, the Brāhmaṇas and the Śrautasūtras*. 's-Gravenhage: Nederlandsche Boek- en Steendrukkerij.

1901 **Hopkins**, E. Washburn, *The Great Epic of India*. New York: Charles Scribner's Sons.

1949–66 **Horner**, Iṣaline B., *The Book of the Discipline* (aka *Vinaya-Piṭaka*). London: Pali Text Society.

1999 **Houben**, Jan E.M., To kill or not to kill. Arguments and perspectives in Brahminical ethical philosophy. In: **Houben** and van **Kooij** 1999: 105–83.

1999 **Houben**, Jan E.M. and Karel van **Kooij** (eds), *Violence Denied. Violence, Non-violence and the Rationalization of Violence in South Asian Cultural History*. Leiden: Brill's Indological Library, 16.

1925 **Hultzsch**, Eugen, *Inscriptions of Aśoka*. Corpus Inscriptionum Indicarum I. Oxford.

1884 **Jacobi**, Hermann, *Jain Sutras* I. Oxford: Clarendon Press (Sacred Books of the East 22).

1984 **Jain**, Jagdish C., *Life in Ancient India as Depicted in Jaina Canon and Commentaries*. Delhi: Munshiram Manoharlal.

1993 **Jaini**, Padmanābh S., Fear of Food? Jain Attitudes toward Eating. In: Smet & Watanabe 1993: 339–354.

2004 **Jha**, Dvijendra N., *The Myth of the Holy Cow*. London: Verso (New Delhi: Matrix Books, 2001).

1930 **Jinasena**, *Harivaṃśapurāṇa*. Bombay: Māṇikyacanda-Digambara-Jain-Granthamālā-samiti 32, 33.

1896 **Jolly**, Julius, *Recht und Sitte*. Strassburg: Karl J. Trübner.

1968–77 **Kane**, Pandurang V., *History of Dharmaśāstra* (*Ancient and Medieval Religious and Civil Law in India*). Poona: Bhandarkar Oriental Research Institute (Government Oriental Series, Class B 6).

1933 **Kapadia**, Hiralal R., Prohibition of flesh-eating in Jainism. In: *Revue of Philosophy and Religion* IV 1933: 232–39.

1941 ——, *A History of the Canonical Literature of the Jains*. Surat: H.R. Kapadia.

1922 **Keith**, Arthur B., see **Rapson** 1922.

1926 **Kirfel**, Willibald, *Beiträge zur Literaturwissenschaft und Geistesgeschichte Indiens*. Festgabe Hermann Jacobi. Bonn: Kommissionsverlag Fritz Klopp.

1941 **Lakṣmīdhara**, *Kṛtyakalpataru*. K.V. Rangaswami Aiyangar (ed.). Baroda: GOS 111.

1973 **Lalwani**, Kastur C., *Ārya Sayyambhava's Daśavaikālika sūtra*. Delhi: Motilal Banarsidass.

1958 **Lamotte**, Etienne, *Histoire du Bouddhisme indien des origines à l'ère Śaka*. Louvain: Institut Orientaliste (Bibliothèque du Muséon 43).

1867 **Lassen**, Christian, *Indische Alterthumskunde* I: *Geographie, Ethnographie und älteste Geschichte*. Bonn, Leipzig (repr. Mettingen, 1968: Zeller Verlag).

1990 **Lath**, Mukund, The concept of *ānṛśaṃsya* in the Mahābhārata. In: **Dandekar** 1990: 113–19.

1883 **Leumann**, Ernst, *Das Aupapātika Sūtra*. Leipzig (Abhandlungen für die Kunde des Morgenlandes VIII 2).

1892 ——, Daśavaikālika-sūtra und -niryukti, nach dem Erzählungsgehalt untersucht und herausgegeben. In: *ZDMG* **46**: 581–663.

1917 **Lüders**, Heinrich, *Eine arische Anschauung über den Vertragsbruch*. Berlin: Sitzungsberichte der Preussischen Akademie der Wissenschaften 347–74 = Lüders 1940: 438–463.

1940 ——, *Philologica Indica*. Göttingen: Vandenhoeck & Ruprecht.

1951 ——, *Varuṇa*. Aus dem Nachlass herausgegeben von Ludwig Alsdorf. Göttingen: Vandenhoeck & Ruprecht.

1938 **Mackay**, Ernest J.H., *Die Indus-Kultur Ausgrabungen in Mohenjo-daro und Harappa* I–III. Leipzig: Brockhaus.

2007 **Mallebrein**, Cornelia, When the buffalo becomes a pumpkin: The animal sacrifice contested. In: **Pfeffer** 2007: 443–472.

2008 **Mallebrein**, Cornelia and Heinrich von **Stietencron**, *The Divine Play on Earth: Religious Aesthetics and Ritual in Orissa*. Heidelberg: Synchron Publishers.

1933 **Malliṣeṇa**, *Syādvādamañjarī* with Anyayoga-vyavaccheda-dvātriṃśikā of Hemacandra. A.B. Dhruva (ed.). Bombay: Bombay Sanskrit and Prakrit Series LXXXIII.

1973 **Malvania**, Dalsukh, Jaina theory and practice of non-violence. In: *Sambodhi* **2(1)**: 1–6.

1931 **Marshall**, John, *Mohenjo-Daro and the Indus Civilisation*. London.

1927 **Mayo**, Katherine, *Mother India*. London: Jonathan Cape.

1992 **Mayrhofer**, Manfred, *Etymologisches Wörterbuch des Altindoarischen* I. Heidelberg: Carl Winter Universitätsverlag.

1926 **McCrindle**, *Ancient India as described by Megasthenes and Arrian*. Calcutta.

1974 **Mette**, Adelheid, *Piṇḍ'esaṇā. Das Kapitel der Oha-nijjutti über den Bettelgang übersetzt und kommentiert*. Akademie der Wissenschaften und der Literatur. Mainz. Abh. der geistes- und sozialwissenschaftlichen Klasse 1973: 11. Wiesbaden: Franz Steiner verlag.

1991 ——, *Durch Entsagung zum Heil. Eine Anthologie aus der Literatur der Jaina*. Zürich: Benziger (repr. as: *Die Erlösungslehre der Jaina Legenden Parabeln Erzählungen*. Frankfurt-Main: Verlag der Weltreligionen, 2009).

1927 **Meyer**, Johann J., *Über das Wesen der altindischen Rechtsschriften*. Leipzig: Harrassowitz.

1998 **Michaels**, Axel, *Der Hinduismus. Geschichte und Gegenwart*. München: C.H. Beck.

1955 **Nebesky-Wojkowitz**, René de, *Wo Berge Götter sind. Drei Jahre bei unerforschten Völkern des Himalaya*. Stuttgart: Deutsche Verlags-Anstalt.

1980 **O'Flaherty**, see **Doniger**.

1994 **Ohira**, (Ms) Suzuko, *A Study of the Bhagavatīsūtra. A Chronological Analysis*. Ahmedabad: Prakrit Text Society 28.

1878 **Oldenberg**, Hermann, Das Śāṅkhāyanagṛhyam. In: **Weber** 1878: 1–166.

1903 ——, *Die Litteratur des alten Indien*. Stuttgart: Cotta; 2nd edn. ibid. 1923.

1919 ——, *Vorwissenschaftliche Wissenschaft*. Die Weltanschauung der Brāhmaṇa-Texte. Göttingen: Vandenhoeck & Ruprecht.

1961 **Om Prakash**, *Food and Drinks in Ancient India*. Delhi: Munshiram Manohar Lal.

1938 **Patel**, G.J., Mahāvīra-svāmino māṃsâhāra. In: *Prasthāna* **XXVI(1)**: 66–74.

1946 **Patil**, Devendra R., *Cultural History from the Vāyu Purāṇa*. Poona: Deccan College (reprint Delhi: Motilal Banarsidass, 1973).

1933–36 **Patwardhan**, Madhao V., *The Daśavaikālikasūtra: A Study*. 2 vols. Sangli. (2nd Edn. Revised and Enlarged by Kāśināth V. Abhyankar. Available only in the British Library, shelfmark: 11856.de 63). non vidi (WB).

2007 **Pfeffer**, Georg (ed.), *Periphery and the Centre. Groups, Categories and Values*. Delhi: Manohar.

1962 **Raghavan**, Venkataraman, the Manu Saṃhitā. In: **De**, S.K. *et al.*, *Cultural Heritage of India* **II**: 335–363.

1951 **Rangaswami Aiyangar**, Kumbakonam V., *Edicts of Aśoka*. Madras: Adyar Library.

1941 ——, *Bṛhaspatismṛti*. Baroda: Gaekwad Oriental Series 85.

1922 **Rapson**, Edward (ed.), *The Cambridge History of India*. Cambridge: Cambridge University Press.

1957 **Rau**, Wilhelm, *Staat und Gesellschaft im alten Indien. Nach den Brāhmaṇa-Texten dargestellt*. Wiesbaden: Otto Harrassowitz.

1930 **Renou**, Louis, *Grammaire sanscrite*. Paris: Adrien-Maisonneuve (repr. 1961).

1968 ——, *Mélanges d'Indianisme à la mémoire de Louis Renou*. Publications de l'Institut de Civilisation indienne 28. Paris: éditions E. de Boccard.

1947–53 **Renou**, Louis et **Filliozat**, Jean, *L'Inde classique*. Manuel des Études Indiennes. Paris: Payot.

1960 **Schlerath**, Bernfried (ed.), *Festschrift für Herman Lommel*. Wiesbaden: Harrassowitz.

1968 **Schmidt**, Hanns-Peter, The Origin of Ahiṃsā. In: **Renou** 1968: 626–655.

1997 ——, Ahiṃsā and Rebirth. In: **Witzel** 1997: 207–234.

1979 **Schreiner**, Peter, Gewaltlosigkeit und Tötungsverbot im Hinduismus. In: **Stietencron** 1979: 287–308.

1932 **Schubring**, Walther, *The Dasaveyāliya Sutta*. Ahmedabad: The Managers of Sheth Ananji Kalianji.

2000 ——, *The Doctrine of the Jains*. Delhi: Motilal Banarsidass.

1933 **Schulze**, Wilhelm, *Kleine Schriften zum 70. Gebutstag*. Göttingen: Vandenhoeck & Ruprecht.

1886 **Schwab**, Julius, *Das altindische Thieropfer*. Erlangen: Andreas Deichert.

1975 **Sen**, Madhu, *A Cultural Study of the Niśītha Cūrṇi*. Amritsar: Sohanlal Jaindharma Pracharak Samiti (Parshvanath Vidyashram Series 21).

1980 **Seyfort Ruegg**, David, Ahiṃsā and Vegetarianism in the History of Buddhism. In: **Balasooriya** 1980: 234–241.

1993 **Smet**, Rudy and Kenji **Watanabe** (eds), *Jain Studies in Honour of Jozef Deleu*. Tokyo: Hon-no-Tomosha.

2007 **Sridhar**, M.K. and Purushottama **Bilimoria**, Animal ethica and ecology in classical India: reflections on a moral tradition. In: **Bilimoria** et al. 2007: 297–328.

1979 **Stietencron**, Heinrich von, *Angst und Gewalt. Ihre Präsenz und ihre Bewältigung in den Religionen*. Düsseldorf: Patmos-Verlag.

1928 **Tawney**, Charles H. and **Penzer**, N.M., *The Ocean of Story*. X. London: Chas. J. Sawyer Ltd.

1957 **Thieme**, Paul, Vorzarathustrisches bei den Zarathustriern und Zarathustra. In: *ZDMG* **107**: 67–104.

1957 ——, Review of Allen 1953. In: *ZDMG* **107**: 664–666.

1971 ——, *Kleine Schriften*. Wiesbaden: Franz Steiner.

1912 **Thurston**, Edgar, *Omens and Superstitions of Southern India*. London: T. Fisher Unwin.

1957 **Tinker**, Hugh, *The Union of Burma*. Oxford: OUP.

1957 **Upadhye**, Ādināth N., Vegetarianism according to Jainism. In: *Souvenir of the XVth World Vegetarian Congress, India*. Bombay: All India Reception Committee, pp. 233–34 reprinted in: *Voice of Ahiṃsā* VIII, 1 (1958): 3–5.

1883 Uvavāiya, see **Leumann**.

1993 **Wagle**, Narendra K. and Fumimaro **Watanabe** (eds), *Studies on Buddhism in Honour of A.K. Warder*. University of Toronto: Centre for South Asian Studies. South Asian Studies Papers, No. 5.

1939 **Waldschmidt**, Ernst, *Beiträge zur Textgeschichte des Mahāpariṇirvāṇasūtra*. Göttingen: Vandenhoeck & Ruprecht.

1960 ——, Indologen-Tagung 1959. Verhandlungen der Indologischen Arbeitstagung in Essen Bredeney, Villa Hügel 13–15 July 1959. Göttingen.

1878 **Weber**, Albrecht, *Indische Studien: Beiträge für die Kunde des indischen Alterthums XV*. Leipzig: F.A. Brockhaus (repr. Hildesheim, 1973: Georg Olms Verlag).

1885 ——, *do* XVII.

1978 **Wezler**, Albrecht, *Die wahren Speiseresteesser, Skt.* vighasâśin. Wiesbaden: Steiner.

1963 **Williams**, Robert, *Jaina Yoga*. London Oriental Series 14. Oxford: Oxford University Press.

1920 **Winternitz**, Moritz, *Geschichte der indischen Literatur* III. Leipzig: C.F. Amelangs Verlag.

1962 ——, Maurice, *History of Indian Literature* I. Calcutta: University of Calcutta.

1963–7 ——, *History of Indian Literature* III. Delhi: Motilal Banarsidass.

1997 **Witzel**, Michael (ed.), *Inside the Texts, Beyond the Texts*. Harvard Oriental Series, Opera Minora 2. Cambridge MA: Harvard University Press.

1987 **Zimmerman**, Francis, *The Jungle and the Aroma of Meats. An ecological Theme in Hindu Medicine*. Berkeley: UCLA.

SUBJECT INDEX

(pages in [ ] refer to German original)

INDEX LOCORUM

(pages in [ ] refer to German original)

Appendix I

REVIEWS

by J.C. Heesterman

Ludwig Alsdorf, *Beiträge zur Geschichte von Vegetarismus und Rinderverehrung in Indien (= Akademie der Wissenschaften und der Literatur in Mainz, Abhn. der Geistes- und Sozialwiss. Klasse*, Jahrg. 1961, Nr. 6). Wiesbaden, in Kommission bei Franz Steiner Verlag GmbH., 1962. 69 pp.

Vegetarianism, or rather *ahiṃsā,* and sanctity of bovine animals (not only the cow, as the author rightly stresses), although never general or even valid for the majority of Hindus, have come to be recognized as the hallmark of Hinduism. Patriots in search of national identity have invoked these doctrines. They can be said to be part of the national ideology of modern India. For all that, they put baffling problems to the administrator and the economic planner. An inquiry into origin and cause of the twin doctrines does not only present an academic interest, it has a bearing on India's present-day reality as well. It is therefore to be welcomed that Professor Alsdorf compressed his findings in an eminently readable essay, that should appeal also to the non-sanskritist.

In accordance with the title the author's viewpoint is purely historical. The problem he has set himself concerns the historical development of the twin doctrines, not their meaning. Paraphrases like 'magisch-ritualistisches Tabu auf das Leben', p. 15, will not be intended as an explanation. Accordingly the author seeks an answer to the question when and in what form the twin doctrines arose and developed; or rather, when and how they manifested thernselves in the texts. The Vedic texts do not know the *ahiṃsā* doctrine and enjoin the killing of cow and bull at certain occasions (e.g. at the ceremonial reception of a guest). It is only in the later *dharma* literature that the *ahiṃsā* doctrine and the inviolability of the cow find full expression. The matter is further complicated by the fact that the *dharma* texts contradictorily contain both the Vedic injunctions and the rigorous demands of *ahiṃsā* and vegetarianism. The historical approach seems to impose itself. In the author's view the contradictions of the texts can mean only one thing: a chronological succession.

The demonstration centres on the relevant part of Manu (V, 5–55), where three successive layers are recognized. The first layer is represented by the discussion on pure and impure food (5–25); there is no question *of ahiṃsā*. This stage is also represented by the *Dharmasūtras*. The next stage comes with the verses 27–44, where *ahiṃsā* is the rule, except the case of Vedic injunctions when meat is allowed or even obligatory. The last stage is reached in 44–55, where *ahiṃsā* and vegetarianism are absolute.

The sanctity of the cow – rightly kept separate from *ahiṃsā* – shows a roughly parallel development. The special position of the bovine is abundantly attested in the Vedic texts. This did not preclude the consumption of beef (not much of an argument, however, for an otherwise unassailable case can be derived from the absence of the cow in the old lists of non-consumable meat, p. 59. The criterion is here, as the author has pointed out previously, impurity. One would hardly expect to find the cow among the impure animals). The next stage is found in some of the older *smṛtis*, where eating beef is restricted to sacrificial occasions. This restriction is then, in the later *smṛtis*, subsumed under the one regarding all meat. (Alsdorf's second layer in the development of *ahiṃsā*, above). Thus the sanctity of the cow has become intimately linked with the *ahiṃsā* doctrine.

This clear-cut chronological frame has much to recommend itself to the Western scholar. I doubt, however, whether it can do justice to the Indian facts, even if we should limit ourselves to the texts. The limitations of the chronological perspective stand out clearly when the author, in his search for historical origins, is forced back away from the texts into the limbo of pre-Aryan civilization and the ruins of Harappa. Although the hypothesis of pre-Aryan origins of Hindu ideas and institutions is far from impossible, this reasoning also means that, because of lack of documentation, the problem is shifted out of sight and rendered all but meaningless. The author further surmises – quite consistently – that not only *ahiṃsā* and sanctity of the bovine, but also their opposite, (ritual) bloodshed, finds its roots in pre-Aryan civilization. Indeed, as the author observes, the juxtaposition of these opposites in pre-Aryan times is no more illogical than their existence side by side in Hinduism until the present day.

Even if, in some cases, we can feel confident that 'kritisch-historischer Betrachtung löst sich also das scheinbare Nebeneinander widersprechender Vorschriften auf in das Nacheinander geschichtlicher Entwicklungsstufen' (p. 17), we must nevertheless admit 'das so typisch indische Nebeneinander nach unserem Empfinden unvereinbarer Gegensätze' (p. 42 n. 1; cf. p. 54). One wonders how, in the Indian view, these opposites are reconciled. Are we forced to consider Indian culture as a meaningless jumble? Here a different line of inquiry can no longer be avoided. Having exhausted the historical question we are faced with the problem of meaning. Here only the beginning of an answer can be indicated. One could start with the apparent persistence of the two opposites. It would seem that, far from presenting an inconsistency, there is a link between them. The link can be illustrated by one of the author's own observations, namely that the monk (who does not kill) can lead a sinless life thanks to the sin of the layman (who does the killing for him).

Going further along this line we note that a similar situation seems to obtain in the Vedic ritual: the sacrificer has to abstain, among other things, from meat; the *ṛtvij* on the other hand is obliged to consume the meat. The sacrificer eats afterwards. The *ṛtvij* who would refuse to eat the sacrificial meat is threatened by Manu with dire consequences. It has been pointed out by Thieme that the basic pattern of the Vedic sacrifice is that of a banquet offered to both divine and human guests. Now the ceremonial reception of the guest (the sacrificial priest is expressly mentioned as such) involves the offering of a cow to the guest. The guest has to give the order for the killing (or he may order to set the animal free), that is, he takes the onus of the killing upon himself, thus enabling the host to partake of the meat. This is probably the reason why Buddhist and Jain monks, though practising *ahiṃsā,* originally could accept meat, on the condition that it was not expressly prepared for them (cf. p. 5ff.).

The ritual texts show a marked aversion to killing. Nevertheless the sacrifice is essential to the maintenance of life. Time and again life has to be rewon out of death. Therefore one party *(ṛtvij,* guest) has to take upon himself the onus of death so that the other may win life. Thus the sacrifice involves the participants in the ever recurring alternation of life and death.

The decisive point in the development is the breakthrough, out of the vicious life-death circle, that is, the rise of the renunciatory way of life, where death is no longer periodically conquered, but permanently eliminated. It would seem that it is in this direction that we have to look for the meaning of *ahiṃsā,* the avoidance of death,

death being otherwise inextricably connected with life. *Ahiṃsā* therefore is proper to the renouncer of the world, its opposite belongs to the sphere of the man-in-the-world. The interaction, as L. Dumont has pointed out, between these two spheres (in Indian terms *nivṛtti* and *pravṛtti*) seems to be central to Hinduism (past as well as present) (cf. L. Dumont, 'Le renoncement dans les religions de l'Inde', *Arch. de Sociologie des Rel.*, no. 7 (1959) 45–69). If I am right this may explain the persistent juxtaposition of the irreconcilable opposites. At the same time it would seem that the search for meaning may deliver a clue to the problem of origin as well.

These few and necessarily sketchy reflections cannot possibly do justice to the author's many interesting and detailed observations (e.g. on the supposed Buddhist and Jain origins of *ahiṃsā;* Buddhism and Jainism are shown, together with brahmanism, to participate in a common movement). The reviewer's reflections are meant as a tribute to the stimulating quality of this interesting study. Professor Alsdorf has given us a most welcome contribution to our knowledge of Indian religious concepts and practices.

J.C. Heesterman, Leiden

Appendix II

THE ORIGIN OF *AHIṂSĀ*

*by Hanns-Peter Schmidt**

I

Ahiṃsā is one of the central ideas of Indian religions, and though the doctrine of 'non-violence' – literally 'non-injury (to living beings)' – is not universally followed in India, there will be only few who do not at least pay lip-service to it. Inspite of its great importance for the religious attitude of the Indians, the history of the idea of ahiṃsā has rarely been investigated, and the handbooks on Indian religions generally devote little space to it.

In modern India ahiṃsā is inseparably connected with vegetarianism, but it is known since long ago and has recently been thrown into relief by L. Alsdorf in his contributions to the history of vegetarianism and cow-worship in India[195] that neither the Buddha nor the Jina were vegetarians though they propagated ahiṃsā. The Buddhist and Jaina monks or ascetics subsisted on begged food, and the main condition was that the food was neither prepared by the monk himself nor prepared especially for him. This applied to any kind of food if it contained meat or not. That originally ahiṃsā had nothing to do with vegetarianism becomes obviously if one considers the strict animism of the Jaina doctrine according to which the whole world is animated – not only animals

---

* The numbers given in square brackets in Schmidt's present article relate to the original page numbers. Mélanges d'Indianisme à la Mémoire de Louis Renou. Publications de l'Institut de Civilisation indienne 28. Paris: Editions E. de Boccard, 1968.

195 'Beiträge zur Geschichte von Vegetarismus und Rinderverehrung in Indien' (Akad. d. Wiss. u.d. Lit. Abh. d. geistes- u. sozialwiss. Kl. 1961. Nr. 6. Wiesbaden 1962), 5 sqq. [J.C. Heesterman's review of Alsdorf's work in IIJ 9, 1966, 147–149, appeared after this paper had been submitted to the editors].

and plants but also the elements earth, fire, water and air consist in atomic individual souls. This involves that the Jaina monk is to avoid beating and heating water, handling fire and using a fan since he would thereby injure water-, fire- and air-souls. He is to accept only food which has been prepared, i.e. killed, by others, including water [626] which must be boiled. Only in this way he is safeguarded against any complicity in depriving an animate being of its life.[196]

Alsdorf (loc. cit., 15) has rightly stressed the fact that the concept of ahiṃsā as we meet it with the Jainas is not based on ethical ideas but on a magico-ritualistic dread of destroying life in any form. He has also realized that the emergence of the 'non-violence' movement is part of the All-Indian religious development and cannot be credited to the reform-religions of the Buddha and the Jina (loc. cit., 49). In his treatment of the Brahmanic sources he begins with Manu's rules on meat-eating. He has convincingly demonstrated (loc. cit., 17 sqq.) that they contain three layers which constitute three successive stages of historical development. In the first layer the eating of kosher animals is taken for granted; in the second meat-eating is prohibited in daily life, but allowed and even compulsory in the ritual; and in the third we find a strict vegetarianism which advises against animal sacrifices.[197] In the earlier juridical texts only the first stage is attested.

Manu's rules against meat-eating are based on the ahiṃsā-doctrine, and this doctrine goes – in Manu's view, too – beyond vegetarianism, since at least plants are included in the category of animate beings. When the most recent layer of Manu's rules proclaims rigid vegetarianism, it would seem that vegetarianism is either a special development of the ahiṃsā-doctrine or is grafted on it.

Concentrating his attention on the history of vegetarianism, Alsdorf has lost sight of the difference between ahiṃsā and vegetarianism. Though, in the discussion of the epic material (loc. cit., 29 sqq.), he does not fail to notice the fact that in these texts the consumption of seeds capable of germination is considered as hiṃsā 'injury', too, he does not attempt to fix the point at which and the reason why vegetarianism became the main-stay of the ahiṃsā-doctrine.

I must admit that I do not know the solution of this problem either. One might think that vegetarianism is the popularized form of the

---

196 Cf. W. SCHUBRING, *Die Lehre der Jainas* (Berlin 1935), § 104.105.154. ALSDORF, loc. cit. 14 sq.

197 Manu does not openly condemn the Vedic sacrifice, but rather propagates the superiority of strict vegetarianism.

ahiṃsā-doctrine which was originally restricted to the ascetic. But this suggestion is a mere guess and remains rather unsatisfactory all the more since I am not able to substantiate it on the basis of our sources.

[627]

Alsdorf (loc. cit., 53 sq.) conjectures that the origin of ahiṃsā and vegetarianism is to be sought in the pre-Aryan Indus-civilization. This is contradicted by the finds of animal bones at the sites of Mohenjo-Daro and Harappa, which rather show that the Indus people were non-vegetarians.[198] Moreover, there are, as far as I see, no traces of similar ideas to be found among the non-Aryan population of India – not influenced by the Brahmanical culture – which could justify the assumption that ahiṃsā and vegetarianism did not originate from conceptions evolved among the Aryans.

It has long been realized that the vows of the Buddhist and Jaina monks, among which the vow of ahiṃsā stands first, closely agree with those of the Brahmanic renouncer.[199] Alsdorf does not enter into a discussion of this matter, obviously, because it does not furnish any material for the history of vegetarianism. If, however, we want to find out the origin of the more comprehensive idea of ahiṃsā and to understand its magico-ritualistic background – which has been recognized but not explained by Alsdorf – we must search for the specific motives on which the rule of ahiṃsā for the Brahmanic renouncer is based.

This I propose to do in the present paper. I take as a starting point all the contexts in which the injunction of ahiṃsā is given by the *Manu-Smṛti*[200] – which reflects a fully developed ahiṃsā-doctrine – and try to trace them back to earlier sources. Among these the *Dharmasūtras* of Āpastamba, Baudhāyana, Vasiṣṭha and

198 Cf. the sources quoted by Alsdorf himself, 1. c., 69 n. 1.

199 Cf. H. Jacobi, *Jaina Sutras* I (Sacred Books of the East XXII, Oxford 1884), XXII sqq., and the earlier authorities quoted there.

200 For the sake of brevity I have refrained from discussing the parallels from the *Mahābhārata*. Much material from this source is found in O. Strauss, 'Ethische Probleme aus dem *Mahābhārata*', *Gior. d. Soc. As. Ital.* 24, 1912, 194–335, and Alsdorf, loc. cit., 29 sqq.

201 The chronology, absolute and relative, of the *Dharmasūtras* is a matter of controversy. It cannot even be asserted that in their present form they are pre-Buddhistic. There is, however, no evidence that they either

Gautama[201] provide the bulk of the material and help to pave the way back to the original source in which the idea of ahiṃsā was conceived. [628]

II

1. According to Manu ahiṃsā is the duty of all the four classes *(varṇa)*: 'Non injury, truth, non-stealing, purity, control of the senses – this Manu has declared to be the comprehensive law for the four classes.'[202]

A similar rule is known to the *Kauṭilīya Arthaśāstra*, which is certainly older than the *Manu-Smṛti*: '(The *svadharma*) of all (classes and orders of life, *āśrama*) are non-injury, truth, purity, freedom from envy, freedom from malice, and indulgence.'[203]

Non-injury as a duty of all is mentioned by Vasiṣṭha,[204] too, but here the sūtra may be either an interpolation or, as Alsdorf (*l. c.*, 29) surmises, a secondary modification of an old śloka which did not contain the word ahiṃsā. At any rate, comparable injunctions do not occur elsewhere in the older law-books.[205]

2. Ahiṃsā-vegetarianism: Animals are not be killed and eaten at all. This is advocated in the third layer of Manu's rules on meat-eating (5, 45–56).[206] The gist of the whole is not so much a condemnation of the Vedic ritual and its animal sacrifices, but rather the propagation of a renouncer-like conduct. This appears in 5, 56: 'There is no sin in eating meat, in (drinking) spirituous liquor and

---

presuppose or oppose Buddhist or Jaina teachings. As to their relative chronology, recent research points to the conclusion that Āpastamba and Baudhāyana are considerably older than Vasiṣṭha and Gautama. Cf. B.K. GHOSH, *Indian Historical Quarterly* 3, 1927, 607 sqq. J.J. MEYER, *Über das Wesen der altindischen Rechtsschriften* (Leipzig 1927), passim. W. GAMPERT, *Die Sühnezeremonien in der altindischen Rechtsliteratur* (Prag 1939), 6 sqq. S.C. BANERJEA, *The Dharma-Sūtras. A study in their origin and development* (Calcutta 1962), 37 sqq.

202 M 10, 63 *ahiṃsā satyam asteyaṃ śaucam indriyanigrahaḥ, etaṃ sāmāsikaṃ dharmaṃ cāturvarṇye 'bravīn manuḥ.*

203 Kauṭ 1, 3, 13 (ed. KANGLE, Bombay 1960) *sarveṣām ahiṃsā satyaṃ śaucam anāsūyānṛśaṃsyaṃ kṣamā ca.*

204 Vas 4, 4 *sarveṣāṃ satyam akrodho dānam ahiṃsā prajananaṃ ca.*

205 BÜHLER, *The Laws of Manu* (SBE XXV. 1886), 416, compares Gaut 8, 23, but this rule refers to a *bahuśruta* and is to be grouped with the ahiṃsā-rules for Brāhmaṇas (below II 4 B).

206 With the exception of 52, which rather belongs to the layer 5, 31–44.

in sexual intercourse; this is the natural way of living beings, but abstention bears great fruits.'[207] Alsdorf (loc. cit., 21) thinks that this śloka has been taken from some other context in order to soften down the glaring contradiction between the demands of strict vegetarianism and the milder opinions of the preceding passages. But it is more probable that it has been added in order to put the whole discussion into its proper context – that of the renunciatory way of life which is the ideal of the Brāhmaṇa.

An attack on the Vedic sacrifice is contained in 5, 53: 'He who for a hundred years annually sacrifices a horse-sacrifice, and he who [629] does not eat meat (at all) – for both of these the fruit of their meritorious deeds is the same.'[208] The author concedes that the sacrifice has its merits, but he insinuates its practical inefficiency and implies that by avoiding meat one attains without effort everything one desires.[209]

In the next śloka we read: 'By eating (only) kosher fruits and roots and by eating (only) the food of silent ascetics, one does not gain the same fruit as by complete avoidance of meat.'[210] If the food of the muni consisted only of vegetarian diet, this injunction would be senseless. Presumably munis were, at Manu's time, still accepting meat and also living on the flesh of animals killed by beasts of prey (cf. below II 5 B).

In 55, a pseudo-etymology of the word *māṃsa* 'meat' is given which reflects the primitive belief that the animal whose meat is eaten in this world will eat, in return, the eater in the next world: 'Me eat will in the next world whose meat I eat in this world; the wise ones proclaim this to be the meatness of meat (= this is why meat is called meat).'[211]

In the earlier sources no trace of strict vegetarianism is found. In modern times vegetarianism has led to substituting effigies of animals made of flour for the sacrificial victim. But this sacrifice

207 M 5, 56 *na māṃsabhakṣaṇe doṣo na madye na ca maithune, pravṛttir eṣā bhūtānāṃ nivṛttis tu mahāphalā.*

208 M. 5, 53 *varṣe-varṣe 'śvamedhena yo yajeta śataṃ samāḥ, māṃsāni ca na khāded yas tayoḥ puṇyaphalaṃ samam.*

209 Cf. M 5, 47 *yad dhyāyati yat kurute dhṛtiṃ badhnāti yatra ca, tad avāpnoty ayatnena yo hinasti na kiṃcana.*

210 M 5, 54 *phalamūlāśanair medhyair munyannānāṃ ca bhojanaiḥ, na tat phalam avāpnoti yan māṃsaparivarjanāt.*

211 M 5, 55 *māṃ sa bhakṣayitā 'mutra yasya māṃsam ihādmy aham, etan māṃsasya māṃsatvaṃ pravadanti manīṣiṇah.* The adaptation of the pun is that of C.R. LANMAN, *A Sanskrit Reader* (Boston 1884), 350.

of *piṣṭapaśu* is unknown even to Manu. He does, however, mention *piṣṭapaśu* in a different context (v. below II 3).

The earlier occurrences of *piṣṭapaśu* have no connection with ahiṃsā or vegetarianism. In the *Śāṅkhāyana-Gṛhyasūtra* an offering of pairs of animals made of flour is prescribed for the full moon of the month Caitra.[212] This sacrifice is completely isolated, and we have no means to tell why the animals were made of flour.

A similar substitute for animals is already known to the Śrauta-ritual. In the Varuṇapraghāsa a ram and a ewe are made of barley, and they are called *anṛtapaśū* 'untrue animals'.[213] In the context of the *Varuṇapraghāsa* there is no allusion to the prohibition [630] of animal-slaughter, and the reason why the animals are made of barley is obviously that barley is the grain belonging to Varuṇa.

3. Ahiṃsā-vegetarianism with the exception of sacrificial victims. Manu 5, 31–44 teaches the duty of eating meat in the sacrifice, but prohibits it on all other occasions: ' "The eating of meat (is ordained) for sacrifice": this is transmitted as a divine rule. But practising (it) on other (occasions) is said to be a demoniac rule.'[214] One does not do wrong by eating meat while honouring the gods, the fathers and guests, irrespective of the way in which the meat was procured.[215] In 33, use is made of the same idea as in 55 (v. above II 2), but the lawful eating of meat is excepted from the evil consequences:

> A twice-born man who knows the rules must not eat meat against the rules unless he is in distress. For, having eaten meat against the rules, he is, when dead, eaten by these (animals) without fail.[216]

In 43, however, hiṃsā is prohibited also if one is in distress, unless it is prescribed in the Veda, and this applies to every Brāhmaṇa, in

---

212 ŚGS 4, 19 *mithunānāṃ ca yathopapādaṃ piṣṭasya kṛtvā*. The later *Vaikhānasa-Smārtasūtra* 4, 8 has a Caitra-offering with totally different offerings.

213 *Maitrāyaṇī-Saṃhitā* 1, 10, 12. *Kāṭhaka* 36, 6.

214 M 5, 31 *yajñāya jagdhir māṃsasyety eṣa daivo vidhiḥ smṛtaḥ, ato 'nyathā pravṛttis tu rākṣaso vidhir ucyate*.

215 M 5, 32 *krītvā svayaṃ vāpy utpādya paropahṛtam eva vā, devān pitṝṃś cārcayitvā khādan māṃsaṃ na duṣyati*. 41 *madhuparke ca yajñe ca pitṛdaivatakarmaṇi, atraiva paśavo hiṃsyā nānyatrety abravīn manuḥ*.

216 M 5, 33 *nādyād avidhinā māṃsaṃ vidhijño 'nāpadi dvijaḥ, jagdhvā hy avidhinā māṃsaṃ pretas tair adyate 'vaśaḥ*.

whichever stage of life *(āśrama)* he may live.[217] This shows that the rules given in 5, 31–44 are not all of the same origin but contain different views.

It is obvious that these rules are only meant for Brāhmaṇas since only they could partake of the sacrificial victim. That the other classes did eat meat and that there was no objection to it, appears from 34 where the sin of a hunter who kills deer for gain is considered to be less grave than that of one – we have to add: Brāhmaṇa – who eats meat at random.[218] If a Brāhmaṇa has the desire for meat he is allowed to make an animal of ghee or flour, but he shall never wish to kill an animal at random.[219]

In 39, it is stated that killing *(vadha)* on ritual occasions is to be considered as non-killing *(avadha)* since animals were created for the sake of sacrifice by Svayambhū, and since the sacrifice is [631] meant for the welfare of the whole world.[220] And injury *(hiṃsā)* to moving and immovable creatures which is enjoined by the Veda is to be known as non-injury *(ahiṃsā)*.[221] The inclusion of immovable beings goes beyond the intentions of the context which is only concerned with meat-eating, but it represents an old conception mentioned also in 40: 'Plants, cattle, trees, (other animals) moving horizontally (like tortoises, etc.), and birds, which have met their death for the sake of sacrifice, attain again higher existences.'[222] The highest bliss is assured to sacrificer and victim alike: 'A twice-born man who knows the true meaning of the Veda and injures animals for these purposes (viz. guest-reception, sacrifice to gods and fathers) makes himself and the animal go to the highest state of existence (in heaven).'[223]

The śloka Manu 5, 41 also occurs in Vasiṣṭha 4, 6 at the beginning of the chapter on impurity. Alsdorf (loc. cit., 24) reasonably suggests

---

217 M 5, 43 *gṛhe gurāv araṇye vā nivasann ātmavān dvijaḥ, nāvedavihitāṃ hiṃsām āpady api samācaret.*

218 M 5, 34 *na tādṛśaṃ bhavaty eno mṛgahantur dhanārthinaḥ, yādṛśaṃ bhavati pretya vṛthāmāṃsāni khādataḥ.*

219 M 5, 37 *kuryād ghṛtapaśuṃ saṅge kuryāt piṣṭapaśuṃ tathā, na tv eva tu vṛthā hantuṃ paśum icchet kadācana.*

220 M 5, 39 *yajñārthaṃ paśavaḥ sṛṣṭāḥ svayam eva svayaṃbhuvā, yajño 'sya bhūtyai sarvasya tasmād yajñe vadho 'vadhaḥ.*

221 M 5, 44 *yā vedavihitā hiṃsā niyatāsmiṃś carācare, ahiṃsām eva tāṃ vidyād vedād dharmo hi nirbabhau.*

222 M 5, 40 *oṣadhyaḥ paśavo vṛkṣās tiryañcaḥ pakṣiṇas tathā, yajñārthaṃ nidhanaṃ prāptāḥ prāpnuvanty ucchritīḥ punaḥ.*

223 M 5, 42 *eṣv artheṣu paśūn hiṃsan vedatattvārthavid dvijaḥ, ātmānaṃ ca paśuṃ caiva gamayaty uttamāṃ gatim.* Cf. 41.

that it is an interpolation. The same holds good, in my opinion, for the occurrence of the śloka in *Śāṅkhāyana-Gṛhyasūtra* 2, 16, 1, where it is quoted in the context of the *madhuparka*, the guest-reception. This (as well as the following) paragraph interrupts the rules referring to the persons to be considered as guests or not.

The older law-books do not mention the restriction of meat-eating to ritual occasions. But we read in the last section of the *Chāndogya-Upaniṣad*:

> This Brahmā said to Prajāpati, Prajāpati to Manu, Manu to his progeny: He, who having returned from the household of his teacher after having learned the Veda and after having done in addition (to the study of the Veda) the work for the teacher according to the rules, and having established himself in a household (of his own) studies (the Veda) for himself in a pure place, raises law-abiding (students); who, having concentrated all his senses on the Self (soul), does not injure any living being except at the right place and time (i.e. in sacrifice); he, indeed, who conducts himself thus as long as he lives enters the world of Brahmā and does not return (i.e., is not reborn).[224]

This restriction of [632] injuring any being to the sacrifice agrees with the idea expressed in *Manu* 5, 40 and 44. And the passage shows that the Brāhmaṇa had to practise ahiṃsā in daily life already in fairly early times.

4. Special injunctions of ahiṃsā are given for the Brāhmaṇa.

A. A Brāhmaṇa must, unless he is in distress, follow a means of livelihood which does not cause injury to living beings, or at least causes only little injury.[225] Actually he shall as far as possible not follow the ways of the world at all for the sake of livelihood.[226]

---

224 ChU 8, 15 *tad dhaitad brahmā prajāpataya uvāca, prajāpatir manave, manuḥ prajābhyah: ācāryakulād vedam adhītya yathāvidhānaṃ guroḥ karma [kṛtvā] atiśeṣeṇābhisamāvṛtya kuṭumbe sthitvā śucau deśe svādhyāyam adhīyāno dharmikān vidadhad ātmani sarvendriyāṇi saṃpratisthāpyāhiṃsant sarvabhūtāny anyatra tīrthebhyaḥ sa khalv evam vartayan yāvad āyuṣaṃ brahmalokam abhisaṃpadyate na ca punar āvartate* – *[kṛtvā]* is BÖHTLINGK's emendation.

225 M 4, 2 *adroheṇaiva bhūtānām alpadroheṇa vā punaḥ, yā vṛttis tāṃ samāsthāya vipro jīved anāpadi.*

226 M 4, 11 *na lokavṛttaṃ varteta vṛttihetoḥ kathaṃcana.*

Thus a Brāhmaṇa must avoid agriculture since it involves doing injury to living beings: 'But a Brāhmaṇa or a Kṣatriya, living by a Vaiśya's occupation, shall avoid with care agriculture which consists mainly in doing injury and depends on others. People think that agriculture is good, (but) this occupation is blamed by the virtuous: (for) the wooden (implement) with iron point injures the earth and the (creatures) living in the earth.'[227] The fact that the Kṣatriya is here mentioned along with the Brāhmaṇa can hardly be interpreted in that way that the Kṣatriya, too, must abstain from agriculture because it involves hiṃsā. Most probably the Kṣatriya is to avoid agriculture since it depends on others (*parādhīna*).

According to Gautama a śrotriya, a Brāhmaṇa well-versed in the Veda, is the final authority in doubtful law-suits 'since he is incapable of injuring or favouring living beings'.[228]

In older times agriculture was not forbidden for Brāhmaṇas, and this rule is preserved by Manu 10, 82. But Gautama gives a restriction: 'agriculture and trade (are allowed to the Brāhmaṇa) if he does not do the work himself.'[229] The motivation for this rule is presumably that being engaged in worldly affairs would impede his proper occupation, the study of the Veda. But the idea of ahiṃsā comes in when Gautama mentions cattle for slaughter among the goods not to be sold by a Brāhmaṇa living by the Vaiśya's mode of subsistence.[230] [633]

Baudhāyana declares that, if a Brāhmaṇa is unable to attend to both, the study of the Veda and agriculture, the latter must be given up.[231] For the Brāhmaṇa it is preferable to be poor in worldly possessions but rich in the knowledge of the Veda, and a verse praising ascetic ideals is added:

> A fat roaring humped bull who does not restrain himself,
> who strikes moving beings, is violent, speaks as he likes,
> does not attain (the world of) the gods; but those who are
> emaciated and (small like) atoms, go there.[232]

---

227 M 10, 83 *vaiśyapravṛttyāpi jīvaṃs tu brāhmaṇaḥ kṣatriyo 'pi vā, hiṃsāprāyāṃ parādhīnāṃ kṛṣiṃ yatnena varjayet. 84 kṛṣiṃ sādhv iti manyante sā vṛttiḥ sadvigarhitā, bhūmim bhūmiśayāṃś caiva hanti kāṣṭham ayomukham.*

228 Gaut 28, 51 *yato 'yam aprabhavo bhūtānāṃ hiṃsānugrahayogeṣu.*

229 Gaut 10, 5 *kṛṣivāṇijye cāsvayaṃkṛte.*

230 Gaut 7, 13 *paśavaś ca hiṃsāsaṃyoge.*

231 Baudh 1, 5, 10, 30.

232 Baudh 1, 5, 10, 31 *na vai devān pīvaro 'saṃyatātmā rorūymāṇaḥ kakudī samaśnute, calattundī rabhasaḥ kāmavādī kṛśāsa ity aṇavas tatra yānti.*

If a Brāhmaṇa lives by agriculture, he shall plough with two bulls whose noses are not pierced and who are not castrated, and he shall not strike them with a goad but only coax them again and again.[233]

Baudhāyana gives the generally accepted rule that a Brāhmaṇa who cannot live by the means proper for his class may live like a Kṣatriya; but he adds that according to Gautama the duties of a Kṣatriya are too cruel for him.[234] The text transmitted under the name of Gautama does not contain this rule, but agrees with Baudhāyana's own view.[235]

Baudhāyana's rule about the way in which a Brāhmaṇa should plough and the view attributed to Gautama show that there was a strong movement which tried to prevent the Brāhmaṇa from becoming involved in any kind of violence.

Under the same aspect an injunction given by Āpastamba may be viewed. In the chapter on murder and homicide he says that 'a Brāhmaṇa shall not take a weapon, not even if he only wants to inspect it'.[236] Presumably this rule is given for the purpose to keep the Brāhmaṇa off from the remotest contact with the means of violence.

B. A Brāhmaṇa who is a snātaka can attain heaven by ahiṃsā and other vows: 'He who is persevering, gentle, controlled, does not associate with people of cruel conduct, does not injure (living beings), shall, if he follows these vows, win heaven by control (of the senses) and by liberality.'[237] [634]

Ahiṃsā belongs to the means by which supernatural faculties are acquired: 'By continuous study of the Veda, by purity, austerities, and non-injury to living beings he remembers his former births.'[238]

From these passages it appears that ahiṃsā is a vow which is treated on the same level as other specifically Brahmanic vows which are, as a rule, not expected of the common man.

---

233 Baudh 2, 2, 4, 21 *asyūtanāsikābhyāṃ samuṣkābhyām atudann ārayā muhur muhur abhyucchandayan*. Cf. Vas 2, 32.

234 Baudh 2, 2, 4, 17 *neti gautamo 'tyugro hi kṣatradharmo brāhmaṇasya.*

235 Gaut 7, 6.

236 Ap 1, 10, 29, 6 *parīkṣārtho 'pi brāhmaṇa āyudhaṃ nādadīta.*

237 M 4, 246 *dṛḍhakārī mṛdur dāntaḥ krūrācārair asaṃvasan, ahiṃsro damadānābhyāṃ jaget svargaṃ tathāvrataḥ*. The other way round the same is formulated in 4, 170: A snātaka, who enjoys doing injury *(hiṃsārata)* does not gain happiness in this world.

238 M 4, 148 *vedābhyāsena satataṃ śaucena tapasaiva ca, adroheṇa ca bhūtānāṃ jātiṃ smarati paurvikīm.*

Ahiṃsā is also one of the vows by which the Brāhmaṇa can attain highest bliss, *niḥśreyasa*, lit. 'the state beyond which there is nothing better':

> The study of the Veda, austerities, knowledge, control of the senses, non-injury, and service for the teacher are the best means to attain highest bliss.[239]

The best means, however, is the knowledge of the universal Self (*ātman*), and the highest bliss is the union with the Self and the cessation of rebirths. The ritual acts prescribed in the karmakāṇḍa of the Veda cause the continuation of rebirths, they are *pravṛtta*, those prescribed in the jñānakāṇḍa cause the cessation of rebirths, they are *nivṛtta*.[240] Therefore a Brāhmaṇa should give up the ritual acts and concentrate himself on the knowledge of the Self.[241] This is virtually identical with renunciation (*sannyāsa*), which was considered to be the ideal conduct of the Brāhmaṇa.

After enumerating the forty sacraments (*saṃskāra*) – that are the ritual duties – of the Brāhmaṇa well-versed in the Veda (*bahuśruta*), Gautama defines the eight qualities of the soul: 'Compassion on all living beings, forbearance, freedom from envy, purity, freedom from exertion (in worldly occupations), auspiciousness, freedom from avarice, and freedom from covetousness.'[242] He who is devoid of these qualities will not be united with Brahman, even if he possesses all the forty sacraments, but he who possesses all the eight qualities of the soul, though only a few of the sacraments, will attain the union with Brahman.[243] Here ahiṃsā is not mentioned but the word *dayā* 'compassion' expresses a similar idea and can be looked upon as one of the positive aspects of ahiṃsā with which it is occasionally used side by side.

[635]

---

239 M 12, 83 *vedābhyāsas tapo jñānam indriyāṇāṃ ca saṃyamaḥ, ahiṃsā gurusevā ca niḥśreyasakaraṃ param.*

240 M 12, 85–93. The Ātman-theory is defined in 91, 118, 125.

241 M 12, 92 *yathoktāny api karmāṇi parihāya dvijottamaḥ, ātmajñāne śame ca syād vedābhyāse ca yatnavān.*

242 Gaut 8, 22–23 *athāṣṭāv ātmaguṇāḥ: dayā sarvabhūteṣu kṣāntir anasūyā śaucam anāyāso maṅgalam akārpaṇyam aspṛheti.*

243 Gaut 8, 24–25 *yasyaite catvāriṃśat saṃskārā na cāṣṭāv ātmaguṇā na sa brahmaṇaḥ sāyujyaṃ sālokyaṃ ca gacchati. yasya tu khalu catvāriṃśat saṃskārāṇām ekadeśo py aṣṭāv ātmaguṇā atha sa brahmaṇaḥ sāyujyaṃ sālokyaṃ ca gacchati.*

Āpastamba recommends the snātaka to avoid all the mistakes like anger, etc. which tend to burn (= hurt) animate beings.[244] This rule is repeated from the introduction to the chapter on penances where it is given in full. It is based on the Ātman-theory and can be compared with Manu's opinion regarding the knowledge of the Self. We shall return to it in the context of the penances (below II 7).

C. Baudhāyana gives special rules for Brāhmaṇa-householders who are called *śālīna* 'living in a hut', *yāyāvara* 'wanderer', and *cakracara* 'circle-goer',[245] and who subject themselves to certain restrictions with regard to their means of subsistence. These modes of life might be looked upon as preliminary stages which finally end in vānaprastha, the life of a hermit in the forest; the tenth mode of life is actually called *vānyā vṛtti*. For a man who has chosen any of these modes of life all worldly duties cease, such as teaching, sacrificing for others, accepting gifts, and performing sacrifices other than those specifically prescribed.

In the context of the rules of purification obligatory for these householders, two verses are quoted which state that the internal purification or that of the self (soul) of creatures consists in ahiṃsā (or *ahiṃsana*).[246]

This shows that they had to abstain from injuring living beings. There is, however, one particular *vṛtti* called *pālanī* 'protecting'[247] or *ahiṃsikā* 'not injuring'. It consists in seeking to obtain from virtuous people husked rice or seeds.[248] Husked rice and seeds are devoid of

---

244 Āp 1, 11, 31, 25 *krodhādīṃś ca bhūtadāhīyān doṣān varjayet*. – Cf. also 2, 2, 5, 13 *sarva-bhūtaparīvādākrośāṃś ca (varjayet)*.

245 Baudh 3, 1–2. That the *śālīnas* and *yāyāvaras* are *gṛhasthas*, and not 'Ermites' and 'Vagants', as J. VARENNE, *Mahā Nārāyaṇa Upaniṣad* (Paris 1960), II, 82, erroneously translates, appears from Vaikh 8, 5. There the *śālīna* is a householder who attends only to his own ritual duties, the *yāyāvara* one who also sacrifices for others and teaches the Veda. *yāyāvara* presumably means 'moving frequently about (in performing sacrifices for others)'. What Baudh is giving are the rules for householders who wish to follow certain ascetic ways of life. Cf. also Baudh 2, 10, 17, 3.

246 Baudh 3, 1, 26 *śrūyate dvividhaṃ śaucaṃ yac chiṣṭaiḥ paryupāsitam, bāhyaṃ nirlepanirgandham antaḥśaucam ahiṃsanam. 27 adbhiḥ śudhyanti gātrāṇi buddhir jñānena śudhyati, ahiṃsayā ca bhūtātmā manaḥ satyena śudhyati*. The latter verse also occurs among the general rules for purification (v. below II 7).

247 HULTZSCH, in his second edition of the text, reads *phālanī*.

248 Baudh 3, 2, 13 *tuṣavihīnāṃs taṇḍulān icchati sajjanebhyo bījāni vā. tuṣavihīna* refers probably to *bījāni*, too.

life – thus the Brāhmaṇa following the *ahiṃsikā vṛtti* accepts only food that has been killed by others.

These *śālīnas* and *yāyāvaras* are sacrificing in the self (*ātmayājin*) by offerings to the vital breaths (*prāṇāhūti*).[249] This mental sacrifice is characteristic for the renouncer.

[636]

5. *A.* The *sannyāsin* 'renouncer' or *parivrājaka (pravrājaka)* 'wandering ascetic' is subjected to the most rigid rules of ahiṃsā.

When entering the Order (*āśrama*) of the sannyāsin, a Brāhmaṇa offers a last sacrifice: 'Having the (sacred) fires in himself, a Brāhmaṇa shall go forth from his house.'[250] He then gives a promise of safety to all the creatures: 'The Brāhmaṇa, who having given fearlessness (= safety) to all the beings goes forth from this house, participates in worlds made of radiance.'[251] This promise will result in his own safety: 'For the twice-born man who has not even caused the slightest fear to living beings there will be no fear from anywhere after he is freed from his body.'[252]

In this context, *abhaya* and *bhaya* are quasi-synonyms of *ahiṃsā* and *hiṃsā*. For, following his promise of *abhaya*, the sannyāsin has to take special safeguards:

> He shall put down his foot purified by sight (i.e. after having made sure that he does not step on any creature), he shall drink water purified (= strained) by a piece of cloth, he shall utter speech purified by truth, his behaviour shall be purified by his mind.[253]

The essence of the sannyāsin's behaviour is described as follows: 'By the restraint of his senses, by the destruction of love and hatred, and by non-injury to living beings he becomes fit for immortality.'[254] The aim of the sannyāsin is the liberation from

---

249 Baudh 2, 7, 12. This and the related texts on the *mānasa yajña* or *prāṇāgnihotra* are collected and commented upon by Varenne, *1. c.*, II, 69 sqq. 53 sqq.

250 M 6, 38 *prājāpatyāṃ nirupyeṣṭiṃ sarvavedasadakṣiṇām, ātmany agnīn samāropya brāhmaṇaḥ pravrajet gṛhāt.*

251 M 6, 39 *yo dattvā sarvabhūtebhyaḥ pravrajaty abhayaṃ gṛhāt, tasya tejomayā lokā bhavanti brahma-vādinaḥ.*

252 M 6, 40 *yasmād aṇv api bhūtānāṃ dvijān notpadyate bhayam, tasya dehād vimuktasya bhayaṃ nāsti kutaścana.*

253 M 6, 46 *dṛṣṭipūtaṃ nyaset pādam vastrapūtaṃ jalam pibet, satyapūtām vaded vācaṃ manaḥpūtaṃ samācaret.* Cf. 68.

transmigration, from the saṃsāra, and the union with the highest Self (*paramātman*) which is present in all creatures: 'By concentration he shall recognize the subtleness of the highest Self and (its) presence in the highest and lowest bodies (= creatures).'[255] This is the same idea we already met with in the context of the ahiṃsā-injunctions for the Brāhmaṇa in general (above II 4 B).

Among the *Dharmasūtras*, the rules for the sannyāsin are given in great detail by Baudhāyana. According to him the vows of true renouncer are non-injury, truth, non-stealing, abstention from [637] sexual intercourse and abandoning (of all possessions). These vows are supplemented by five minor vows, viz. freedom from anger, obedience to the teacher, freedom from negligence, purity and cleanliness in eating.[256]

The ascetic shall not hurt living beings with the weapons (lit. sticks) speech, thought and act.[257] He has to carry with him a piece of cloth for straining water for the purpose of purification.[258]

The rites with which a man enters the order of ascetics are given more fully than in the Manu-Smṛti.[259] They culminate in the promise of safety to all creatures.[260] While Manu (6, 40 v. above) says that the sannyāsin does not experience fear after death, Baudhāyana quotes the following verse: 'The silent ascetic who wanders about after having given fearlessness to all beings – for him no fear arises here on this earth from all the beings either.'[261]

---

254 M 6, 60 *indriyāṇāṃ nirodhena rāgadveṣakṣayeṇa ca, ahiṃsayā ca bhūtānām amṛtatvāya kalpate.* Cf. 75.

255 M 6, 65 *sūkṣmatāṃ cānvavekṣeta yogena paramātmanaḥ, deheṣu ca samutpattim uttameṣu adhameṣu ca.*

256 Baudh 2, 10, 18, 2–3 *athemāni vratāni bhavanti: ahiṃsā satyam astainyaṃ maithuṇasya ca varjanaṃ tyāga ity eva. pañcaivopavratāni bhavanti: akrodho guruśuśrūṣāpramādaḥ śaucam āhāraśuddhiś ceti.*

257 Baudh 2, 6, 11, 23 *vāṅmanaḥkarmadaṇḍair bhūtānām adrohī, daṇḍa* has here hardly the connotation 'means of punishment', as BÜHLER, The Sacred Laws of the Āryas II (SBE XIV.1882), 260, translates.

258 Baudh 2, 6, 11, 24 *pavitraṃ bibhṛyāc chaucārtham.* Cf. *jalapavitram* 2, 10, 17, 12.33.43.

259 Baudh 2, 10, 17 The details can be passed over here. The mantras used for repositing the fires in the self are taken from TS 3, 4, 10, 5; TB 2. 5. 8. 8. where they refer to the Agnyupasthāna; the sannyāsic rite is a reinterpretation of the older ritual, where the sacrificer makes the fire mount himself so that he may not loose it.

260 Baudh 2, 10, 17, 29 *abhayaṃ sarvabhūtebhyo mattaḥ.*

261 Baudh 2, 10, 17, 30 *abhayaṃ sarvabhūtebhyo dattvā yaś carate muniḥ, na tasya sarvabhūtebhyo bhayaṃ cāpīha jāyate.*

The sannyāsin does not sacrifice anymore as the gṛhastha does since he has himself become identical with the sacrificial fires which consist in his vital breaths (*prāṇa*). His sacrifice is an *ātmayajña*, a sacrifice in his self,[262] and it consists of the food he has begged. His detachment from all sensual pleasure requires that he eats his food like a medicine, i.e. without tasting it, after having given portions to the creatures out of compassion.[263]

Vasiṣṭha and Gautama teach that the ascetic has to be indifferent towards the creatures by avoiding injury as well as favour.[264]

Of great importance are Gautama's rules that the ascetic shall not take any limb of plants and trees if it is not (already) separated [638] and that he shall avoid the destruction of seeds.[265] This means that he has to subsist on food devoid of life.

The idea that the sannyāsin must live only on food that is abandoned voluntarily and spontaneously is already present in the Īśopaniṣad:

> All this that moves on earth (= all living beings) is to be dwelled in by (= is the abode of) the Lord. Therefore you should nourish yourself with what is abandoned (voluntarily ceded to you); you should not covet anybody's property. [266]

At the same time this verse is another instance for the conception that the Self (*Ātman*) – here identified with the Lord – dwells in all living beings. This conception is, moreover, again connected with the idea of ahiṃsā: '"Demoniac" are called those worlds, they are covered with blind darkness – to them those people go after death who are killers of souls (or: "a soul").' – 'Who however sees all beings in his own self, and his self in all beings – from him it (the one) does not strive to protect (hide) itself (= to him it reveals itself readily).'[267]

---

262 Baudh 2, 10, 18, 8–9.

263 Baudh 2, 10, 18, 10 *bhūtebhyo dayāpūrvaṃ saṃvibhajya śeṣam adbhiḥ saṃspṛśyauṣadhavat prāśnīyāt.*

264 Vas 10, 29 *upekṣakaḥ sarvabhūtṣu hiṃsānugrahaparihāreṇa*. Gaut 3, 24 *samo bhūteṣu hiṃsānugrahayoḥ.*

265 Gaut 3, 20 *nāviprayuktam oṣadhivanaspatīnām aṅgam upādadīta. 23 varjayed bījavadham.*

266 Īśop 1 *īśāvāsyam idaṃ sarvaṃ yat kiṃ ca jagatyāṃ jagat, tena tyaktena bhuñjīthā mā gṛdhaḥ kasya svid dhanam.* The translations from Īśop are those of P. THIEME, *JAOS* 85, 1965, 89 sqq.

B. The *vānaprastha*, the hermit living in a hut in the forest,[268] is also subjected to a number of restrictions which presuppose ahiṃsā though Manu does not use the term in this context. 'The hermit is to give up all food coming from the village[269] and everything grown on ploughed land.[270] He may eat what is either cooked with fire or ripened by time.'[271] Or, following the rule of the Vaikhānasas, he shall always subsist on flowers, roots and fruits alone which are ripened by time and fallen spontaneously.[272] The hermit shall be compassionate towards all living beings.[273]

Gautama teaches that the vānaprastha has to live on forest [639] produce alone which includes the meat of animals killed by beasts of prey.[274]

Baudhāyana divides the vānaprasthas into two categories – those who cook and those who do not. Among those who cook are those who eat what is generated from semen, viz. the flesh of animals killed by tigers, wolves, falcons and other beasts of prey.[275] The general rule for all Brahma-Vaikhānasas is as follows: 'He shall not injure gnats and flies, he shall endure cold and heat, staying in the forest, contented, enjoying bark and skin (as dress), and water (alone as drink).'[276]

Āpastamba does not explicitly refer to ahiṃsā, but he possibly implies it when he says that the hermit shall enter water slowly and bathe without beating it.[277] This reminds one of the rule for the Jaina monk who is not to beat water either.

---

267 Īśop 3 *asuryā nāma te lokā andhena tamasāvṛtāḥ, tāṃs te pretyābhigacchanti ye ke cātmahano janāḥ.* 6 *yas tu sarvāṇi bhūtāny ātmann evânupaśyati, sarvabhūteṣu cātmānaṃ tato na vijigupsate.*

268 I leave aside the hermit living without hut (M 6, 25 sqq.), who is called *araṇyanityah* by Vas 10, 15, and who is a special type of sannyāsin whose rules apply to him mutatis mutandis.

269 M 6, 3 *saṃtyajya grāmyam āhāram.*

270 M 6, 16 *phālakṛṣṭam.*

271 M 6, 17 *agnipakvāśano vā syāl kālapakvabhug eva vā.*

272 M 6, 21 *puṣpamūlaphalair vâpi kevalair vartayet sadā, kālapakvaiḥ svayaṃśīrṇair vaikhānasamate sthitaḥ.*

273 M 6, 8 *saruabhiitnnukampalea.*

274 Gaut 3, 31 *baiṣka.*

275 Baudh 3, 3, 6 *retovasiktā nāma māṃsam vyāghravṛkaśyenādibhir anyatamena vā hatam.* Cf. 2, 6, 11, 15 *baiṣkam apy upayuñjīta.*

276 Baudh 3, 3, 18–19 *śāstraparigrahaḥ sarveṣāṃ brahmavaikhānasānām: na druhyed daṃśamaśakān himavāṃs tāpaso bhavet, vanapratiṣṭhaḥ saṃtuṣṭaś cīracarmajalapriyaḥ. tāpasa* is here to be taken as opposite of *himavant*, not in the sense of 'performing austerities' as BÜHLER (SBE XIV, 293) has it.

277 Āp 2, 9, 22, 13 *śanair apo 'bhyaveyād anabhighnan.*

6. Among other vows the *brahmacārin*, the Vedic student has to keep that of ahiṃsā: 'He is to avoid honey, meat, perfumes, garlands, spices, women, everything turned sour and injury to animate beings.'[278]

Hiṃsā is mentioned in the same context by Gautama: The student has to abstain from gambling, low service, taking something not offered to him, and injury.[279]

Though ahiṃsā is not referred to by the older Dharmasūtras in connection with the rules for the brahmacārin, it is presupposed in Pāraskara-Gṛhyasūtra where the student is to fetch fire-wood from the woods without injuring trees.[280] The condition that the fire-wood must not be cut off from living trees but must have fallen spontaneously is not mentioned elsewhere, but it can be assumed that the vow of ahiṃsā is implied by the initiation ceremony. On this occasion the teacher commits the pupil to all the gods and to all the beings so that he may not be hurt.[281] These formulas [640] occur already in the Śatapatha-Brāhmaṇa, where the sentence is added: 'Thus his disciple does not suffer any harm.'[282]

It is true that in these passages the brahmacārin's practising ahiṃsā is not explicitly stated; they only say that the student himself is to be protected from injury. But from Pāraskara's rule it can be inferred that the student, in his turn, had to avoid injuring any animate being.

7. Ahiṃsā is one of the means to remove sins, one of the austerities (*tapas*) or penances to be performed by the penitent:

> An oblation in the fire together with the 'great utterances' (*bhūr bhuvaḥ svaḥ*) must daily be made by (the penitent) himself. He must practise non-injury, truth, freedom from anger, and uprightness.[283]

Baudhāyana, too, mentions ahiṃsā as one of the means of penance:

---

278 M 2, 177 *varjayen madhu māṃsaṃ ca gandhaṃ mālyaṃ rasān striyaḥ, śuktāni yāni sarvāṇi prāṇināṃ caiva hiṃsanam.*

279 Gaut 2, 17 *dyūtaṃ hīnasevām adattādānaṃ hiṃsām.* Cf. M 2, 179.

280 PGS 2, 5, 9 *ahiṃsann araṇyāt samidha āhṛtya.*

281 PGS 2, 2, 21 *athainaṃ bhūtebhyaḥ paridadāti … viśvebhyas tvā devebhyaḥ paridadāmi sarvebhyas tvā bhūtebhyaḥ paridadāmi ariṣṭyā iti.*

282 ŚB 11, 5, 4, 3–4 *tathā hāsya brahmacārī na kāñcanārtim ārcchati.*

283 M 11, 223 *mahāvyāhṛtibhir homaḥ kartavyaḥ svayam anvaham, ahiṃsāṃ satyam akrodham ārjavaṃ ca samācaret.*

> Non-injury, truth, non-stealing, ablutions in water in the morning, at noon, and in the evening, obedience towards the teacher, continence, sleeping on the ground, wearing one garment only, and fasting – that are the austerities (penances).[284]

This rule closely agrees with the vows of the sannyāsin (v. above II 5A), and Baudhāyana and Manu obviously presuppose that following some of the sannyāsin's vows for a limited time can free from minor sins. Entering the order of sannyāsa after going through the other three *āśramas* is, according to Manu, the means to remove all sins.[285]

Āpastamba inserts before the chapter on penances a passage on the knowledge of the ātman, and the means by which this knowledge is attained, imply ahiṃsā, though the term is not used:

He shall attend to the methods of concentration which lead to the Self, are accompanied by the abandoning (of passions) and instrumental in not bringing (the passions) forth (again). There is found nothing higher than the attainment of the Self. Therefore we shall quote as examples verses which refer to the attainment of the Self: 'All animate beings are the castle of the (Self), who is lying in concealment, who is not killed, who is spotless; those who attend to the immovable (Self) who lives in a movable dwelling (become) immortal.' [641] 'Despising all what is called an object (of the senses) in this world, the wise man shall attend to that one who is lying in concealment.'[286] 'The wise one who sees all beings in the Self, who reflecting (upon this) does not become perplexed, and who sees the Self everywhere, that Brahman, in truth, shines in heaven ... From him (the Self), the highest, who divides himself, spring all the bodies; he is the root, permanent, eternal.'[287] 'But, the extinction

---

284 Baudh 3, 10, 13 *ahiṃsā satyam astainyaṃ savaneṣūdakopasparśanaṃ guruśuśrūṣā brahmacaryam adhaḥśayanam ekavastratānāśaka iti tapāṃsi*. Cf. also the śloka on purification 1, 5, 8, 2 (the soul is purified by ahiṃsā) which recurs in the chapter on ascetic householders 3, 2, 27 (v. above II 4 C).

285 Cf. M 6, 85.96.

286 Āp 1, 8, 22, 1 *adhyātmikān yogān anutiṣṭhen nyāsasaṃhitān anaiścārikān. 2 ātmalābhān na paraṃ vidyate. 3 tatrātmalābhīyāñ cchlokān udāhariṣyāmaḥ. 4 pūḥ prāṇinaḥ sarva eva guhāśayasyāhanyamānasya, vikalmaṣasyācalaṃ calaniketaṃ ye 'nutiṣṭhanti te 'mṛtāḥ. 5 yad idam id ihed iha loke viṣayam ucyate, vidhūya kavir etad anutiṣṭhed guhāśayam.*

287 Āp 1, 8, 23, 1 *ātman paśyan sarvabhūtāni na muhyec cintayan kaviḥ, ātmānaṃ caiva sarvatra paśyet sa vai brahmā nākapṛṣṭhe virājati. 2 ... parameṣṭhī vibhājaḥ, tasmāt kāyāḥ prabhavanti sarve sa mūlaṃ śāśvatikaḥ sa nityaḥ.*

of the faults in this life has its root in concentration. Having removed the faults which tend to burn (= injure) the animate beings, a wise man goes to (final) peace.

Now we shall exemplify the faults which tend to burn the animate beings: Anger, delight, wrath, greed, perplexity, perfidy, deceit (or: injury), lying, gluttony, slander, envy, lust and rage, disinterest in the Self, non-concentration: the extinction of these (faults) has its root in concentration.

Freedom from anger, from delight, from wrath, from greed, from perplexity, from perfidy, from deceit (or injury), speaking the truth, moderate eating, freedom from slander, from envy, sharing with others, abandoning (all possessions), uprightness, affability, tranquillity, self-control, freedom from conflict with all the animate beings, concentration, honourable conduct, freedom from malice, contentedness – these (virtues) have been agreed upon for all the āśramas; attending to them according to the rules one becomes possessed of that one who is going everywhere (= one becomes united with the universal Self).'[288]

The description of the universal Self closely corresponds to that given in the *Īśopaniṣad* quoted above (II 5 A). The passages cited are presumably taken from an Upaniṣad, which is not preserved [642]. This Upaniṣad was related to or even partly dependent on the *Īśopaniṣad*.[289]

We have seen above (II 4 B), that Āpastamba refers to this section in the context of the duties of the snātaka. In general the attainment of the ātman is a prerogative of the sannyāsin,[290] but it is the aim of every Brāhmaṇa whose whole conduct is guided by sannyāsic ideals. Āpastamba has put the passage on the knowledge of the ātman at the head of the chapter on penances, obviously because he

288 Āp 1, 8, 23, 3 *dosāṇāṃ tu nirghāto yogamūla iha jīvite, nirhṛtya bhūtadāhīyān kṣemaṃ gacchati paṇḍitaḥ. 4 atha bhūtadāhīyān doṣān udāhariṣyāmaḥ. 5 krodho harṣo roṣo lobho moho dambho droho mṛṣodyam atyāśaparīvādāv asūyā kāmamanyū anātmyam ayogas teṣāṃ yogamūlo nirghātaḥ. 6 akrodho 'harṣo 'roṣo 'lobho 'moho 'dambho 'drohaḥ satyavacanam anatyāśo 'paiśunam anāsūyā saṃvibhāgas tyāga ārjavaṃ mārdavaṃ śamo damaḥ sarvabhūtair avirodho yoga āryam ānṛśaṃsaṃ tuṣṭir iti sarvāsramāṇāṃ samayapadāni tāny anutiṣṭhan vidhinā sārvagāmī bhavati.*

289 Cf. Āp. 1, 8, 23, 1 *ātman paśyan sarvabhūtāni na muhyet* with Īśop 7: *yasmint sarvāṇi bhūtāny ātmaivābhūd vijānataḥ, tatra ko mohaḥ kaḥ śoka ekatvam anupaśyataḥ*. Cf. also Yājñavalkya's *na vā are 'haṃ mohaḥ bravīmi* BĀU 2, 4, 13. 4, 5, 14.

290 Cf. Āp 2, 9, 21, 13 sqq.

was of the firm conviction that the sannyāsin-like conduct is the highest penance and safeguards the Brāhmaṇa against committing sins and crimes.

III

From a casual survey of the material collected in the preceding paragraphs it might appear that the idea of ahiṃsā originated among the world-renouncers, was gradually adopted by the Brāhmaṇas and was finally considered to be a rule for the whole society whose values were determined by the precedent of the Brāhmaṇas.

In the *Dharmasūtras* as well as in the *Manu-Smṛti* the prohibition of injuring animate beings is mainly based on the ātman-theory. This theory which is first connected with the ahimsā-idea in the *Īśopaniṣad*, goes – in the fully developed form we are concerned with – back to Yājñavalkya. In the *Bṛhadāraṇyaka-Upaniṣad* he says of the man who has desires: 'Having obtained the end of his action, whatever he does in this world, he comes again from that world to this world for (further) action.'[291] This means that acts, be they good or bad, lead to a new birth in this world. The man however who has no desires anymore (*akāma*) except that for the Self (*ātmakāma*) becomes united with the Brahman (*brahmāpyeti*) and is not reborn.

> This (ātman = Brahman) the Brāhmaṇas wish to know by recitation of the Veda, by sacrifice, by liberality, by austerities, by fasting. Knowing this (ātman) one becomes a silent ascetic. Seeking him as their world the wandering ascetics wander forth.... These two (thoughts) do not overcome him: 'Therefore I did something bad' and 'therefore I did something good' – he overcomes them both; both what he has [643] done and what he has not done do not burn him.... Therefore one who knows thus – after becoming appeased, self-controlled, enduring, indifferent, concentrated – sees the Self in (his) self, sees the Self as everything ... becomes a Brāhmaṇa (in the real sense, viz. a knower

291 BĀU 4, 4, 6 *prāpyāntaṃ karmaṇas tasya yat kiṃ ceha karoty ayam, tasmāt lokāt punar aity asmai lokāya karmaṇe.*

> of Brahman = ātman) who has no doubt (anymore): He is one whose world is Brahman.[292]

Yājñavalkya does not mention ahiṃsā as one of the virtues of the ascetic, but the knowledge of the Self is inseparably connected with renunciation. Renunciation is for him the result of the knowledge that every deed done in this world bears its fruits in the next world and in future births. This fate can be overcome only by realizing the unity of all beings in the universal Self. It would be easily conceivable that the idea of ahiṃsā sprang from the conception that the same Self which dwells in oneself also dwells in all the other beings and that by injuring other beings one would injure oneself. Nevertheless this conclusion would be a fallacy since it does not explain the significance of ahiṃsā in the animistic and pluralistic religion of the Jainas. The Jainas however know a karman-doctrine which is similar to that of Yājñavalkya, and so do the Buddhists who do not recognize a universal Self either.

The *Manu-Smṛti* adduces besides the ātman-theory another motivation for the ahiṃsā-doctrine – the popular belief that the eater of the meat of an animal will be eaten by this animal in the next world (5, 33.55). This conception could easily be connected with the karman-doctrine. But it is older than this theory, and we must consider the attitude taken to it by the theoreticians of the Vedic ritual.

IV

In the *Śāṅkhāyana-Brāhmaṇa* the triṣṭubh meter used in the morning-litany of the Soma-sacrifice is identified with force (*bala*) and strength (*vīrya*), the bṛhatī and uṣṇih with large and small cattle, respectively. By using the triṣṭubh before and after, the bṛhatī and uṣṇih cattle is encircled by strength and force:

> In the middle are cattle connected with the bṛhatī and the uṣṇih; having encircled cattle from both sides with force and

292 BĀU 4, 4, 22–23 . . . *tam etaṃ vedānuvacanena brāhmaṇā vividiṣanti yajñena dānena tapasānāśakenaitam eva viditvā munir bhavati, etam eva pravrājino lokam icchantaḥ pravrājanti . . . etam u haivaite na tarata ity ataḥ pāpam akaravam ity ataḥ kalyāṇam akaravam ity ubhe u haivaiṣa ete tarati nainaṃ kṛtākṛte tapataḥ . . . tasmād evaṃvic chānto dānta uparatas titikṣuḥ samāhito bhūtvātmany evātmānaṃ paśyati sarvam ātmānam paśyati . . . avicikitso brāhmaṇo bhavaty eṣa brahmalokaḥ*. Cf. also BĀU 3, 4 and 5.

> strength, he (the hotṛ) puts (cattle) into the sacrificer. Thus cattle do not run away [644] from the sacrificer. Just as men eat cattle in this world, partake of them, so cattle eat men in yonder world, partake of them. He (the sacrificer) seizes them in this world through the morning-litany; they, seized in this world, do not eat him in yonder world, do not partake of him; just as he eats them in this world, partakes of them, so he eats them in yonder world, partakes of them.[293]

Being eaten in yonder world is considered as common fate. But one can evade this fate by magical means, in this case by the morning-litany of the Soma-sacrifice. Generally the magical power consists in the knowledge of an equivalence or correspondence between the object and the means. The correspondence Śāṅkhāyana establishes refers to the 'seizing' of cattle and has no immediate connection with the eating of cattle, but it is implied that 'seizing' means winning power over cattle in this and the next world.

Another example is furnished by the Śatapatha-Brāhmaṇa:

> From this sacrifice, in truth, the man (= the sacrificer) is born. What food a man consumes in this world, that consumes him, in return, in yonder world. This sacrifice is, in truth, performed as one of fermenting (= intoxicating) drink, and fermenting drink is not to be consumed by a Brāhmaṇa. He is born from what is not to be consumed, and the food does not, in return, consume him in yonder world. Therefore the Sautrāmaṇī is the sacrifice of a Brāhmaṇa.[294]

Here the author argues that being born from something unconsumable guarantees that the sacrificer cannot be consumed either in yonder world.

---

293 ŚāṅkhB 11, 3 *madhye bārhatāś cauṣṇīhāś ca paśavo balenaiva tad vīryeṇobhayataḥ paśūn parigṛhya yajamāne dadhāti tathā ha yajamānāt paśavo 'nutkrāmukā bhavanti tad yathā ha vā asmiṁl loke manuṣyāḥ paśūn aśnanti yathaibhir bhuñjata evam evāmuṣmiṁl loke paśavo manuṣyān aśnanty evam ebhir bhuñjate sa enān iha prātaranuvākenāvarunddhe tam ihāvaruddhā amuṣmiṁl loke nāśnanti nainena pratibhuñjate yathaivainān asmiṁl loke 'śnāti yathaibhir bhuṅkta evam evainān amuṣmiṁl loke 'śnāty evam ebhir bhuṅkte.*

294 ŚB 12, 9, 1, 1 *etasmād vai yajñāt puruṣo jāyate, sa yad dha vā asmiṁl loke puruṣo 'nnam atti tad enam amuṣmiṁl loke pratyatti sa vā eṣa parisruto yajñas tāyate 'nādyā vai brāhmaṇena parisrut sa etasmād anādyāj jāyate taṃ hāmuṣmiṁl loke 'nnaṃ na pratyatti tasmād eṣa brāhmaṇayajña eva yat sautrāmaṇī.*

The fullest account of this conception is found in the story of Bhṛgu's visit to yonder world.[295] Bhṛgu considered himself superior in knowledge to his father Varuṇa. To teach him a lesson, Varuṇa sends him to yonder world. There Bhṛgu sees: (1) a man cutting a man apiece; (2) a man eating a man who is crying aloud; and (3) a man eating a man who is silent. Asking for the reason [645] of these horrible happenings, Bhṛgu is told to ask his father. Varuṇa gives him the following explanations: The first man is a tree which was cut in this world and is now doing the same to the wood-cutter, the remedy (*niṣkṛti* JB, *prāyaścitta* ŚB) for this is to put fire-wood on the fire in the daily Agnihotra, thus one evades being cut by trees in yonder world. The second man is an animal which was slaughtered and eaten and is now eating the eater; the remedy is the offering of milk in the Agnihotra – milk being an equivalent of the cow and then of cattle in general – (ŚB) or offering the first offering with loud recitation (JB). The third man is a plant which was eaten and is now eating the eater; the remedy is the illumination of the Agnihotra milk with a straw in order to see in the dark of the early morning or late evening and to be able to prevent the milk from boiling over – (ŚB) or to offer the last offering with silent recitation (JB).

H. Lommel[296] has shown that the legend is based on the conception of yonder world as an inverted world where everything of this world is turned into its opposite. He has further drawn the convincing conclusion that originally this conception has nothing to do with ethical ideas and that the fate man undergoes in yonder world is not to be considered as a punishment. The idea of the inverted world is a simple and naive conception of the inevitable course of the world, for which Lommel has adduced a great number of ethnological and folkloristic parallels.

Viewed from this standpoint, the remedies given in the Brāhmaṇas appear to be arbitrary and unsatisfactory. But they are in perfect consonance with the magical theory of the Vedic ritualists. That man suffers in the next world the same fate he has caused to his victims in this world was probably common belief. In the ritual texts it is only rarely mentioned presumably because it was of little consequence for the ritualist who, by establishing symbolical equivalences for all the ritual acts, was able to secure any end for the sacrificer in this and the next world.

295 ŚB 11, 6, 1. JB I, 42–44. I confine myself to giving a short description of the points essential for my purpose.

296 Paideuma 4, 1950, 93–109.

The ritualists were however deeply concerned with the killing and injuring of animate beings which occurs in the sacrifice itself. It appears from the Bhṛgu-legend that they were animists who treated trees, plants and the elements (water is mentioned in the legend) on a par with men and animals. Killing and hurting creatures had undesirable consequences which must be eliminated. [646]

V

The most general theory for eliminating the killing in the sacrifice is the conception that the victim or the offering is reborn from the fire in which it is offered:

> They kill, in truth, this sacrifice when they perform it; and when they press out the King (Soma), then they kill him; and when they make an animal consent and cut it up, then they kill it; by pestle and mortar and by the two millstones they kill the haviryajña. After having killed the sacrifice he (the adhvaryu) pours it which has become seed into the fire as its womb, for the womb of the sacrifice is, in truth, the fire; from that (the fire) it (the sacrifice) is reborn.[297]

In general the words 'to kill' and 'to die' are not used. For leading the animal up for sacrifice and killing it *ā labhate* '"he takes hold of" is substituted, for killing alone *saṃ jñapayati* "he makes consent"'.[298] The slaughterer is called *śamitṛ* 'appeaser'.[299] And where the killing and dying is explicitly stated – as in the passage just cited, it is done only in order to nullify or to deny it on the spot. The idea that the animal does not die, but goes to the gods whose herd it joins, is attested already in the *Ṛgveda*.[300] And a Brāhmaṇa says: 'Not to

297 ŚB 11, 1, 2, 1–2 *ghnanti vā etad yajñam, yad enaṃ tanvate yan nv eva rājānam abhiṣuṇvanti tat taṃ ghnanti yat paśuṃ saṃjñapayanti viśāsati tat taṃ ghnanty ulūkhalamusalābhyāṃ dṛṣadupalābhyāṃ haviryajñaṃ ghnanti. taṃ hatvā yajñam, agnāv eva yonau reto bhūtaṃ siñcaty agnir vai yonir yajñasya sa tataḥ prajāyate.*

298 Cf. H. OERTEL, 'Euphemismen in der vedischen Prosa', *Sitzungsber. d. Bayer. Akad. d. Wiss. Phil.-hist. Abt.* 1942. 8, 6 sqq. Add *ā sthāpayati* 'to make stop' and *gamayati* 'to make go'.

299 *śamāyati* in the connotation 'to kill' is not used for the killing of the victim in the Brāhrnaṇa-texts: cf. OERTEL, loc. cit., 8 sq.; it occurs in this context first in *Vaitāna Sūtra* 10, 18.

300 ṚV 1, 162, 21.

death, in truth, do they lead (the animal) which they lead to the sacrifice.'[301]

But apart from these more general conceptions the whole ritual is pervaded by acts meant for immediately eliminating any killing and injury – the acts of appeasing (*śānti*).[302] They do not refer only to the offerings but to any kind of injury committed in the course of the sacrifice. These rites are of special interest for the problem under discussion since in their and similar contexts we meet with the earliest occurrences of the word *ahiṃsā* (attested only in the final dative *ahiṃsāyai*). A few examples will suffice to illustrate the working of these rites.

[647]

When the tree that is to serve as the sacrificial post in the animal-sacrifice is felled, precautionary measures are taken to prevent it from being injured:

> 'O plant, protect it', he (the adhvaryu) says in order to protect it. 'O axe, do not injure it' – with these words he puts this (blade of darbha[303] – grass) between it (the tree) and the thunderbolt – the axe is, in truth, a thunderbolt – so that there be no injury.[304]

In a parallel text *śāntyai* is given in place of *ahiṃsāyai*.[305] Here the injury done to the tree is diverted to the blade of grass.

The tree itself, when falling down, is liable to injure the worlds:

> The sacrificial post is, in truth, a thunderbolt; these worlds are afraid of it when it is being hurled down since being hurled down unappeased it is capable of injuring these worlds. When he says: 'With your top do not injure the sky, with your middle (do not injure) the intermediate world, become united with the earth, go to radiance', he thus

301 ŚB 3, 8, 1, 10 *na vā etaṃ mṛtyave nayanti yaṃ yajñāya nayanti.*

302 The material has been collected and discussed in detail by D. J. HOENS, *Śānti I* (Thesis Utrecht 1951).

303 Read: *kuśa-* (WB).

304 MS 3, 9, 3 *oṣadhe trāyasvainam, ity āha trātyā eva svadhite mainaṃ hiṃsīr iti vajro vai svadhitir vajrād vāvāsmā etad antardadhāty ahiṃsāyai.*

305 TS 6, 3, 3, 2.

> appeases it; thus appeased, it is hurled down so that it does not do injury to these worlds.[306]

When the victim has been killed by suffocation, the apertures of its body are sprinkled with water:

> Burning pain hits the vital breaths of the animal being killed. When he says: 'Do not injure its voice, do not injure its breath', he thus frees its vital breaths by water from burning pain. With the words: 'Whatever of you is wounded, whatever of you is stopped (= killed), of that become purified, beautify yourself for the gods', he has made unwounded whatever they have wounded by making it go (= by killing it), that he appeases.[307]

The rest of the water used for this purpose is poured on the earth. Since the burning pain has been transferred from the vital breaths of the animal to the water, the pain now enters the earth: 'When he says: 'Hail to the waters', he thus appeases (them). They thus hit this (earth) appeased so that they do not do injury (to the earth).'[308]

[648]

When the victim is cut open, the same procedure is followed as in the case of felling the tree: The knife is not to injure the animal.[309]

After the offering of the omentum the sacrificer, his wife, and the priests have to cleanse themselves with water: 'That, in truth, they wound what they make consent, what they cut up. Water is (a means of) appeasing, they appease it by water as (a means of) appeasing, they put it together (= heal it) by water.'[310]

---

306 MS 3, 9, 3 *vajro vai yūpas tasmād vā ime lokā nīryamāṇād bibhyatīśvaro hy eṣo 'śānto nīryamāṇa imāṁl lokān hiṃsitor yad āha divam agreṇa mā hiṃsīr antarikṣaṃ madhyena pṛthivyāḥ saṃbhava bhrājaṃ gaccheti śamayaty eva śānta eva nīryata eṣāṃ, lokānām ahiṃsāyai.*

307 MS 3, 10, 1 *paśor vai māryamāṇasya prāṇāñ śug ṛcchati yad āha vācam asya mā hiṃsīḥ prāṇam asya mā hiṃsīr ity adbhir vāvāsyaitat prāṇāñ śuco muñcati yat te krūraṃ yad āsthitaṃ tad etena śundhasva devebhyaḥ śumbahasveti yad evāsya gamayantaḥ krūram akraṃs tad akrūram akas tac śamayati.*

308 MS 3, 10, 1 *yad āha śam adbhya iti śamayaty eva śāntā evemām ṛcchanty ahiṃsāyai.*

309 MS ibid.

310 ŚB 3, 8, 2, 30 *krūrī vā etat kurvanti yat saṃjñāpayanti yad viśāsati śāntir āpas tad adbhiḥ śāntyā śamayante tad adbhiḥ saṃdadhate.*

Water is the most common means of appeasing (*śānti*) or healing (*bheṣaja, niṣkṛti*), and the same or similar formulations are used in other contexts too, for example, when the grain for the sacrificial cakes is threshed and ground and thereby injured or killed,[311] and when the earth is dug up for the construction of the vedi[312] or for the erection of the sacrificial post.[313]

Another way of avoiding injury is found in the symbolical identifications. To prevent the fire-pan from being injured by the fire, the adhvaryu

> fumigates it with horse-dung so that it is not injured, for the horse, in truth, belongs to Prajāpati, (and) Agni is Prajāpati, (and) oneself does not, in truth, injure oneself. That (he does) with dung since that is what was eaten (and therefore) useless. Thus he does not injure the horse nor the other animals.[314]

A pit is dug for depositing the fire-pan while a yajus is recited for which the following motivation is given:

> Prajāpati thought: 'He who will dig her (the earth) up first, will suffer harm.' He saw this yajus: 'Aditi . . . shall dig you in the lap of the earth, o pit'; Aditi . . . is, in truth, this (earth); with her, in truth, he dug that (pit) in her so as to do no injury (to her), for oneself does not injure oneself.[315]

From the last passage it appears that the precautionary measure is taken in order to prevent the being injured from taking revenge on the sacrificer. In a number of instances *ahiṃsāyai* refers to the prevention of injury to the sacrificer, his progeny and cattle. [649] Preventing or healing every possible injury to any being is

311 ŚB 1, 2, 2, 11.14.

312 MS 3, 2, 3.

313 TS 6, 3, 4, 1. KS 26, 5.

314 ŚB 6, 5, 3, 9 *aśvaśakair dhūpayati, prājāpatyo vā aśvaḥ prajāpatir agnir na vā ātmātmānaṃ hinasty ahiṃsāyai tad vai śaknaiva tad dhi jagdhaṃ yātayāma tatho ha naivāśvaṃ hinasti netarān paśūn.*

315 MS 3, 1, 8 *prajāpatir amanyata: yo va asyā agre vikhaniṣyaty ārtiṃ, sa āriṣyatīti. sa etad yajur apaśyad: aditis tvā . . . pṛthivyāḥ sadhasthe . . . khanatv avaṭetīyaṃ vā aditis . . . anayā vai sa tad asyām akhanad ahiṃsāyai na hi svaḥ svaṃ hinasti.*

one of the principles of the ritualistic theory of the Brāhmaṇas. The sacrificer, being instrumental – mostly through the agency of his priests – in every ritual act and therefore responsible, must be safeguarded against any conceivable retaliation.

One might even speak of a ritual ahiṃsā-theory. Though *ahiṃsā* is not used as a terminus technicus in the Brāhmaṇa-texts, the verb *hiṃs* is the most general expression for 'to injure'.

Occasionally *ahiṃsāyai* is used in more general contexts without any reference to the injury done by the sacrificer in the ritual. In a passage relating to the verses addressed to Pūṣan in the Agnyupasthāna, 'the worship of the fires', which follows the Agnihotra, we read:

> 'Pūṣan, the Lord of the paths, protect me', (this is equivalent to) this (earth); 'Pūṣan, the lord of cattle, protect me', (this is equivalent to) the intermediate world; 'Pūṣan, the overlord, protect me', (this is equivalent to) yonder (world): Thus he approached these worlds, he commits himself to these worlds so as not to be injured.[316]

I have selected this passage since its wording closely agrees with the formula used by the teacher when he commits the pupil to all the gods and all the beings 'for not being hurt' (*ariṣṭyai*, v. above II 6).[317] Considering the fact that in a Gṛhyasūtra the student is to avoid injuring trees, it was suggested above that the student, who was to be protected from getting hurt by the beings, had in his turn to avoid hurting the beings. That this is not explicitly stated in the Śatapatha-Brāhmaṇa, is mere coincidence. It was certainly presupposed since it is a logical consequence of the ritual ahiṃsā-theory: The student who did not yet sacrifice and did not yet know how to eliminate by magical means the evil consequences of injuring animate beings had to practise ahiṃsā.

---

316 MS 1, 5, 1 I *pūṣā mā pathipāḥ pātv itīyam eva pūṣā mā paśupāḥ pātv ity antarikṣam eva pūṣā mādhipāḥ pātu ity asā evemān eva Iokān upāsarad ebhyo lokebhyo ātmānaṃ paridhatte 'hiṃsāyai. paridhatte* stands for *paridatte* – a confusion which already occurs in the Ṛgveda.

317 For *ariṣṭyai* used in similar contexts as *ahiṃsāyai* cf. ŚB 13, 4, 15. PB 8, 5, 16. 16, 10, 10.

VI

The animistic world-conception of the Vedic ritualists resembles that of the Jainas, and the ahiṃsā-rules for the Jaina monk apply to the same objects to which the ritual ahiṃsā-theory is applied. The conclusion suggests itself that the ritual ahiṃsā-theory is the ultimate source of the later renunciatory ahiṃsā-[650]doctrine.[318] It is the Vedic ritual which makes us understand the magico-ritualistic background of the ahiṃsā-movement. But it is still a far cry from the theory of the ritualists who believed in being able to compensate for every injury by magical means to that of the renouncer who did not share this belief. The ahiṃsā-doctrine of the renouncer is, in fact, a complete reversal of the ritual theory. Since the reform-religions of the Jina and the Buddha cannot have initiated this development, it is necessary to look for other factors which could have brought it about.

Since its earliest occurrence the ahiṃsā-doctrine is connected with the belief in metempsychosis. The conception of transmigration was gradually developed in the time of the Brāhmaṇa texts. There we meet with the problem of recurring death (*punarmṛtyu*):[319] One began to wonder if the life in yonder world was permanent or if it ended with a new death which resulted in a rebirth in this world. First one tried to solve this problem with the usual magical means; by specific sacrifices it was possible to escape punarmṛtyu. But once doubts were raised they persisted and led to the further question if the effect of ritual acts was permanent and final or if the fruits of these acts could be used up. This idea has certainly contributed to the development of the karman-doctrine which applied the same argument not only to ritual acts, but to every action. The future births

---

318 This was first hinted at by me in *Ztschr. f. vgl. Sprachf.* 78, 1963, 46 n. 1. – M. BLOOMFIELD, *The New World. A Quarterly Review of Religion, Ethics and Theology* 1, 1892, 262 (cf. *ZDMG* 48, 1894, 556 n. 3) connected the formula *svadhite mainam hiṃsīḥ* with the idea of ahimsā. He was, however, biased by the opinion that Buddhist ahiṃsā was identical with vegetarianism and thus stopped short of the correct solution of the problem.

319 Cf. H. OLDENBERG, *Die Lehre der Upanishaden* (Göttingen 1915), 28 sqq. With regard to the development of the transmigration doctrine I agree in principle with E. FRAUWALLNER, *Geschichte der indischen Philosophie* I (Salzburg 1953), 50 sq. 65 sq. It is not possible to go into details here, but it can be maintained that the attempts to derive the idea of metemphychosis from pre-Aryan sources neglect the evidence available in the ritual texts.

depend on the good and bad actions done in this life. Since the fruits of good deeds are being used up and since even sacrifices, by which one attains a blissfull existence in heaven, are only of temporary effect, the conclusion is finally drawn that solely by renouncing all actions, be they good or bad, release from transmigration is possible. Among the actions which produce the most undesirable consequences, the injury done to living beings, quite naturally, stood first, and ahiṃsā became one of the foremost duties of the renouncer.

In the *Dharmasūtras* the life of a man is divided into four successive stages [651]: those of the student, the householder, the hermit in the forest, and the wandering ascetic or renouncer. It has often been suggested that this āśrama-system was an attempt of the orthodox Brāhmaṇas to assimilate and to bring under their control ascetic movements which originated outside their fold and threatened to undermine the social order.[320] There are, however, as pointed out by J.C. Heesterman,[321] in the Vedic ritual some significant details to be found which can be regarded as precursors of the later vānaprastha and pārivrājaka. At the abhijit and viśvajit sacrifices the sacrificer gives all his possessions as dakṣiṇās, retires with his wife to the forest to live on roots and fruits, then procedes to various people to be entertained as a guest in order to regain what he has spent, and finally returns home. In the sarvamedha the sacrificer spends all he has conquered in dakṣiṇās, resumes the sacred fires in himself, goes to the forest and does not return anymore. The brahmacārin corresponds to the dīkṣita whose observances and dress are similar. Thus the three modes outside the world correspond, according to Heesterman, to the stages through which the sacrificer has to pass.

The similarity between brahmacārin and sannyāsin is, I think, equally significant.[322] The student and the renouncer are celibates, live on begged food, carry a staff, recite the Veda,[323] do not perform

---

320 On the āśrama-system cf. M. WINTERNITZ, *Festgabe H. Jacobi* (Bonn 1926), 215–227. F. WEINRICH, *Arch. f. Religionswiss.* 27, 1929, 77–92. B. LIEBICH, *Die vier indischen āsramas* (Breslau 1936). On asceticism cf. L. SKURZAK, 'Etudes sur l'origine de l'ascétisme indien', *Travaux de la Société des Sciences et des Lettres de Wroclaw.* A 15. 1948, who tries to prove the pre-Aryan origin of the wandering ascetics.

321 Wiener Ztschr. f. d. Kunde Süd- und Ostasiens 8, 1964, 24 sqq.

322 The parallelism has been recognized since long ago. Cf. e.g. the survey by S.B. DEO, *History of Jain Monachism* (Poona 1956), 40 sqq.

323 The recitation of the Veda is compulsory for the sannyāsin: Āp 2, 9, 21, 10. Baudh 2, 10, 18, 24. Vas 10, 4–5. M 6, 83.

sacrifices and practise ahiṃsā. Probably the vows of the sannyāsin were partly modelled after those of the brahmacārin. It is striking that Baudhāyana mentions obedience towards the teacher among the duties of the ascetic (v. above II 5 A). Attention must also be drawn to the correspondence between the initiation of the student and the rites with which the ascetic renounces the world: The teacher commits the student to the beings so that they do not hurt him (v. above II 6); the renouncer gives the promise of fearlessness to the beings. Both involve reciprocity. The student is not to hurt the beings, and the renouncer will not experience fear. It was suggested above (V end) that the student had, originally, to avoid injuring beings because he did not yet know how to compensate for injuries. The sannyāsin avoids injury for the [652] opposite reason. He does not apply magical means anymore since he knows that their effect is not permanent. Both modes of life are preparatory stages; their main aim is the acquisition of knowledge. The student strives for the knowledge of the Veda, the renouncer for the knowledge of the ātman. In the course of development both stages could even coalesce. It is possible to remain a lifelong student in the teacher's house,[324] and according to Manu this permanent student will be united with Brahman and will not be reborn, i.e. he attains the same aim as the renouncer.

Sannyāsa can thus be regarded as a return to brahmacarya. In the *Śatapatha-Brāhmaṇa* the brahmacārin's life is equated to a long sacrificial session *(sattra)*.[325] The student does not perform sacrifices, but his duties are identified with the ritual acts. The sannyāsin is an ātmayājin, who sacrifices, while taking his food, in his self, the sacred fires being identified with his vital breaths (v. above II 5 A). The whole ritual is resumed in and absorbed by the individual. This process of individualization and interiorization of the sacrifice is already clearly discernible in the development of the ritual theory itself.[326] The meta-ritualism – to use a term coined by L. Renou[327] – of the Upaniṣads works with the same means as the older ritualism, viz. the knowledge of equivalences. While the ritual makes the sacrificer dependent not only on other men, the officiants, but also on other beings, the victim, offerings, etc., and thus liable to retribution, the meta-ritual eliminates all these factors.

324 Āp 2, 9, 21, 6. Vas 7, 4–6. Gaut 3, 4–9. M 2, 242–244. 247–249
325 ŚB 11, 3, 3, 2.
326 Cf. Heesterman, loc. cit., 14 sqq. 22 sq.
327 Renou-Filliozat, *L'Inde classique* I (Paris 1947), § 578.

The step from external to internal sacrifice certainly preceded the emergence of absolute renunciation. An example for the internal sacrifice is the daily self-study of the Veda (*svādhyāya*), which is a great sacrificial session (*mahāsattra*) called the sacrifice to the *brahman*, the totality of Vedic knowledge and as such the universal principle.[328] He who attends to the daily self-study of the Veda and knows the equivalences with the ritual acts of the sattra 'is, in truth, freed from recurring death, goes to the union with (lit.: to the state of having the self of) brahman'.[329] By depending solely on himself the sacrificer is able to overcome recurring death.

Against the same background must be judged the teaching of Ghora Āṅgirasa in the *Chāndogya-Upaniṣad* in which the word [653] *ahiṃsā* occurs for the first time in the sense of the new doctrine. Ghora equates the whole life of a man to the Soma-sacrifice, and he assigns to pleasures and progeneration their proper place without depreciating them. But he has a kind of moral code: the dakṣiṇās, the gifts to the priests, are identified with austerity, giving (alms), uprightness, non-injury and speaking the truth.[330] Since also the other identifications are based on similarities, there is no reason to suppose that this particular one is arbitrary. The similarity between giving alms and dakṣiṇā is obvious. But what have the other virtues in common with the gift? I think that Ghora interpreted them as varieties of self-denial. By austerity one becomes emasciated, gives of one's own substance; thus the offerings of the *dīkṣita* who is practising *tapas* consist in that which is growing less of his body.[331] Speaking the truth is not a matter of course: one speaks lies in anger, in drunkenness, and even while dreaming.[332] Therefore the Vedic sacrificer has to enter on the vow of truth since men speak untruth, the gods truth, and in the sacrifice a man goes from the world of men to the world of the gods.[333] Continuously speaking the truth is thus a severe kind of self-restraint. Ahiṃsā is not the rule in daily life either; by practising it one saves the life of creatures and denies oneself the natural tendency to live on the other beings. According to the ritual ahiṃsā-theory the creature injured or killed is healed

328 ŚB 11, 5, 6, 3–9. (cf. 7, 3–9).

329 ŚB 11, 5, 6, 9 *ati ha vai mucyate gacchati brahmaṇaḥ sātmatām.*

330 ChU 3, 17, 4 *atha yat tapo dānam ārjavam ahiṃsā satyavacanam iti tā asya dakṣiṇāḥ.*

331 MS 3, 6, 6.

332 Cf. ṚV 7, 86, 6.

333 Cf. ŚB 1, 1, 1.

and restored to life by magical means. By interiorizing the sacrifice in order to become independent from the other beings such external acts are excluded, and this leads to the logical conclusion that injury to living beings had to be avoided altogether.

It is not possible to determine the exact place of Ghora's teaching in the development of Upaniṣadic thought. From his words it seems to appear that he did not yet know the karman-doctrine and the ātman-theory. He seems to have believed in the rebirth of the father in the son,[334] and at the same time in a personal release after death which was the result of the dying man's last wish.[335]

[654]

Ghora imagined the state of release to be in the realm of the light of the primeval seed (*pratnasya retaso jyotis*) which is kindled beyond the sky and the sun; the primeval seed is truth.[336] We do not know if he believed in the survival of the individual soul in after-life or its complete mergence in the light of truth. If the first is the case, he would approximately belong to the period which preceded that of the precursors of the Jina who taught that the released souls rise to the summit of the cosmos and stay there for ever.

Ghora did not yet teach complete renunciation as Yājñavalkya did whose doctrine has become the basis of the renunciatory ideology prevalent among the Brāhmaṇas (v. above III). The austerities Ghora

---

334 ChU 3, 17, 5 . . . *soṣyaty asoṣṭeti punarutpādanam evāsya* '"He will press Soma (= his wife will bear); he has pressed Soma (= his wife has born)" – that is his rebirth.' I am, however, not certain if this is the correct interpretation. – J. NARTEN, *Die sigmatischen Aoriste im Veda* (Wiesbaden, 1964), 268, doubts the ambiguous use of *soṣyaty asoṣṭa*. – Senart, Ganganath Jha and Swāmi Swāhānanda translate 'his mother has born' (WB).

335 ChU 3, 17, 6 . . . *apipāsa eva sa babhūva so 'ntavelāyām etat trayaṃ pratipadyetākṣitam asi acyutam asi prāṇasaṃśitam asīti* 'A man has become really without thirst (desire); he shall, in the hour of death, take refuge to this triad: "You are imperishable, you are immovable, you are the peak of breath (= life)."' On the decisive importance of the last wish for a man's future fate, a notion which was combined with the karman-doctrine by the Buddhists, cf. F. EDGERTON, *Ann. Bhandarkar Or. Inst.* 8, 1927, 219–249.

336 Ghora's idea is derived from ṚV 8, 6, 30 and 1, 50, 10 (both originally referring to the rising of the sun) which are quoted in the Upaniṣad. For *pratnasya retas* = *ṛta* cf. H. LÜDERS, *Varuṇa* (Göttingen 1951–59), 620 sq., whose decisive argument is the verse BĀU 5, 15, 1 = Īśop 15 *hiraṇmayena pātreṇa satyasyāpihitaṃ mukham* 'The face of truth is covered by a golden bowl (= the sun).' This verse, too, occurs in the context of a dying man's prayer.

337 Cf. e.g. the legend of Agastya and Lopāmudrā (ṚV 1, 179) and the frog-hymn (7, 103).

practised were probably of a temporary nature, just as the austerities already practised by the Vedic poets in order to attain higher knowledge.[337] At the close of his life he became without thirst (*apipāsa*: v. p. 653, n. 6), i.e. had renounced all desires and, in the hour of death, took refuge to the truth he had recognized in order not to be reborn. It would seem that his attitude agreed, in essence, with that of the later āśrama-system in which renunciation is the last stage of life. There is, however, one difference: Ghora regarded the whole life as an internal sacrifice, did apparently not perform real sacrifices, while the later doctrine restricted the internal sacrifice to the sannyāsin.

The conclusion that only absolute renunciation can lead to final release from transmigration was presumably drawn soon afterwards. In theory this conclusion was generally accepted, and renunciation became the ideal mode of life for the Brāhmaṇa. In practice many compromises were made. For a long time the old ritual held its position; it was considered to be of limited and relative effect only, but it had its merits for the man who was not yet prepared to recognize the ultimate truth. Ahiṃsā was one of the most prominent values established by the meta-ritualists, and [655] it was adopted as a general rule of conduct for the Brāhmaṇa. Avoiding during the whole life all the faults which hurt living beings is the best means to attain the union with the universal Self, as Āpastamba teaches (v. above II 7). These faults and the virtues opposed to them are moral qualities which predominantly refer to social intercourse, and one can perhaps see here the transition of the idea of ahiṃsā (Āpastamba does not use the term), which was mainly concerned with bodily injury, to that of a general fellow feeling for all living beings as it is often understood in modern India. This also appears from Gautama's putting *dayā* 'compassion' at the head of the eight qualities of the soul (v. above II 4B).[338] The primitive idea of the inverted world (IV), where one suffers the same fate one has caused to other beings, and the transmigration doctrine, both of which Manu adduces in order to justify the injunction of ahiṃsā, will however have contributed more to the spread of 'non-violence' than any ethical motive. The ethical motivation is secondary, the original motive was fear, a fear that resulted from the breakdown of the magico-ritualistic world-conception, but paved the way for establishing higher values.

Tübingen.

---

338 Cf. also Baudh 2, 10, 18, 10 (above p. 637, n. 8).

Appendix III

AHIṂSĀ AND REBIRTH

Hanns-Peter Schmidt

I

[207]

Ahiṃsā 'non-violence', or, more literally, 'non-injury', and the doctrine of metempsychosis are two ideas common to the three Indian religions, Hinduism, Buddhism and Jainism. It is reasonable to assume that these ideas go back to a common source. Whether *ahiṃsā* and metempsychosis depend on each other, are causally related, is an important problem. In an article published in 1968 I have attempted to answer the question of the origin of *ahiṃsā* and its connection with metempsychosis on the basis of the earliest literary evidence.

The relation of *ahiṃsā* to vegetarianism, which is considered its most important expression, was not investigated by me at that time. I only offered the suggestion that vegetarianism may be a popularized form of *ahiṃsā*. Originally strict *ahiṃsā* was probably restricted to the ascetic since it encompasses the abstention from injuring any living creature, be it animal or plant, and with the Jainas even of the elements water, fire and air. In a way my suggestion is corroborated by the view of the Jainas according to which there are two kinds of *ahiṃsā*, viz., the gross (*sthūla*) and the subtle (*sūkṣma*) one. *Sthūla-ahiṃsā* is that of the layman who must refrain from injuring beings with two to five sense-organs, *sūkṣma-ahiṃsā* that of the monk who must avoid injuring any being (cf. Williams 54.64ff. Tähtinen 113). Also in Buddhism injuring lower beings is a lesser sin than injuring higher beings (Tähtinen 113. McDermott 272). In Hindu sources this is not explicitly stated, at least not in connection with the rule of *ahiṃsā*. But Manu 11.109ff. offers a hierarchy of beings which implicitly says the same thing. It comes out most clearly in 141ff.: the killing of small animals with bones requires more severe penance than that of animals without bones; these are followed by the cutting of fruit-trees, etc., living creatures in food, spices, fruits and flowers.

A few words about the meaning and derivation of the word *hiṃsā* are called for since there is still some difference of opinions. In the last century the word was generally explained as an abstract noun derived from the verb *hiṃsati* which was analyzed as a truncated desiderative of *han* 'to strike, slay, kill'. This interpretation is still upheld by some scholars (e.g. Biardeau, Malamoud, Dumont, Zimmermann, Schreiner). It is even assumed that the desiderative meaning is still present in the abstract *hiṃsā* as 'wish to kill or hurt'. This attempt at literal precision is however ill-advised: the verb *hiṃsati* does not show desiderative meaning anywhere. The grammarians who proposed the derivation had to assume that the verb had already lost the desiderative force. The derivation from the [208] desiderative of *han* was first rejected by Wackernagel nearly a hundred years ago and definitively demolished by Liiders (775ff.).

The main objection against deriving *hiṃs* from *han* is the fact that the loss of the root syllable is simply inexplicable. Other truncated desideratives do not offer any analogy: They are all due to the loss of the initial of the zero-grade root due to reduction of an unpronouncable consonant cluster (*dipsati* < *dabh*, *śikṣati* < *śak*, *sīkṣati* < *sah*, *lipsati* < *labh*, *ripsati* < *rabh*, *pitsati* < *pad*, *dhīkṣati* < *dah*). A zero-grade desiderative from *han* could only have resulted in **jighasati*; moreover, we have already in the Ṛgveda the *vṛddhi* desiderative of *jighāṃsati*. Bartholomae believed that a perfect analogy was found in Avestan *jihāt* (Nyāyišn 1.1) which he explained as a desiderative of *gam*, but this should rather have been **jijahāt*, **jijaŋhāt*; it is therefore preferable to adopt the variant reading *jahāt* which is regular sigmatic aorist (Kellens 398 n. 2).

Wackernagel and Lüders derive *hiṃsati* from a root *hiṣ* 'to injure'. Although the present stem-form *híṃsa* occurs earlier than the expected older form *hinás*, it is the latter which is almost exclusively used in the rest of Vedic literature. The objection – still raised by some linguists – that from a root *hiṣ* one should expect **hináṣṭi* and **hiṃṣánti* (cf. *pináṣṭi*, *piṃṣánti*), has plausibly been countered by Lüders: in the case of *hinásti*, the assimilation has worked in the opposite direction. The shift of accent in the ṚV form *híṃsanti* has parallels in *ínvanti*, *jínvanti*, and *pínvanti*, from which secondary present stems were formed just as from *híṃsanti*.

In the following I am giving a shortened version of my earlier paper with some changes and additions (in particular III); in VI–VIII I discuss some of the work published on the subject since 1968 and advance some arguments which may support my original thesis.

II

In order to find out how and in which context the uncompromising absolute value of *ahiṃsā* emerged, I adopted the same method Alsdorf (17ff.) had applied in separating the three historical layers to be distinguished in Manu's rules on meat-eating. In the first stage there is no prohibition, in the second, prohibition in daily life but obligation in the ritual, and in the third, absolute prohibition and advocacy of pure vegetarianism.

Regarding *ahiṃsā* we come to the following result:

1. The rule that *ahiṃsā* belongs to the duties of all four classes (M 10.63) is not known to sources older than Kauṭalya (1.3.13); on Vasiṣṭha 4.4 cf. Alsdorf 29.

2. Vegetarianism as expression of *ahiṃsā* (M 5.45–56). This may be less a rejection of the Vedic animal sacrifice than rather the recommendation of *sannyāsin*-like conduct. In the older sources there is no mention of consistent vegetarianism.

3. Vegetarianism with the exception of sacrificial animals (M 5.31–44). Killing in sacrifice was considered as non-killing since the creator has created the animals for sacrifice and the sacrifice serves the whole world (39). *Hiṃsā* in ritual is considered to be *ahiṃsā* (44). Plants and animals [209] killed in sacrifice attain higher existences (40). The older legal texts do not mention the restriction of meat-eating to the sacrifice (on Vas 4.6 cf. Alsdorf 23f.). But in the last section of the Chāndogya-Upaniṣad (8.15) – which is probably a very late addition – we read:

> He who has returned from the house of his teacher, established himself in his own household, raised law-abiding students, concentrated his senses on the self (*ātman*), did not injure any living being except on ritual occasions, enters the world of *brahman* and is not reborn.

This passage appears to be a polemic against the doctrine according to which rebirth can only be overcome by the renouncer who has given up the material sacrifice which yields only transitory fruits.

Since repeatedly meat-eating in the ritual is opposed to the illegal or random meat-eating (cf. M 5.33; 36; 38), the question arises whether in ancient India animals were slaughtered for food without consecration. According to the interpretation of Keith and Heesterman (1962: 19) the different ways of tying the animal to the sacrificial pole (TS 6.3.6.3) reflect the difference of sacral and profane killing. I do not think that this is cogent since it is also possible to assume a difference between *gṛhya-* and *śrauta*-ritual. Misgivings regarding the assumption that random killing was common arise also from the fact that in hunting the idea of sacrifice is involved. In Mbh 1.109.13 the Ṛṣi Agastya, who is on a hunt in connection with a great sacrificial session (*sattra*), sprinkles the wild animals and dedicates them to the gods. In Mbh 3.37.41 the Pāṇḍavas go hunting with pure arrows and sacrifice to the fathers, gods and brahmins; in 3.79.8 they kill many kinds of wild animals for the sake of the brahmins. The opinion of Zimmermann (180ff.) that on the whole meat was consecrated seems to be justified.

It could of course be objected that in a Buddhist Jātaka (no. 199; cf. Alsdorf 61) and in Kauṭalya's Arthaśāstra (2.26) the slaughter of animals is mentioned without any reference to consecration. Furthermore, also Aśoka, in the first rock edict, does not say anything about the consecration of the animals slaughtered for the imperial kitchen. He even explicitly prohibits the sacrifice of animals in the residence. Since, however, the three animals (two peacocks and one antelope), which were still slaughtered at the time of the edict, were probably connected with a dynastic cult (cf. Schmidt 1980: 48), a consecration of some kind probably took place.

After all, it would be surprising if in India unceremonial slaughter had been widespread while it was taboo in related cultures.

In classical Greece meat sold on the market had to come from animals sacrificed to a deity (Detienne-Vernant 11. Barthiaume 65).

The Zoroastrians have similar rules. He who eats unconsecrated meat will be delivered to the demons (Pahlavi Texts p. 126 § 32–33); the hairs of an unlawfully slaughtered animal become tips of arrows killing the slaughterer (Śāyast-nē-šāyast 10.8); if the head of the animal is not consecrated, the god Hōm will not allow the soul to pass the bridge of the judge to paradise (Persian Rivayats of Hormazyar Framarz, trsl. Dhabhar, 264). Boyce (150) mentions that certain religious rites were prescribed at the killing even of wild animals without, however, giving the source of this rule. [210]

I think it is improbable that we can deduce a general toleration of random slaughter from the lack of reference to the consecration of the victim in certain Indian sources. Unlawful slaughter will certainly have occurred, but the reaction will have been similar to what we know from the African Nuer: bad conscience and shame (Evans-Pritchard 263f.).

4. For the brahmin there are many rules which depend on *ahiṃsā*. Thus he is to earn his living only in professions which do not or do

only little *hiṃsā* (M 4.2). The brahmin and the warrior should avoid agriculture because by ploughing one injures living beings and is made dependent on others (M 10.83–84). In older times agriculture was not prohibited to the brahmin (cf. M 10.82), but Gautama 10.5 gives a restriction: agriculture and trade are allowed only if the brahmin does not do the work himself. He is also prohibited from selling animals for slaughter (Gaut 7.13), which may include sacrificial animals.

Ahiṃsā is one of the means to attain heaven (M 4.246), eternal bliss (M 12.83). The best means, however, is to give up the sacrifices prescribed in the *karmakāṇḍa* of the Veda, since they lead to rebirth, and to follow the spiritual practices of the *jñānakāṇḍa* which lead to knowledge of the *ātman* and union with it and thus overcome rebirth (M 12.85–93; 118; 125). This agrees in essence with renunciation considered as the ideal conduct for the brahmin.

5. The renouncer (*sannyāsin*) or wandering ascetic (*pravrājaka, parivrājaka*) is subjected to the strictest rules of *ahiṃsā*. Upon entering this stage of life one performs a sacrifice whose *dakṣiṇā*s are one's whole possessions, and one reposits the sacred fires in oneself. One gives the promise of fearlessness (*abhaya*) to all beings which guarantees one's own fearlessness (M 6.38–40). Here *abhaya* is a quasi-synonym of *ahiṃsā*. The *sannyāsin* prepares himself for immortality by *ahiṃsā* (M 6.60; cf. 75). His aim is union with the highest self (*paramātman*) which is present in all beings (M 6.65). *Ahiṃsā* as a vow of the renouncer occurs in Baudh (2.10.18.2). The ascetic is to avoid injuring beings by word, thought and deed (2.6.11.23). The consecration culminates in the giving of *abhaya* to all beings (2.10.17.29–30). The renouncer should subsist only on food offered voluntarily and spontaneously, an idea attested already in Īśopaniṣad 1, probably the oldest metrical Upaniṣad.

Rules similar to those for the *sannyāsin* apply to the *vānaprastha*, the hermit in the forest. He should live on flowers, roots and fruits which are ripe and fallen spontaneously (M 6.21) and show compassion towards all beings (M 6.8). Some hermits live on the meat of animals killed by beasts of prey (Baudh 3.3.6; 2.6.11.15; Gaut 3.31). The hermit shall enter water slowly and bathe without beating it (Āp 2.9.22.13). This reminds one of the rule for the Jaina monk, who is not to beat water either.

6. The *brahmacārin*, the Veda student has to avoid honey, meat, perfumes, garlands, spices, women, everything turned sour and injury to living beings (M 2.177). In an earlier text he has to abstain from gambling, low service, taking something not offered to him and

injury (Gaut 2.17; cf. M 2.179). *Ahiṃsā* is also presupposed in a domestic *sūtra* where the student is to fetch fire-wood without injuring trees (PGS 2.5.9). The student's vow [211] of *ahiṃsā* may be implied by the initiation ceremony where the teacher commits the pupil to all the gods and all the beings so that he may not be hurt (PGS 2.2.21). The same formula occurs already in ŚB 11.5.4.3–4. It seems obvious that the student in his turn had to avoid hurting beings.

7. *Ahiṃsā* is one of the means to remove sins, one of the austerities or penances (*tapas*) to be performed by the penitent (M 11.223). Baudhāyana knows this rule, too (3.10.13; cf. 1.5.8.2 which recurs in the chapter on ascetic householders 3.2.27). This actually agrees closely with the vows of the renouncer. Following some of the renouncer's vows for a limited time was obviously considered a means to free oneself from minor sins. Entering the order of *sannyāsa* is the means to remove all sins (M 6.85; 96).

Āpastamba inserts before the chapter on penances a passage on the knowledge of the *ātman* (1.8.22–23), implying that *ahiṃsā* is one of the preconditions for attaining final peace in the universal *ātman*. The description of the *ātman* is similar to that in the Īśopaniṣad (cf. especially Īśop 7 with Āp 1.8.23.1).

Āpastamba refers to this section in the context of the duties of the *snātaka* (1.11.31.25; cf. 2.2.5.13). In general the attainment of the *ātman* is considered a prerogative of the *sannyāsin* (cf. Āp 2.9.21.13ff.), but it is the aim of every brahmin whose whole conduct is guided by sannyāsic ideals.

III

Forerunners of vegetarianism have been assumed in certain substitutions mentioned in the Brāhmaṇas.

1. In the new- and full-moon sacrifice a cake made of barley and rice is identified with the animal victim. The reason given is that when the five standard victims – man, horse, cow, sheep, goat – were offered, the sacrificial sap (*medha*) left them and entered the next in line while the victims themselves became different animals: *kiṃpuruṣa* (mostly interpreted as monkey, but cf. now Parpola *apud* Staal II 62ff. who identifies him as an aboriginal who, like the other animals unfit for sacrifice, belongs to the wilderness), bos gaurus, gayal, camel and *śarabha* (four-horned gazelle). When the sap leaves the goat, the last in line, it enters barley and rice which, since they contain the sap of all the victims, equal them, and their offering

accordingly equals an animal sacrifice (AB 2.8–9. ŚB 1.2.3.6–9. MS 3.10.2). The Vādhūla-Sūtra (IV 19a, cf. Heesterman 1985: 62) explicitly connects this with the creation of agriculture. It is of course tempting to see here at least the beginning of an abolition of animal sacrifices, and this conclusion was drawn by Max Müller (cf. Eggeling's note on ŚB; Lévi 136ff.). In my opinion it is, however, more than doubtful that the general replacement of animal sacrifice by vegetal sacrifice was intended. The fact that the *kiṃpuruṣa*, etc. are declared unfit for sacrifice and therefore also inedible implies that the original victims remained edible in principle, fit for sacrifice. Also the use of the cake in the real animal sacrifice militates against the vegetarian interpretation; the cake here serves to put the sacrificial sap into the animals (ŚB 3.8.3.1–2. KB 10.5. AB 2.8–9. MS 3.10.2). I should [212] infer from the story only an upgrading of the vegetal sacrifice, caused probably by economic changes. The farmer will have kept only a few cattle, mainly as draught animals and milk-producers. When the solemn sacrifice was no longer the privilege of the rich magnates, and also the less affluent brahmin wanted to make his contribution and obtain the merit of the sacrifice, an upgrading of the more modest sacrifices had to follow. The Vādhūla version, in which two fishes bring the agricultural implements and warn the gods not to sacrifice before rice and barley have multiplied, gives an ecological argument. Ecological concern is also attested in Mbh 3.244 where the Pāṇḍavas move from a forest whose herds have been reduced by hunting to another one where there is plentiful game. Economic and ecological considerations may later have favoured vegetarianism, but were hardly its ultimate cause.

2. Vādhūla IV 74 teaches the equivalence of the *soma* with barley and rice and of the *agniṣṭoma* with the *brahmaudana*; at the end Vādhūla says that he prefers twelve rice-mess bowls to the *soma*-sacrifice and the *dakṣiṇā*s. It is difficult to guess Vādhūla's motives, but possibly he advocates a more modest sacrifice.

3. Vādhūla IV 108 (cf. Witzel 391f.) reports that formerly one offered a human victim at the *agnicayana*; it was successively substituted by a horse and a hornless goat. The original five victims – man, horse, bull, ram, goat – whose heads had to be built into the fire-altar were released and substituted by effigies made of rice and barley (or in case of a long *dīkṣā* of clay or gravel: Vādhūla III 59). Since the human head is talked about at length in III 59, one wonders where it comes from. Actually, the systematizers of the ritual were in a dilemma as the many contradictory versions in the other texts show, on which we have the illuminating exposition of Heesterman

(1985: 51f. with n. 41 and 42). The use of the head had been outlawed because it was asuric practice (ŚB 3.8.3.28–29), and the original beheading of the victim was replaced by strangulation. For whatever reason, the heads for the altar were not eliminated, but it became difficult to produce them. Originally they probably came from outside the sacrifice proper. According to BaudhŚS 10.9 the human head and that of the horse were to be taken from battle victims.

Heesterman persuasively argues that the heads of the bull, the ram and the goat came from the dicing and banquet revelry mentioned immediately following. The variants are then attempts to fit the killings of the victims into the standardized form of the animal sacrifice, by necessity resulting in equations which always leave a remainder. Heesterman suggests that the freeing of the animals in Vādhūla IV 108 means being let out of the sacrificial context and beheaded. If this is correct, the substitutes are only a face-saving device to keep the decapitation out of the reformed ritual (in Vādhūla III 59 the effigies are set free, according to Caland thrown away, not offered). Then the Vādhūla passage cannot be considered as evidence for the progress on the way to *ahiṃsā* as Witzel seems to think. However, the evidence about the *agnicayana* heads, contradictory as it is, can be considered 'humanization' of the sacrifice inasmuch as it rejects human sacrifice.

4. In the ritual of the purchase of *soma* the *somakrayiṇī* cow was, as Heesterman (1989: 352ff.) argues, originally the victim for the guest [213] reception of King Soma and, as can be concluded from the identification with the goddess Vāc and Īḍā, Manu's wife who was sacrificed, substitute for the sacrificer's wife. In BaudhŚS (6.17 end) the offering of the *madhuparka* and the cow are mentioned, followed by the words *tam adhvaryur viśāsti* 'the *adhvaryu* gives the various directions concerning her (the cow)', which could however also mean 'the *adhvaryu* cuts her up'. In 21.13 we read that according to Bodhāyana there should be a cake and a cow, according to Śālīki only a cake. Since no further details about the treatment of the cow are given, we do not know for certain whether Bodhayana still practised the sacrifice of the cow.

Heesterman thinks that the mysterious associations of the *somakrayiṇī* were too horrible to be acted out ritually. There may be another reason for the release of the cow. In the myth told in the *gonāmika* (MS 4.2.3; cf. Heesterman 355) it is the female of the opposing party whose head is to be cut off. I should therefore consider it possible that the *somakrayiṇī* was let go because she was the sacrificer's own, and the cow sacrifice had to be dropped because the rival's cow had been eliminated together with the rival himself. In ĀpŚS 10.27.5 the *somakrayiṇī* is ransomed by another cow and sent to the sacrificer's cow-pen. Apparently the *soma*-seller is to keep the substitute cow. Whether here a trace of the original two cows set against each other is preserved remains doubtful since the older sources are silent. At any rate, the *ātithyeṣṭi*, a vegetal substitute for an original animal sacrifice, cannot be counted as evidence for the progress of vegetarianism since the motives are specific and unrelated to the reluctance to kill animals. The animal offering is, after all, made up for by the *agniṣomīya paśu* the next day.

5. The *anṛtapaśū* 'untrue, false animals' in the Varuṇapraghāsa of the *cāturmāsyas* consist of effigies of a ram and a ewe made of barley and are offered respectively to Varuṇa and the Maruts (MS 1.10.12. KS 36.6). The myth connected with the offerings relates that the creatures treated Prajāpati with contempt and left him after he had created them. Prajāpati became Varuṇa and seized them (TB 1.6.4.1; cf. MS 1.10.10. KS 36.5); it is also said that the creatures or Prajāpati's sacrifice were attacked by the Maruts (TB 1.6.4.2; cf. MS 1.10.6;10. KS 36.5). While the contempt and the infidelity of the creatures can be considered as *anṛta* 'untruth', this does not give a satisfactory reason for the *anṛtapaśū* even if we interpret the word as 'animals (destined to atone) for untruth' since the substitution by effigies made of barley would remain unexplained. A concrete reason for the barley is given in the White Yajurveda: Varuṇa is winter, and barley, the winter corn, belongs to him; the creatures ate the barley and were therefore seized by Varuṇa (ŚB 2.5.2.15–16). Thus it becomes clear why the offerings consist of barley – the stolen goods are returned.

However, also here the question why the offerings are animal effigies remains unanswered. One is reminded of the Greek βουφόνια where a bull eats the grain sacrifice on the altar and is consequently slaughtered (Burkert 137f.). It cannot be excluded that in the Varuṇapraghāsa an original animal sacrifice was replaced by the effigies because of some reinterpretation. The offerings for Varuṇa and the Maruts, the ram and the ewe, represent the relationship between king and people (*viś*), and the pairing (*mithuna*) is their reconciliation [214]. For further aspects of this episode I refer to the remarks of Heesterman (1985: 135ff.). In general the *cāturmāsyas* do not contain animal sacrifices, but occasionally they are combined with them (cf. Bhide 172ff.), which shows that no vegetarian reform was connected with the *anṛtapaśū*.

6. The animals made of flour in the *caitra*-sacrifice (ŚGS 4.19) are supposed to be birds (*cakravākas*, etc.) according to the native

commentary. Something similar is mentioned at the Phālgunīkarman (MGS 2.10.1ff. KGS 70). Motives for the substitution cannot be ascertained, and it would be rash to assume a vegetarian tendency.

Figures made of flour (*piṣṭa*) and other material as substitutes for animal victims occur in the Veda only in very specific cases, which can hardly be considered to be at the root of an incipient vegetarian movement. To judge from the known evidence, vegetal substitutes for animals became current only rather late when a vegetarian movement unrelated to the old ritual had emerged.

IV

At the time of the Brāhmaṇa-texts it was believed that the animal whose meat one eats will eat the eater in the other world (KB 11.3); the same idea is even applied to every kind of food (ŚB 12.9.1.1). In order to escape this fate ritual, magical means are applied which usually consist of equivalences or analogies between object and means. The most impressive example is found in the Bhṛgu legend (ŚB 11.6.1. JB 1.42–44); here it is assumed that one can escape from being cut up by trees, eaten by animals and plants by correctly performing the daily *agnihotra*. The means for forestalling are called expiation (*prāyaścitta* or *niṣkṛti*); accordingly the killing and destroying of creatures by which man lives was considered a sin. Every injury occurring in the ritual must be eliminated or nullified.

A very general solution was the assumption that something of the offering, animal or vegetal, that has become 'semen' is poured into the fire, the 'womb' of the sacrifice, so that the sacrifice is reborn from this fire (ŚB 11.1.2.1–2). The sacrifice is full of rites meant to eliminate death and injury, viz., the appeasement rites (*śānti*). In this context we also meet for the first time the word *ahiṃsā*: this or that action is performed so that there may be no injury (*ahiṃsāyai*). By putting a dry blade of grass between the axe and the tree one averts the injury from the living tree to the dead blade (MS 3.9.3). Not enough, the falling tree may injure the worlds and must therefore be appeased (M 3.9.3). When the animal has been suffocated, the body orifices are sprinkled with water while an *ahiṃsā* formula is recited; thereby the vital breaths of the victim are freed from burning pain (MS 3.10.1). The rest of the water is poured on the earth which would be injured if the waters were not appeased before (MS 3.10.1). Of the pain arising during the killing it is also said that it concentrates in the heart and passes from there into the spit for roasting the heart;

the spit is not thrown on the ground or into the water, but buried in wet ground with *ahiṃsā* formulas. In this way one is [215] delivered from Varuṇa who is here the guardian over the sin of killing (ŚB 3.8.5.8–10).

Similar feelings are today still expressed by those who sacrifice goats to Durgā (E. Dimock *apud* O'Flaherty 176):

> One does not usually eat meat because the animal does not want to be killed; it struggles and becomes angry, and so its body becomes full of tempestuous poisons that infect the meat so that it poisons anyone who eats it. But one can eat the meat of a goat sacrificed to Durgā, for the priest pacifies the goat until it is willing to die; and so its meat has none of the poison of hate.

This modern example can also be considered a good illustration of the motivation for the use of the root *śam* 'to appease' as a euphemism for 'to kill'.

Frequently we hear that the sacrifices and creatures in general shall not be injured (e.g. TS 5.2.8.7; ŚB 2.5.1.14). Particular rites are meant to save the sacrificer's cattle from injury (KapKS 31.1: this passage does not refer to *ahiṃsā* in the later sense, viz., the prohibition of killing animals, as Tähtinen 3 thinks).

In the *agnyupasthāna* the sacrificer commits himself to the three worlds in order not to be injured (MS 1.5.11). This is probably the most general form of precautionary measures to protect oneself in all circumstances. The passage is of special interest since also the teacher commits the student to all beings so that he is not harmed (ŚB 11.5.4.3–4). The student is in need of this protection, especially since he cannot yet prevent possible consequences by ritual means.

In the constant reference to prevention of and atonement for death and destruction a principle is recognizable which runs through the whole ritual: the sacrifice with all the destruction it involves is meant to create an intact world. Everything hurt, everything killed is either reborn or healed or sent to the gods alive.

V

The idea that the eater is eaten by the eaten in the other world presupposes that he suffers a second death in the beyond. The texts do not tell us whether one visualized this as an eternal cycle or as a single process. It is not clear either where the person killed in the other world goes. The closest idea we find in the sources is that of recurrent death (*punarmṛtyu*) which occurs rather late in the Brāhmaṇa period and soon disappears again since it is replaced by the doctrine of reincarnation whose precursor it can be understood to be (for a detailed discussion cf. Horsch 1971: 136ff.). Also in this context the sources usually do not tell us whereto the recurrent death leads, whether to a new birth on earth or in yonder world. Probably it is the latter since in one instance (ŚB 2.3.3.8) it is said that he who enters yonder world without having freed himself from death, dies again and again in yonder world. Only in the latest text which mentions *punarmṛtyu* is it equated with *punarājāti*, rebirth (GB 1.1.15; 1.3.22). All instances have in common that recurrent death should be struck off, destroyed by ritual acts, especially by the knowledge of such acts. In the end the ritual is pushed aside altogether. Recurrent death is averted when one knows that death is the self (BĀU 1.2.7), the sacrifices are meant for the self [216] (BĀU 1.5.2), when one knows the water that extinguishes the fire of death (BĀU 3.2.20), or the secret of the wind (BĀU 3.3.2).

At the same time we find the idea that the fruits of the sacrificial work are transitory, are consumed in yonder world. Their destruction can be prevented by faith (*śraddhā*: JB 2.53–54).

He who goes into the wilderness and worships with the words 'faith is our asceticism' reaches the *brahman*, the highest principle and fundament of the world, on the path of the gods. But he who worships in the village with the words 'sacrifice and donations are our gift' reaches, on the path of the fathers, the moon, King Soma, who is the food of the gods; he remains there up to the dregs, i.e. the new moon, and then returns on the same way to earth, is reborn as a plant, an existence he can escape only if he is eaten by somebody and is reborn from that person's semen, according to his conduct as a brahmin, *kṣatriya* or *vaiśya*, or even as a dog, a pig or a *caṇḍāla*. The worst sinners go to a third place and become minute beings of whom it is said 'be born and die', and who return incessantly, with no chance of salvation (ChU 5.3–10. BĀU 6.2). [Similar ideas are attested in Borneo (Hertz 60f.)].

This passage is of special interest since it combines several ideas which are of importance in our context. It contrasts the ascetic in the wilderness with the sacrificer in the village; only the former attains salvation, the latter faces a doubtful future which does not depend only on his sacrificial work, but also on his conduct and even on chance. Thus salvation from transmigration is possible only for him who renounces the world.

The *karman*-theory is also implied here. It was first suggested (BĀU 3.2.13) and then further developed by Yājñavalkya. In the discussion with King Janaka he says that the *ātman* is the ruler of the universe who does not increase by the good (*sādhu*) and does not decrease by the non-good (*asādhu*); he who knows this is not affected by good or bad work (BĀU 4.4.22–23). The following shows that Yājñavalkya considers the striving for the *ātman* as the highest goal for the brahmin. The wandering ascetics (*pravrājaka*) go to the *ātman* as their own world. The ancient wise men knew this and did not desire progeny, nor property, nor the world. At the end of the passage we meet the term *abhaya* 'fearlessness', known from the consecration of the *sannyāsin*. According to Yājñavalkya the brahman is *abhaya*, the state of salvation in which one need not fear any longer (cf. BĀU 4.2.4).

In BĀU 1.4.2 we hear that fear is there where there is a second. This statement is probably to be ascribed to Yājñavalkya who thereby gives a clear formulation of his *brahman-ātman* monism.

When Yājñavalkya decided to become a wandering ascetic himself, he wanted to divide his possessions between his two wives. Maitreyī, who was a *brahmavādinī*, a woman learned in the Veda, asked whether the whole world with all its riches would make her immortal. When Yājñavalkya denied this, she asked him to tell her all he knew, and he taught her his *ātman*-theory (BĀU 4.5).

At the end of his life Yājñavalkya goes into the wilderness. Here we can recognize a first step towards the later doctrine of the four stages of life [217] (*āśrama*), *pravrajyā* later being the fourth and last stage. Since he mentions indifference to progeny as characteristic for the *pravrājaka*, he probably considered renunciation permissible at every period of life, although he himself took this step only in old age. From the reference to earlier wise men we can conclude that there were already outsiders who had withdrawn from the world. Although we do not know what their ideas were, it is probable that they were among those thinkers who sought to overcome recurrent death by knowledge.

Yājñavalkya's thoughts move already on a higher level of philosophical abstraction. The devaluation of the traditional ritual started already earlier as we have seen in the context of the doctrine of recurrent death. More examples for this are found among those passages which imply the interiorization of the ritual. Without questioning the authority of the Veda, the ritual is interiorized by substituting the practical performance by pure knowledge. For instance, he who applies himself to the private recitation of the Veda (*svādhyāya*), performs a great sacrificial session (*mahāsattra*), the sacrifice for the *brahman*, the totality of Vedic knowledge and as such the universal principle; he is freed from recurrent death, becomes of the same self as the *brahman* if he knows the equivalences of the ritual acts of the *sattra* (ŚB 11.5.6.3–9).

The life of the *brahmacārin* is also identified with a long sacrificial session; the *brahmacārin* does not sacrifice, but his duties are identified with the ritual acts (ŚB 11.3.3.2). The renouncer is an *ātmayājin* who, when he eats, sacrifices in himself, and the sacred fires are identified with the vital breaths (Baudh 2.10.18.8–9). The teacher commits his pupil to all beings in order to protect him from harm (ŚB 11.5.4.3–4); in turn the pupil has to abstain from harming the beings (cf. above II 6). The *sannyāsin* gives the beings the promise of fearlessness, and thus has nothing to fear from the beings.

In the same sense of the interiorization of the ritual we must understand the source in which the term *ahiṃsā* occurs for the first time in the sense of the new doctrine (ChU 3.17.4–6). Ghora Āṅgirasa equates the whole life with a *soma*-sacrifice. He assigns to pleasures and progeneration their proper place without depreciating them. He identifies the *dakṣiṇā*s with asceticism, alms-giving, uprightness, non-injury and speaking the truth. The common denominator of these virtues is self-denial. By asceticism one gives of one's own substance; thus the offerings of the *dīkṣita* are what is growing less of his body (MS 3.6.6). By alms-giving one gives of one's property. Uprightness and speaking the truth are not matters of course either. To cheat and lie, be it consciously or unconsciously, belongs to everyday life; one lies in anger, in drunkenness and while dreaming (ṚV 7.86.6). Therefore man, who (by nature) speaks untruth, has to take the vow of truth in the ritual since he thereby enters the world of the gods, who (by nature) speak the truth (ŚB 1.1.1).

Non-injury is not the rule in daily life either; by practising it one denies oneself the natural tendency to live on other beings. Apparently Ghora did not perform real sacrifices. In the end he (actually: Ghora's addressee, Kṛṣṇa Devakīputra; WB) became without thirst and wished for release by entering the realm of the light of the primeval seed, truth, which lies beyond the sky and the sun. It [218] is not clear whether complete mergence in the light of truth or the survival of the individual soul is meant. On the whole it seems that Ghora's attitude agrees with the last stage of life inasmuch as he renounces all desires. By conducting his life as an interiorized sacrifice he actually anticipates the way of the later householder who follows the sannyāsic ideal according to the possibilities of worldly life. Later doctrine, however, restricted the internal sacrifice to the *sannyāsin*, a doctrine which did of course not go unchallenged.

The idea that only renunciation and withdrawal from the world can lead to salvation from transmigration was already conceived by Yājñavalkya or the *munis* he refers to as his predecessors. Although he does not mention *ahiṃsā*, it can be inferred that it went as a matter of course with his identification of the *brahman-ātman* with *abhaya* 'fearlessness' which is also the gift or promise the *sannyāsin* gives to the creatures when undergoing his *dīkṣā*. Every *karman*, every deed produces a fruit, a result, which must be consumed. The good ritual work which was once believed to lead to heaven and immortality was now viewed to be transitory. Once the merit had been used up, a rebirth in this world resulted which was more and more considered to be undesirable because it was unpleasant, full of pain and grief. The generalization of the ritual *karman*-doctrine to one which included all deeds of man intensified the pressure and thus the desire to evade one's fate. If the sacrifice could secure only a temporary stay in heaven, it was devalued, became meaningless for the truly knowing one, and with it also the magical means by which one had believed it possible to annul death and injury. *Ahiṃsā* became by necessity one of the main demands of the thinkers who transcended the ritual. Once one has lost confidence in the magical manipulations, the fear of the revenge of the victim which is repeatedly adduced as a reason for *ahiṃsā* comes to the fore again (cf. M 5.55).

Especially for the brahmins *ahiṃsā* became a general rule. To avoid during the whole life all those mistakes which hurt living beings is the best means to attain the union with the universal *ātman* (ĀpDhS 1.8.23.4). The mistakes and the opposing virtues which are mentioned in this context refer especially to social intercourse, and here one can perhaps see the transition of the idea of *ahiṃsā* which was mainly concerned with physical injury to an ethical idea in a broader sense, to compassion with all beings. Gautama (8.22–23) puts compassion (*dayā*) at the head of the eight qualities of the soul. For Vasiṣṭha (10.5) compassion counts more than giving. The *sannyāsin* does not eat before having given a share to the beings out of compassion (Baudh 2.10.18.10). *Ahiṃsā*, non-injury, *abhaya*, fearlessness and *dayā*, compassion, are ideals which the brahmin in general is to follow, probably after the model of the *sannyāsin*.

VI

Two monographs on *ahiṃsā*, both rich in material, appeared in the 1970s; the work of Alsdorf and myself remained unknown to them. The book of Walli does not offer any historical perspectives. Tähtinen discusses [219] the question of origins in an appendix (132ff.). Although he has recognized the ritual *ahiṃsā*-theory, he wants to separate it from that of the *śramaṇas*, the ascetics. Following earlier scholars he assumes that there were non-Vedic and non-brahmanic sages (*muni*) and ascetics (*yati*). The older Upaniṣads are supposed to represent a partial fusion of sacrificial culture and ascetic culture, of ritual thought and moral thought. Jainism is considered as an old non-brahmanic tradition which historically goes back at least to Pārśva, the 23rd Tīrthaṅkara (ca. 9th–8th century BC). Also the eight-fold path of the Buddha is called the old path which has been followed by previous Buddhas; *ahiṃsā* is one of the virtues included in it. Some authors look for pre-Aryan origins of, or at least influences in, Buddhism and Jainism although concrete proof for this assumption is lacking. Jaini (169) argues that the Jainas have no memory of a time when they fell within the Vedic fold and could accordingly not have started as an *ahiṃsā* oriented sect within the Vedic tradition. Even if one concedes the rather vague possibility that Buddhism and Jainism originated in a completely different milieu than Vedism, the question remains against which practices the ascetic movements were directed.

The Buddhists and the Jainas stress the *kṣatriya* descent of their founders and the opposition to the brahmins. Their followers came mainly from the upper classes (Oldenberg 74; Gombrich 56ff.). The motives which induced especially *kṣatriya*s to renounce the world are not yet known (see, however, Dundas 2002: 153ff.; WB). Urbanization has been made responsible, and also plagues have been considered as an inducement to withdrawal from the world (Gombrich). Since our sources are silent about this, such guesses should not be taken too seriously. But we can assume with some plausibility that in *kṣatriya* circles an independent world view was developed which was opposed to many brahmanic ideas rooted in ritualistic thinking. As is well-known, in the Upaniṣads new ideas, especially the doctrine of transmigration, were introduced by *kṣatriya*s, and brahmins became their willing students. The problem was last summarized by Horsch (1966: 427–448). It will not be too far from the truth if one assumes that the Buddha and the Jina belonged to the same line of tradition, but went beyond the royal sages of the Upaniṣads by rejecting the Veda and the ritual based on it. That Buddhism was a reaction against late Vedic ideas would appear from the *anātman*-doctrine which can hardly be anything but a criticism of the *ātman*-doctrine.

In the brahmanic sources we can follow the evolution of the ideas of *ahiṃsā* and renunciation, in Buddhism and Jainism they are there right from the beginning, it is true, in opposition to Vedic ritualism, but a ritualism which had already been superseded by the meta-ritualists who interiorized the sacrifice. The Buddhists and Jainas could do what the meta-ritualists could not: they could deny the validity of the Veda whose rituals were kept alive by the representatives of the *karmakāṇḍa*.

My article has partly found approval, partly been received with reserve. Della Casa follows my interpretation nearly to the letter. Schreiner (302 n. 23) thinks that Della Casa differs from me in assuming that *ahiṃsā* was practised not because one gave up atonement, but because one doubted the possibility of atonement; this is wrong since I had stated exactly the [220] latter view (650; 652). Spera, who deals mainly with *ahiṃsā* in the Mahābhārata, the Purāṇas, and in Jainism, refers to my work without criticism. But he thinks that the way of the Jainas is parallel to that of the Hindus, but different. The Jainas are supposed to be pre-Aryan, animistic and sedentary, the Hindus polytheistic (with magical tendencies) and nomadic. This view is without foundation just as similar ones already mentioned. I have shown that there are animistic ideas in the Veda; moreover, animism and polytheism do not exclude each other. At the time when the ideas we are concerned with arose, the Vedic people were not nomadic any longer.

Wezler (87 n. 252), who seems to agree with my main arguments, doubts that the 'magico-ritual fear of destroying life in any form' was the only root of strict *ahiṃsā* and the asceticism resulting from it. He especially objects to the 'monocausal' interpretation. Such an interpretation was not intended, and I have not claimed that asceticism is derived from *ahiṃsā*. After all, *ahiṃsā* is only part of the ascetic practices, and asceticism existed long before the development of the strict *ahiṃsā*-doctrine. My work had the aim to follow the development of the idea of *ahiṃsā* in the sources extant and to abstain from general hypotheses as far as possible. I do not at all exclude the possibility that the further investigation of the complex of renunciation and asceticism can uncover other aspects which contributed to the spread of *ahiṃsā*. So general a criticism as that of Wezler is not very helpful since there is not even a suggestion where the other causes might be sought.

Incidentally it should be mentioned that Wezler (110f.) has misrepresented my position regarding the genesis of the *āśramas*. I explicitly stated (651) that I do not share the opinion that the *āśramas* were created by the brahmins in order to bring ascetic movements under their control.

Schmithausen concedes (116) that my hypothesis shows at least one of the roots of *ahiṃsā* in the whole ascetic tradition of India. He repeats Wezler's objection to 'monocausal' explanations (n. 95). He points out that archaic hunting societies often restrict the killing of animals to a minimum or pacify the lords of the animals, for which he refers to an example from South America. Not only the fear of the animal's revenge is a motive, but also the awe of taking life and the respect for life, and furthermore the realization of the relationship of all living creatures and an ecological instinct. But he immediately concedes that these notions were not necessarily differentiated by those people. With these remarks nothing new is added to my thesis.

The behaviour of the hunting societies agrees closely with that of the Vedic ritualists as will be shown below (VIII). Schmithausen thinks that the close connection of *ahiṃsā* with compassion cannot be derived from the fear of revenge, but it can be derived from awe which can also be considered as evidence for an explicit ethicization of *ahiṃsā*. I cannot see such a difference between fear and awe since awe is sublimated fear, and compassion in its most literal sense causes fear. Schmithausen deals with Buddhism in which *ahiṃsā* and compassion tend to coalesce, but he should have mentioned that also in Hinduism and Jainism both concepts [221] are closely linked. The central importance of fearlessness for the *sannyāsin* must be stressed since it brings out the close connection of fear with *hiṃsā*.

Halbfass (87–129), to whom we owe a valuable exposition of the Pūrvamīmāṃsā view of the ritual *hiṃsā*, doubts that the Vedic ritualists' fear of committing *hiṃsā* was the ultimate source of the later renunciatory *ahiṃsā*-doctrine (113). He thinks the concern about the harming and killing was not intrinsic to, or inseparable from, their ritualism. He rather wants to make external factors responsible for the development which led to the sharp antagonism between Vedic ritualism and *ahiṃsā*. The ritualists 'may have been concerned that certain means employed in the ritual might violate rules that were not those of the rituals themselves, and unleash forces that might turn against the ritualists'. But he adds that we do not know the nature and origin of such fears. These remarks can hardly be accepted as a refutation of my hypothesis.

That the magico-ritual elimination of killing and injury was an integral part of the world-view of the ritualists cannot be denied unless one denies the ritualists' credibility. It is obvious that the emancipation from the magical approach has to be sought in the ritualists' own circle. This appears clearly from the ethicization of the *karman*-concept in the Upaniṣads which reflect the views of the meta-ritualists. Halbfass's position is all the more surprising since in the course of his investigation of the Pūrvamīmāṃsā standpoint (92) he quotes the Upaniṣad doctrine of the way of the fathers, which leads to rebirth, and the way of the gods, which leads to the liberation from transmigration. This doctrine was developed in ritualistic circles. For the Upaniṣadic thinkers the way of the ritual was the lesser one, that of the knowledge of the unity of the world in *ātman-brahman* the higher one. The brahmins themselves were divided into the conservative ritualist party and the renunciatory philosopher party. This division has survived to this day, whichever concessions many or most ritualists may have made to vegetarianism.

Proudfoot discusses Alsdorf's and my work in his Canberra dissertation of 1977 which was published in 1987. He rejects Alsdorf's interpretation of Manu 5.5–56. He thinks (8f.) that

> Alsdorf conjures up the image of a collision between the newly emerging values of vegetarianism-cum-*ahiṃsā* and the conservative inertia of tradition. Alsdorf makes nothing of the fact that the author of Manu saw all the rules as having an element in common: all are concerned with governing the consumption of food. If nothing else, this is suggestive of how practice may be instrumental in creating linkages between ideologically unrelated institutions. However because of his commitment to a simple causal relationship between vegetarianism and *ahiṃsā*, Alsdorf is precluded from exploring more subtle patterns of multiple causation.

Since the author does not reveal how he views the linkages and multiple causation, nothing can be gained from this criticism. It is certainly legitimate to ask why Manu composed the section on food in the way he did, but whatever the answer may be, it will not change anything in Alsdorf's demonstration of historical layers.

While Proudfoot calls Alsdorf's work an 'a priori interpretation' of causality, he labels mine as an 'unstructured description'. By this characterization he means that in contrast to Alsdorf I do 'not set out to organize the material around a consistent theme or portray a pattern which [222] will account for the evolution of the *ahiṃsā* ideal or any aspect of its practice'. When he continues by stating that I rather submit to the judgement of Manu, this is a patent error, since I took Manu's list only as a convenient starting-point for the historical investigation. Accordingly it goes without saying that soon questions arise to which Manu has no answer. My conclusions are therefore not drawn from Manu's material, but from older sources. Proudfoot also objects to my inclination to attribute to ethical motives less influence on the spread of *ahiṃsā* than to the fear of revenge or punishment in the hereafter or a future birth. He tries to marginalize the retribution mentioned in M 5.55 – the eater is eaten by the food in the hereafter – but since it is also mentioned in 5.33, it will have played a role which cannot be neglected all the more since it goes back to old models. The fact that Manu prefers the ethical motivation does not speak against this: it is not surprising that the learned brahmin makes use of the more sublime interpretation.

Proudfoot suggests that the idea of rebirth 'arose as a new social philosophy rationalizing disparities of wealth or a crystallizing social structure' since transmigration has ethical implications. This would turn my conclusions on its head. By letting Manu's guiding hand slip I am supposed to lack the basis for refuting it. I do not understand how anyone can get the idea that I intended to refute Manu. My concern was historical and accordingly different from Manu's summary of views existing at his time. Proudfoot does not make any suggestion how the new social philosophy is supposed to have looked. Just as in the criticism of Alsdorf he leaves it at pseudo-theoretical remarks. The lack of substantiation makes a discussion impossible.

In his summary (151) Proudfoot states that in Mbh 12.255:

> *ahiṃsā* is identified with a fundamental conception of the life-process and of the relationship between life in this world and the next, which controverted the view that life is dynamically sustained through a circulatory exchange between this world and the hereafter in which sacrifice was an essential link.

He maintains that this 'puts a new complexion upon the reaction' I proposed between transmigration and the devaluation of the sacrifice in favour of renunciatory *ahiṃsā*, because in the episode the intermediation of ascetic values is not involved. I wonder how this late source can be used for the purpose to refute or change conclusions drawn from earlier material. Moreover, the episode does contain references to renunciatory values as Proudfoot himself has noted (128). His summary does not properly reflect the results of his own analysis.

Brian K. Smith (1990, 196 n. 33, repeated in Doniger and Smith 1990: XXXII n. 39) objects to my opinion on the ground that concern for the victim is universal and that therefore there is no 'ritual *ahiṃsā*'. In the ritual texts *ahiṃsā* also refers to the prevention of injury to the sacrificer, his progeny and cattle. Smith remarks: 'such a self-interested *ahiṃsā* in relation to oneself and one's possessions is of course a desideratum in Vedism, but that is certainly not the *ahiṃsā* of post-Vedism.' The later conception of *ahiṃsā*, it is true, differs from the Vedic one, but this does not exclude that the one is derived from the other. I have argued that the ritual *ahiṃsā* [223] was turned on its head by the later thinkers. Hindu, Jain and Buddhist *ahiṃsā* also remained self-interested, though the motivation changed.

Chapple (4ff.) has the impression that Alsdorf and myself minimize the importance of Jainism in the development of *ahiṃsā* and vegetarianism. He also states that both of us 'claim that Mahāvīra was not a vegetarian, a claim that has been contradicted by the Jaina scholar H. R. Kapadia'. He does not attempt to refute Alsdorf's (8ff.) demonstration that two of the oldest canonical Jaina texts unambigously show that Jaina monks did eat meat and fish when they received it as alms, and that in another canonical text the sick Mahāvīra refuses to accept two pidgeons prepared especially for himself, but asks for meat of a chicken killed by a cat. Thus Mahāvīra's attitude towards meat-eating agreed with that of the Buddha who did allow it if the animal was not killed specifically for the monk. Alsdorf (53f.) looked for the origins of *ahiṃsā* and vegetarianism in the pre-Aryan Indus civilization.

I disagreed (627). It is true that the presence of animal bones in the refuse of Mohenjo-daro is by itself not a cogent argument for the absence of vegetarianism in that culture. My main argument was and is that the Vedic sources do allow us to reconstruct a development within the Vedic culture. Chapple is of the opinion that recent scholarly investigations tend to refute my conclusions. The evidence he quotes is far from cogent. Even if one assumes that the animals on the Indus civilization seals and amulets were worshipped, this does not imply that all of them were inviolable and not sacrificed. The possible links between the figures in postures similar to those of yoga in [229] Jainism and Hinduism have no bearing on the *ahiṃsā* problem since yoga is not inseparably connected with *ahiṃsā*.

VII

The *dīkṣita*, the *brahmacārin* and the *sannyāsin* all undergo a consecration (*dīkṣā*), subject themselves to severe restrictions which to a large extent are the same for all of them. In order to determine to which of the three the vegetarianism of the brahmin can be traced back, we must consider the differences. I myself stated (1968: 651) that the vows of the *sannyāsin* are probably modelled after those of the *brahmacārin* and that *sannyāsa* can be considered as a return to *brahmacarya*. The difference between the two is essentially that the *brahmacārin* strives for the knowledge of the Veda, the *sannyāsin* for the knowledge of the *ātman*. The prohibition of meat for the *brahmacārin* and the *dīkṣita* had originally nothing to do with vegetarianism and the later *ahiṃsā*-doctrine. Avoidance of meat and sex belongs to the preparation for sacrifice also elsewhere (e.g. Greece: Burkert 60f. Rome: Ovid, Fasti IV 657–658). For the *brahmacārin* and the *dīkṣita* the restrictions are temporary, for the *sannyāsin* permanent. The *dīkṣita* prepares himself for the sacrifice which he must perform once he has entered upon this road. The *sannyāsin* divests himself of his ritual utensils before he undergoes the *dīkṣā* for the new *āśrama*. The strictly vegetarian brahmin will originally have hardly undergone the *dīkṣā* for the *soma* sacrifice, but will, as far as possible, have followed the rules for the *sannyāsin* for whom the private recitation of the Veda (*svādhyāya*) remains a duty (Baudh 2.10.18.22; 24. Āp 2.9.21.10). The *brahmacārin* acquires the knowledge of the Veda by repetition, the *sannyāsin* preserves it for himself by repetition.

Vegetarianism has become the cornerstone of *ahiṃsā* because abstaining from meat is possible, from vegetal food not. That the *hiṃsā*, which cannot be avoided even in the vegetarian mode of life, was a deep concern for the brahmin appears from Manu 3.68: The householder has five butcheries, viz., hearth, grinding stone, broom, mortar and pestle, water vessel. Atonements for the *hiṃsā* caused by these implements are the five daily 'great sacrifices' for the gods, fathers, creatures, men and the *brahman* (the Veda in form of the private recitation).

These sacrifices are first mentioned in ŚB 11.5.6.1ff., a passage already mentioned above in Section V. Kane (II 697) says they are morally and spiritually more progressive than the *śrauta* sacrifices; he also thinks that they were introduced because everybody could afford them. I leave it open whether these sacrifices are a late development or rather an ancient custom. That they occur in the sources in contexts which presuppose the interiorization of the ritual is probably due to the fact that they had no place in the *śrauta* ritual and could gain their importance only in those circles that devalued the sacrifice on a grand scale.

[230] A more detailed version of the last and most eminent of the 'great sacrifices', the *svādhyāya*, is found in TA 2.10ff. As in ŚB it is said that by the *svādhyāya* one gains an imperishable world, the liberation from recurring death and becomes united with the *brahman* (2.14.3; cf. 2.19.4). In 2.15.5 we read:

> when the fire was born, evil (*pāpman*) took hold of it, by the oblations the gods warded the evil off, by the sacrifice the evil of the oblations, by the *dakṣiṇā*s the evil of the sacrifice, by the brahmin the evil of the *dakṣiṇās*, by the metres the evil of the brahmin, by the *svādhyāya* the evil of the metres; the *s v ā d h y ā y a* is free from evil, it is a divine purifier.

According to 2.16–17, officiating at the sacrifice and accepting *dakṣiṇā*s leaves the brahmin empty, and he must fill himself again by thrice reciting the Veda. By officiating one milks the metres, and by *svādhyāya* of the words of the ceremonies concerned on a pure place in the wilderness the metres are filled up again. Then follow the identifications which make the *svādhyāya* an interiorized sacrifice.

In this text there is not yet any mention of renunciation, but the pre-eminence of the *svādhyāya*, which outweighs the whole sacrificial ritual, is clearly expressed. The evil the brahmin takes upon himself by the priestly office can be atoned by the *svādhyāya*. A further step will lead to rejecting the priestly office and also to giving up own sacrifices. One may ask why then still *sannyāsa* was needed if one could attain the liberation from recurring death already by the *svādhyāya*. This question was asked already in early times. We can infer this from a Dharmasūtra (Āp 2.9.21.2) where it is stated that one can attain peace (*kṣema*) if one lives in all stages of life according to the laws; that *kṣema* refers here to salvation appears from the fact that shortly afterwards (14) the word is used of the goal of the *sannyāsin*. Also Vasiṣṭha 8.17 is of the opinion that by doing one's duties (among them that to sacrifice) one never forfeits the world of *brahman*.

Repeatedly the Dharmasūtras polemize against *sannyāsa*; the Vedic sacrifices, including animal sacrifices, are obligatory, and only one *āśrama*, that of the householder, is recognized because the others do not produce progeny (Āp 2.9.23.9–10. Baudh 2.6.11.27ff. Gaut 3.36). Implicitly the view of some teachers that one can renounce immediately after *brahmacarya* is rejected; renunciation is restricted to childless persons, widowers and generally to septuagenarians whose children are independent (Baudh 2.10.17.2–5). The resistance is not so much directed against renunciation as such, but against withdrawal from the world before one has done one's social duties. Since not everybody could hope to live long enough to qualify for *sannyāsa*, it was nearly unavoidable for the teachers of *dharma* to hold out the prospect of salvation to everybody, in whichever stage of life he may be.

The attitude of the Dharmasūtras is also represented in the epic story of the young forest hermits and Indra in the form of a golden bird (Mbh 12.11), which Wezler (95ff.) has dealt with. Indra teaches the boys that it is not they who are the true eaters of food remnants, but rather the householder who offers the five 'great sacrifices' and eats the remnants. The story has a parallel in the Buddhist Vighāsajātaka (393) in which the ascetics live on remnants of flesh which beasts of prey have left. This [231] corresponds to the rule of the Dharmasūtras according to which the *vānaprastha*s, or certain *vānaprastha*s, live on such remnants of prey, even though the Jātaka, by using the word *kuṇapa* 'carrion', views the conduct of the ascetics not only as foolish, but also as reprehensible or at least disgusting. Wezler has aptly characterized the conduct of the *gṛhastha*, the true eater of food remnants, as innerworldly asceticism whose propagation is a criticism of the asceticism of those who withdraw from the world.

The true eaters of food remnants were not all vegetarians; at least Yudhiṣṭhira and the Pāṇḍavas were not, and probably not the brahmins either who followed them (Mbh 3.2.2; 8; 55ff.). The Pāṇḍavas were not *vānaprastha*s in the sense of the *āśrama* doctrine; *vānaprastha* as *āśrama* involves *ahiṃsā*, but not in principle vegetarianism. In contradistinction to the *vānaprastha*, who must live on food he has gathered himself, the *sannyāsin* is allowed to beg. It is noteworthy that nowhere in the brahmanic literature is anything said about the question of whether the *sannyāsin* is allowed to accept meat or not. Remembering the agreements between the rules for the *sannyāsin* and those for the *brahmacārin* we may conclude that the *sannyāsin* had to avoid meat.

In an article first published in 1964 (reprinted 1985: 41ff.) Heesterman has pointed out that the ideal brahmin is a renouncer. Among the five categories of brahmins mentioned in Mbh 12.77.2–6 the first, the *brahmasama*, is concerned only with learning and the preservation of the tradition. The *devasama*, who possesses the knowledge of the three Vedas, is also engaged in his own sacrificial work. The *kṣatrasama* serves princes as sacrificial priest and as housepriest and is probably also officiating at animal sacrifices. Heesterman correctly states that the *brahmasama* follows the *jñānamārga*, the *devasama* the *karmamārga*; but it must be added that also the *kṣatrasama* follows the *karmamārga*, and takes on himself more evil or defilement because he does not only carry his own, but also that of his patron. To keep free from evil and defilement to a large extent is possible only for the *brahmasama*. He follows the path inaugurated by the Upaniṣads, contemplates the *brahman*, the totality of the Veda which is identical with the absolute. The interiorization of the ritual was the achievement of an intellectual élite that absolutized *ahiṃsā* which finally resulted in vegetarianism. The prestige of the renouncing sage has certainly contributed to the spread of vegetarianism; the aspiration towards higher spiritual and social status has played a role alongside the hope for a better rebirth and eventual salvation.

Although the respect for life is attested with many peoples and the inhibition to kill is universal, outside India fundamental vegetarianism was not common in antiquity nor is it at present. In Greece animal sacrifice was rejected and vegetarianism advocated by the Orphics and Pythagoreans; other philosophers criticized animal sacrifice, but vegetarianism has found only isolated following. It is remarkable that, just like in India, it appears in philosophical circles, and especially in those which also teach metempsychosis. Empedocles (fragment 115) mentions bloodshed among the causes of irksome rebirths.

VIII

The only critic who has offered a counter-thesis to my thesis is Heesterman (1984). He concedes that bloody sacrifices were performed and even required the world over in spite of the universal awe and fear of killing (122). But he continues: 'It would seem, however, that it is only in India that we find an overwhelming concern with the technical-ritualistic means to take away the sting of sacrificial death and to undo the injury.' This is manifestly erroneous. On the contrary it could be said that the consciousness of guilt and the tendency to shift the blame from one's shoulders was greater in ancient Greece since there we hear even of the stoning – symbolic or not – of the actual performers (Burkert 165f.). The magical means by which one tried to neutralize and annul the actual killing are attested with many peoples, and the agreements with details of the Vedic animal sacrifice are striking. Therefore it cannot be said with Heesterman (123) that the obsessive concern about the ritual undoing of the injury points to the impending collapse of the violent sacrifice.

It will be useful and instructive to quote here the main similarities which exist between the hunting and sacrificial customs of North Asiatic and other peoples collected by Meuli and the Vedic animal sacrifice. Quite generally it is said that in previous times men and animals lived in peace (Meuli 225). This has a parallel in the Indian legend of the ages of the world: in the *kṛtayuga*, the golden age, animals were inviolable (*ahiṃsya*), only in the *tretayuga* the animal sacrifice was introduced (Mbh 12.137.73–74). From India Meuli only quoted the victim's agreement to its own sacrifice (267 n. 2). 'Causing to agree' (*saṃjñapana*) is used in the Brāhmaṇas as a euphemism for 'killing'; also the consent of the parents, brother and companion of the victim is required (ŚB 3.7.4.5). The victim's shivering and shuddering, caused by the sprinkling with water, is taken as consent (Meuli 264f.); this is also known in Greece (266f.). Although the animal is sprinkled with water in Vedic India, this particular interpretation is not attested in the sources, but we know it in recent times from Nepal (Witzel 391 n.54). With Hindukush tribes shaking the head three times counts as consent of the goat (Jettmar 212); here the additional question is asked whether the offering is welcome to the gods, and the victim's shuddering is interpreted as a positive sign of the gods (cf. 254). With the Cheremis the orifices of the horse's body are closed at the killing so that the soul is kept inside (Meuli 259). This can be compared to the purification of the vital breaths (*prāṇa*), i.e. the body orifices, of the victim by the sacrificer's wife; here the *prāṇa*s are identified with the waters, and thus the food of the gods goes to them alive (ŚB 3.8.2.4; cf. Schwab 110f.). While dismembering the animal the bones must be kept undamaged (Meuli 259).

The same is the case in the Vedic animal sacrifice and of course also in the *aśvamedha* (Schwab 105); for the *aśvamedha* the earliest reference is found in ṚV 1.162.18–20. With the North Asiatic peoples animals (and men) have several souls of which one remains with the bones and dies only when the [224] bones disintegrate. In the sacrifice the bones must remain undamaged; a god or spirit collects them; with the two other souls the animals join the herd of the gods (Friedrich 193). This reminds us of ṚV 1.162.2 and 7 where the horse joins the herd of the gods and many other, also post-Vedic, instances which state that the animal goes to the gods in heaven. Certain parts of the animal – they vary from place to place – are considered to be the seat of life (Meuli 246f.). These parts are either preserved and buried with the bones or offered to the spirit; swallowed raw or cooked; partly offered to the spirits and partly eaten by elect people or the whole community (256f.). The *iḍā* of the Vedic animal sacrifice (Schwab 128; 138ff.; 148f.) is a perfect parallel: it consists of parts of the heart, the tongue, the liver and the kidneys (some sources add other pieces of meat). Meuli (248) quotes as general motives for the relation of the hunter to the animal fear of the animal, compassion with and concern for it. This agrees with what Schmithausen has adduced from South America.

Heesterman is of the opinion that the classical ritual of the brahmins has replaced an agonal ritual which was permeated by violence. The adversary or rival, who was an integral participant in the pre-classical ritual, is supposed to have been eliminated, the sacrificer to have united in himself the roles of the two rivals and thereby created a non-violent, private and transcendent universe, isolated from the reality of society. Heesterman believes that in the course of the elimination of violence from the ritual the death of the victim came to be regarded as a ritual mistake. The original method of killing by beheading was replaced by suffocation, strangulation. I think it is rather questionable to view killing by suffocation as a step towards a less violent and cruel sacrifice, and thereby towards *ahiṃsā*. The passage which Heesterman (1962: 23f.) adduces in order to show that the killing was a ritual mistake cannot carry the burden of proof (KS 29.4. MS 4.8.6). For the mistake – the cutting of the victim's head – would have to be corrected by the sacrifice of another victim, the cow for Mitra and Varuṇa – a rather unbelievable procedure. There is no reason to assume that here killing is redeemed by killing since in the context an opposition between the two victims is not recognizable. It is not demonstrable that the 'head of the sacrifice' refers to the head of the animal victim.

Before I pursue this question, it may be noted that Heesterman's thesis of the progressing reduction of violence might suit the competing sacrifice in TS 2.2.9.7. Somebody whose rival performs a *soma*-sacrifice in order to harm him should offer a counter sacrifice in which a sacrificial cake is substituted for the cow to Mitra and Varuṇa. Here an animal sacrifice is replaced by a vegetal one. But we should not draw any far-reaching conclusions from this passage. It does not amount to a step towards *ahiṃsā* since the *agniṣomīya paśu* is not eliminated. It is rather an attempt to foil an expensive sacrifice by a less expensive one.

In the passage quoted by Heesterman we read that the head of the sacrifice was cut off and the sacrificial essence had flowed into the cow (KS 29.4). With the sacrifice of the cow one provides the sacrificer with sacrificial essence. Mitra took what was sacrificed well, and Varuṇa what was sacrificed badly. Thereby the sacrificer is freed from Mitra and Varuṇa, and the cow serves to pacify the sacrifice. The text does not identify the head, [225] MS and TS 6.6.7 do not mention it at all. MS ends with the statement that with the sacrifice of the cow the sacrificer puts right everything done incorrectly in the ritual. From this Heesterman concludes that here the idea of killing has been replaced by the concept of the mistake. But there is no indication that what is incorrectly done refers to the animal sacrifice.

Possibly TS can lead us to the identification of the head of the sacrifice in this instance. Here the passage ends with the statement that the metres of the sacrificer were exhausted and that the cow is the essence of the metres by whose sacrifice the metres regain their essence. A comparison with TS 2.1.7 (cf. KS 13.8. MS 2.5.7) would seem to confirm the conclusion that the metres are the head of the sacrifice. We read that the *vaṣat*-call split the head of the Gāyatrī. Bṛhaspati seized the sap which flowed out first, and it became a white-backed cow; Mitra and Varuṇa seized the second part of the sap, and it became a two-coloured cow; the All-gods seized the third part, and it became a many-coloured cow; the fourth part fell on the earth, Bṛhaspati seized it, and it became a bull-calf; Rudra seized the blood, it became a fierce red cow. Here we have several bovines which are the sap of the metres; each of them is to gain specific favours from the gods concerned. The general sense seems to be that by sacrificing the cows one brings the sap of the metres in circulation again.

Although I agree with Heesterman insofar as the original decapitation of the victim at the pole – as presupposed by ṚV 1.162.9 – was replaced by strangulation, I think that the reason for this was not the progressing elimination of violence, but rather a change in the relation to blood. It is well-known that the blood is offered to the demons (*rākṣasa*) and at different occasions also to Rudra and his cohorts (*aśvamedha* TS 1.4.36. ŚB 13.3.4.2ff. *śūlagava* PGS 3.8.11). The blood must remain outside the place of sacrifice, quite in contrast to ancient Greek ritual where the altar is swimming in blood. The cause for this change cannot be deduced from our sources, but one can surmise that it is based on a reaction against the customs of inimical neighbours, be they Aryan or non-Aryan. Decapitation is still today the rule in non-Vedic Hindu ritual.

Even if we concede that the use of the head in the sacrifice was abandoned and, as Heesterman (1967, reprinted 1985: 45–58) has argued, procuring the head of the victim posed difficulties for the later ritualists in specific cases, this does not account for the metaphoric use of the 'head of the sacrifice' in the context of the cow for Mitra and Varuṇa. This cow is killed in atonement for cutting off the 'head of the sacrifice' identifiable as the metres. There is no indication that here the ritualists replaced the *agniṣomīya paśu* by the metres, and thus took a step toward non-violence.

It should not be overlooked that the Vedic ritualists were quite aware of the violence and cruelty involved in strangulation. Amends had to be made when the victim uttered a cry or beat its breast with its feet (TS 3.1.4.3; 3.1.5.2). The fact that the possibility of long suffering was greater in the case of strangulation than in case of decapitation certainly did not escape the notice of the ritualists.

Heesterman proceeds from his rather shaky basis to turn the development of the *ahiṃsā* idea I had reconstructed on its head. He thinks that it started from an originally violent pattern of sacrifice of the *kṣatriya*s [226] which was replaced by a ritualistic system of the brahmins which reduced violence to a minimum. For this purpose he wants to take the argument further back than the ritual *ahiṃsā*-theory.

It is not Heesterman's aim to prove that the ritual *ahiṃsā*-theory is young, but rather to determine the source in which *ahiṃsā* and vegetarianism have united. He believes to have found it in the *dīkṣita*, the person consecrated for the sacrifice. The state of the *dīkṣita* lasts 'till . . . the sacrificer empties himself of his accumulated power in gifts (*dakṣiṇā*) and sacrificial offerings'. In the stereotyped animal and *soma* sacrifices the *dīkṣā* period is rather short and does not allow extensive activities. Furthermore the *dīkṣita* must stay in his hut, but he can send out others to beg or rob goods for him which he later distributes as *dakṣiṇā*s (cf. Heesterman 1959: 248). In the more complicated rituals of the *rājasūya* and the *aśvamedha* the time of the *dīkṣā* lasts a whole year and thus allows extensive raids. If the king stayed at home in the classical ritual, this does not mean that he did not lead the raids himself in the pre-classical ritual.

In his article on the *vrātya*s (1962: 11ff.) Heesterman has adduced plausible reasons for this development: the *vrātya* is in certain respects the precursor of the *dīkṣita* (Falk 49ff. discusses other aspects of the *vrātya* problem). The *vrātya*s give everything they have gained. Also the *dīkṣita* divests himself of at least part of his property. The descriptions of the *dīkṣita* are ambivalent: partly they are positive by emphasizing his purity and his power accumulated by asceticism (*tapas*) which prepares him for a new birth; partly they are negative, emphasizing his impurity and the fact that he can be considered dead – he has, after all, entered the world of the gods. As far as the embryonal state is concerned it should be noted that the food of the *dīkṣita* consists exclusively of milk.

Another plausible proposal of Heesterman is that what appears to be a violent raid is connected with the annual transhumance which naturally occurred when one's own land was fully grazed and one had to look for fatter pastures to feed one's cattle and to increase the flock. If, then, the *dīkṣita* or his forerunner, the *vrātya*, left 'this world' of home for 'that world' of the wilderness, he had to adopt a different lifestyle. When he took his herd out with the purpose of increasing it, be it by natural propagation, be it by raiding the neighbours, he had to abstain from slaughtering his own animals for food.

Heesterman (1984: 126) views the classical ritual as an attempt to create a peaceful and orderly world of its own, isolated from the social world. The ritual thus became a rudiment, was no longer in the centre of religious life and was pushed into a rather shadowy marginal existence precariously preserved by learned brahmins on the fringe of the spreading later forms of Hinduism. The tortuous attempts to preserve the 'authority of the Veda' would attest to that.

The performance of the great Vedic sacrifices was certainly a prerogative of men of affluence and influence. In a way the ritual became a mere merit feast. While originally depending on loot and conquest, it was later continued by the wealthy who distributed the wealth acquired by other means and either knew how to make new fortunes or would withdraw from [227] the world. The privatization of the sacrifices, which from the *soma*-sacrifice upwards were originally reserved to kings and chieftains, was probably introduced by the brahmins when the economic conditions for the pre-classical ritual had disappeared.

Heesterman thinks that as soon as the alternation of warlike and peaceful phases was not given any longer the consecrated warrior changed into the harmless *dīkṣita* who was at the same time to be the completely peaceful *gṛhastha*. From now on the vegetarian rule was valid not only for the *dīkṣita*, but also for the *gṛhastha*. The first requirement to become a *dīkṣita* and sacrificer is to be a married householder. In this way we can, in Heesterman's opinion, understand how the merger of *ahiṃsā* and vegetarianism occurred, and also that the combined rule became a universal one which bound both, the worldly *gṛhastha* and the other-worldly *sannyāsin*.

Heesterman takes this a step further by maintaining 'that the typical fusion of *ahiṃsā* and vegetarianism arose from brahmanic ritual thought, while Buddhists and Jainas, though stressing non-violence, originally had no particular use for vegetarianism'. This is an obvious fallacy. The brahmanic forest hermit, *vānaprastha*, followed the same principle as the early Buddhists and Jainas: meat was acceptable for him when the animal had not been killed by himself or for him. Heesterman overlooks the fact that the Jainas have become the strictest vegetarians while certainly not all believers in the revelation, the *śruti*, as interpreted by the brahmins, are vegetarians, nor even all brahmins.

Heesterman's conclusions result in a veritable dilemma: while on the one hand he recognizes the similarity of the *dīkṣita* and the *sannyāsin* and even sees the *dīkṣita* as the forerunner of the *sannyāsin*, he at the same time assumes the fusion of *dīkṣita* and *gṛhastha*. We must take into consideration that the emergence of renunciation falls into a time when the classical ritual was already developed and the old ritual order was remembered only in semi-historical stories which were hardly understood. We have to reconstruct the older stages with considerable ingenuity and difficulties. Especially since vegetarianism spread among the brahmins only slowly, at least in that form which also prohibits animal sacrifices, it seems improbable that the temporary vegetarianism of the *dīkṣita* in the sense of the old ritual order was the model for the vegetarian brahmin.

Strict vegetarianism applied originally only to a special category of brahmins to which I shall return later. For the orthodox brahmin there was the rule that killing in sacrifice is no killing just as intercourse with one's wife during the period most favourable for conception (*ṛtu*) is no breach of celibacy (M 3.50). The vegetarian tendency spread only slowly, and orthodox scholars resisted for a long time, even to the present, the abolition of the animal sacrifice. In spite of all the evidence the Mahābhārata provides for the opposition against the animal sacrifice, this institution has not been completely suppressed until the present day. The logician Viśvanātha (seventeenth century) accused those who prohibited meat-eating to be Buddhists (after Kane III 946). In this he was probably depending on older sources. In the [228] Viṣṇupurāṇa 3.18 we find a story about the fight between gods and demons. First the demons win because they perform the Vedic ritual. Finally Viṣṇu makes them become heretics (Buddhists and Jainas) by deception. They are being convinced of the absurdity of the opinion that the victim goes to heaven by the objection that then one should also sacrifice one's own father. It is noteworthy that this story occurs in a Vaiṣṇava source, considering that the Vaiṣṇavas have been the champions of vegetarianism among the Hindus for a long time. Also in the Bhāgavatapurāṇa 4.26.6 the killing of game for the ancestor worship is still mentioned as permitted or required, significantly enough in a context which condemns the excesses of hunting. The guilty King Purañjara is chopped up in yonder world by the murdered animals (4.28.26).

The Vedānta philosopher Śaṅkara (on Brahmasūtra 3.1.25 and 3.4.28) rejects the opinion that the animal sacrifice is sinful. The Vaiṣṇava philosopher Madhva (twelfth century) is often credited with the introduction of the *piṣṭapaśu*, the substitute animal made of flour, but in his commentary on Brahmasūtra 3.1.27 he does not consider the Vedic animal sacrifice as sinful. Substitute animals were only introduced by his followers as is apparent from an interpolation in the Kumbakona edition of the Mahābhārata (in the crit. ed. 806* after 12.123.15). Borrowing from the Jainas is improbable since they reject the offering of substitutes because it involves the wish to kill (cf. von Glasenapp 84 and *27). In the first quarter of this century there was a dispute between orthodox ritualists and Mādhvas (Parpola and Kashikar in Staal II 247). The poet Śrīharṣa (twelfth century) devoted a whole canto of his Naiṣadhīyacarita to the praise and defence of orthodox brahmanic values, among them the animal sacrifice, even the sacrifice of a cow (17.177; 200).

[232]

WORKS CITED AND THEIR ABRREVIATIONS

Sources

AB	Aitareya-Brāhmaṇa
Āp	Āpastamba Dharmasūtra
ĀpŚS	Āpastamba Śrautasūtra
Baudh	Baudhāyana Dharmasūtra
BaudhŚS	Baudhāyana Śrautasūtra
BĀU	Bṛhadāraṇyaka-Upaniṣad
Bhāgavatapurāṇa	
ChU	Chāndogya-Upaniṣad
Gaut	Gautama Dharmasūtra
GB	Gopatha-Brāhmaṇa
Kauṭalya, Arthaśāstra	
KB	Kauṣītaki-Brāhmaṇa
KapKS	Kapiṣṭhala-Kaṭha-Saṃhitā
KGS	Kāṭhaka Gṛhyasūtra
KS	Kāṭhaka-Saṃhitā
M	Manusmṛti
Mbh	Mahābhārata
MGS	Mānava Gṛhyasūtra
MS	Maitrāyaṇī Saṃhitā
Pahlavi Texts, ed. J.M. Jamasp-Asana. Bombay, 1897–1913	
PGS	Pāraskara Gṛhyasūtra
ṚV	Ṛgveda
Šayast-nē-šāyast, ed. and trsl. J.C. Tavadia. Hamburg, 1930	
ŚB	Śatapatha-Brāhmaṇa
ŚGS	Śaṅkhāyana Gṛhyasūtra
Śrīharṣa, Naiṣadhīyacarita	
TĀ	Taittirīya-Āraṇyaka
TB	Taittirīya-Brāhmaṇa
TS	Taittirīya-Saṃhitā
Vādh	Vādhūlasūtra, Ed. Caland, Acta Orientalia 4 (1926), 6 (1928)
Vās	Vāsiṣṭha Dharmasūtra
Viṣṇupurāṇa	

Secondary Literature of the Appendices

Alsdorf, Ludwig. 1962. *Beiträge zur Geschichte von Vegetarismus und Rinderverehrung in Indien,* Abhandlungen der Akademie der Wissenschaften und der Literatur. Geistes- und sozialwissenschaftliche Klasse 1961 Nr. 6. Wiesbaden.

[233]

Barthiaume, Guy. 1982. *Les rôles du mageiros. Etude sur la boucherie, la cuisine et le sacrifice dans la Grèce ancienne.* Leiden.
Bhide, V.V. 1979. *The Cāturmāsya Sacrifices.* Pune.
Biardeau, Madeleine and Charles Malamoud. 1976. *Le sacrifice dans l'Inde ancienne.* Paris.
Boyce, Mary. 1975. *A History of Zoroastrianism* I. Leiden.
Burkert, Walter. 1983. *Homo necans.* Berkeley-Los Angeles.
Chapple, Christopher Key. 1993. *Nonviolence to Animals, Earth and Self in Asian Traditions.* Albany.
Della Casa, Carlo. 1976. Ahiṃsā: Significato e ambito originari della non violenza. *Indologica Taurinensia* 3/4.187–196.
Detienne, M. et J.-P. Vernant. 1979. *La cuisine du sacrifice en pays grec.* Paris.
Dhabhar, B.N. 1932. *The Persian Rivāyats of Hormazyār Frāmarz.* Bombay.
Doniger, Wendy and Brian K. Smith. 1990. *The Laws of Manu.* Harmondsworth: Penguin.
Dumont, Louis. 1980. *Homo hierarchicus.* Chicago-London.
Dundas, Paul. 2002. *The Jains.* London-New York.
Evans-Pritchard, E.E. 1956. *Nuer Religion.* Oxford.
Falk, Harry. 1986. *Bruderschaft und Würfelspiel.* Freiburg/Breisgau.
Friedrich, Adolf. 1943. Knochen und Skelett in der Vorstellungswelt Nordasiens. *Wiener Beiträge zur Kulturgeschichte und Linguistik* 5.189–247.
Glasenapp, Helmuth von. 1923. *Madhva's Philosophie des Viṣṇuglaubens.* Bonn.
Gombrich, Richard. 1988. *Theravada Buddhism. A Social History from Ancient Benares to Modern Colombo.* London-New York.
Halbfass, Wilhelm. 1991. *Tradition and Reflection. Explorations in Indian Thought.* Albany.
Heesterman, J.C. 1959. Reflections on the Significance of the dakṣiṇā. *Indo-Iranian Journal.* 3.241–258.
——. 1962. Vrātya and Sacrifice. *Indo-Iranian Journal.* 6.1–37.
——. 1984. Non-violence and Sacrifice. *Indologica Taurinensia.* 12.119–127.
——. 1985. *The Inner Conflict of Tradition.* Chicago.
——. 1989. Somakuh und Danaergabe. XIII. *Deutscher Orientalistentag. Ausgewählte Vorträge.* Hsg. v. Einar von Schuler. Stuttgart.
Hertz, Robert. 1960. *Death and the Right Hand.* London.
Horsch, Paul. 1966. *Die vedische Gāthā- und Śloka-Literatur.* Bern.
——. 1971. Vorstufen der indischen Seelenwanderungslehre. Asiatische Studien. 25.99–157.
Jaini, Padmanabh S. 1979. *The Jaina Path of Purification.* Berkeley-Los Angeles.
Jettmar, Karl. 1975. *Die Religionen des Hindukush.* Stuttgart.
Kane, V.P. 1930–1966. *History of Dharmaśāstra* I-V. Poona.
Kellens, Jean. 1984. *Le verbe avestique.* Wiesbaden.
[234]
Lévi, Sylvain. 1899. *La doctrine du sacrifice selon les Brāhmaṇas.* Paris.
Liiders, Heinrich. 1940. *Philologica Indica.* Göttingen.

McDermott, James F. 1989. Animals and Humans in Early Buddhism. *Indo-Iranian Journal*. 32: 269–280.

Meuli, Karl. 1946. Griechische Opferbräuche. *Philobolia. Für Peter von der Mühll*, 185–288. Basel.

O'Flaherty, Wendy Doniger. 1987. The Good and Evil Shepherd. *Gilgul. Essays . . . dedicated to R.J. Zwi Werblowsky*, 169–191. Leiden.

Oldenberg, Hermann. 1923. *Buddha. Sein Leben, seine Lehre, seine Gemeinde.* Stuttgart-Berlin.

Proudfoot, Ian. 1987. *Ahiṃsā and a Mahābhārata Story*. Canberra.

Schmidt, Hanns-Peter. 1968. *The Origin of Ahiṃsā. Mélanges d'Indianisme à la mémoire de Louis Renou*. 625–655. Paris.

——. 1980. The Sēnmurw. Of birds and dogs and bats. *Persica* 9.1–85.

Schmithausen, Lambert. 1985. Buddhismus und Natur. *Die Verantwortung des Menschen für eine bewohnbare Welt im Christentum, Hinduismus und Buddhismus*. Hsg. v. Raimondo Panikkar und Walter Strolz, 100–133. Freiburg/Breisgau.

Schreiner, Peter. 1979. Gewaltlosigkeit und Tötungsverbot im Hinduismus. *Angst und Gewalt, ihre Präsenz und ihre Bewältigung in den Religionen*. Hsg. v. Heinrich von Stietencron, 287–308. Düsseldorf.

Schwab, Julius. 1886. *Das altindische Thieropfer*. Erlangen.

Smith, Brian K. 1990. Eaters, food and social hierarchy in ancient India. *Journal of the American Academy of Religion*. 58.177–208.

Spera, Giuseppe. 1982. *Notes on Ahiṃsā*. Torino.

Staal, Frits. 1983. *Agni. The Vedic Ritual of the Fire Altar* I–II. Berkeley.

Tähtinen, Unto. 1976. *Ahiṃsā. Non-Violence in Indian Tradition*. London.

Walli, Koshelya. 1974. *The Conception of Ahiṃsā in Indian Thought (According to Sanskrit Sources)*. Varanasi.

Wezler, Albrecht. 1978. *Die wahren 'Speiseresteesser'* (Skt. *vighasâśin*). Abhandlungen der Akademie der Wissenschaften und der Literatur. Geistes- und Sozialwissenschaftliche Klasse 1978 Nr. 5. Wiesbaden.

Williams, R. 1963. *Jaina Yoga: A Survey of the Medieval Śrāvakācāras*. London.

Witzel, Michael. 1987. The case of the shattered head. *Studien zur Indologie und Iranistik*. 13–14.363–415.

Zimmermann, Francis. 1987. *The Jungle and the Aroma of Meats. An Ecological Theme in Hindu Medicine*. Berkeley-Los Angeles.

Appendix IV

PROHIBITION OF FLESH-EATING IN JAINISM

By H.R. Kapadia

Diet plays an important part in human life; for, not only does the physical constitution depend on it but even the mental equanimity and moral achievements are practically governed by it.

This seems to be the reason why Indian philosophers in particular have pronounced their judgement in favour of or against some of the eatables[339] and drinks. Side by side, the time[340] when one should take one's meals and the quantity[341] to be taken at the time are also specifically mentioned in Jainism. But this is not the place to deal with Jaina diet in all its details. The main object of writing this article is (1) to point out that the verdict of Jainism goes emphatically against flesh-eating and (2) to answer the question whether it is permitted under any special circumstances.

According to Jainism penance (*tapas*) is of two types: (1) the external and (2) the internal, the former being considered useful in preparing the ground for the latter.[342] The external penance like the

---

339 In Pravacanasāroddhāra (v. 1411–1412, p. 411), its author Nemicandra Sūri II mentions 18 articles of food (*bhakṣya bhojana*) current in the world.

340 Jainism advises us to refrain from taking meals after sunset. This rule is to be scrupulously observed by Jaina saints for whom this is looked upon as the sixth vow, in addition to the five mahāvratas they are bound to observe. See Daśavaikālikasūtra (IV, 8).

341 32 morsels are considered sufficient for a man and 28 for a woman, each morsel being in size equal to that of the egg of a hen. See Haribhadra Sūri's comm. (p. 27) to Daśavaikālikasūtraniryukti (v. 47). – No one so far seems to have stumbled over the fact that the Jains, who allegedly never ate meat or eggs, express a mouthful of food just by means of a hen's egg, of all things, instead of a fruit, as could rather be expected. The same holds true for Jacobi's compromise of *maṃsa* and *maccha* as a metaphorical expression (see below; WB).

342 Compare the views of Mahātmā Gandhi on the observance of a fast leading to *ātmaśuddhi*.

internal one is of six kinds,[343] one of them being *rasaparityāga* which means that whatever article is likely to lead the senses astray when consumed should be given up. Accordingly liquor (*madya*), flesh (*māṃsa*), honey, butter etc.[344] are to be discarded. From this it will be easily inferred that flesh-eating [233] is against the very spirit of Jainism, especially when it lays stress on *ahiṃsā*, *saṃyama* and *tapas* as its three essential features. It will not be amiss to mention in this connection what are called *vikṛtis*. A student conversant with Jainism needs hardly to be reminded that out of the 10 *vikṛtis* viz. milk, curds, ghee, oil of sesamum etc., treacle, *pakvānna*, honey, liquor, flesh and butter, the last four are styled as *abhakṣya* or those that are unfit for consumption. The first six are called *bhakṣya*; but after all, they, too, are *vikṛtis*, although less harmful, and should therefore be avoided as far as possible.

Before I actually refer to passages in the Jaina canon and point out how they denounce flesh-eating, I shall have to define the term 'Jaina'. A true 'Jaina' is he who firmly believes that: (1) true God (*Paramātman*) is one who is completely free from attachment and aversion; (2) that the real guru is he who strictly observes celibacy; and (3) that the real *dharma* is that which has *ahiṃsā* as its chief characteristic. It is a truth generally admitted that conviction is not always immediately followed by action. Hence a Jaina though a firm believer in the principles of Jainism may not be seen actually following them in practice. There is a possibility of such a person being a slave of passions, and hence being addicted even to the worst types of the seven *vyasanas*[345] viz., (1) gambling, (2) flesh, (3) wine, (4) a prostitute, (5) hunting, (6) theft; and (7) debauchery. It may be remarked that so long as such a person considers this conduct to be contrary to the holy precepts of Jainism and sincerely repents for it, that person does not cease to be a Jaina, though such a person may be actually seen taking flesh. But, this does not mean that flesh-eating goes uncondemned in Jainism. For, there is a higher stage than this for a Jaina layman who takes a vow of refraining from the *abhakṣyas*.[346] The question of a Jaina saint taking flesh never arises, since he is spiritually on a higher plane than even this type of Jaina

343 Cf. the Niryukti (v. 47) to Daśavaikālikasūtra (1, 1).

344 See Vācakavarya Umāsvāti's Bhāṣya (p. 238) to Tattvārthādhigamasūtra (IX, 19) and Siddhasena Gaṇi's comm. (p. 238) to it.

345 *'dyūtaṃ ca māṃsaṃ ca surā ca veśyā pāparddhi-caurye paradāra-sevā | etāni sapta vyasanāni loke ghorātighoraṃ narakaṃ nayanti ||'*

346 They are 22 in number. See Pravacanasāroddhāra (v. 245, 246; p. 58).

layman. That is why we find in Sūtrakṛtāṅga (II, 2; p. 96), the second *aṅga* of the Jainas, Jaina saints styled as *'amajjamāṃsāsiṇo'* or those who do not take *madya* and *māṃsa*. The seventh verse of the second *cūlikā*[347] of Daśavaikālikasūtra too, supports this statement for it says:

> not taking [234] *madya* and *māṃsa*, free from jealousy, and frequently desisting even from pure (*nirvikṛti*) food, and observing *kāyotsarga* from time to time, a Jaina saint should be always exerting for *svādhyāya*. It may be mentioned *en passant* that *svādhyāya* is prohibited in a place where there is flesh.[348]

From these remarks it must have been realized by the reader that Jainism differs from other religions in its view about flesh-eating. This is further borne out by the fact that it has pointed out in unequivocal terms the penalty one has to pay for eating flesh. For instance, in Sthānāṅga (IV), the third *aṅga*, it is said: an individual amalgamates *nāraka-nāma-karman*, i.e. becomes doomed to be born in hell, for four reasons, viz.: (1) *mahārambha*; (2) *mahāparigraha*; (3) killing a five-organed being; and (4) *kūṇimāhāra* or flesh-eating. This very fact is mentioned in Bhagavatīsūtra (VIII, 9, p. 80), the fifth *aṅga*, and in Aupapātikasūtra, (*sūtra* 56), generally referred to as the *upāṅga* of Ācārāṅga. Uttarādhyayanasūtra, too, looked upon as one of the four *Mūlasūtras*, denounces flesh-eating, as could be seen from its ch. V, v. 9–10; ch. VII, v. 6–7 and ch. XIX v. 70–71. These verses are translated in S.B.E. Series (vol. XLV) as under:

'An ignorant man kills, lies, deceives, calumniates, dissembles, drinks liquor and eats meat, thinking that this is the right thing to do. (9)'

'Overbearing in acts and words, desirous for wealth and women, he accumulates sins in two ways, just as a young snake gathers dust (both on and in its body). (10)'

'He is desirous of women and pleasures, he enters on undertakings and business, drinks liquor, eats meat, becomes strong, a subduer of foes. (6)'

'He eats crisp goat's meat, his belly grows, and his veins swell with blood – but he gained nothing but life in hell, just as the ram is only fed to be killed for the sake of a guest. (7)'

---

347 The authorship of this *cūlikā* is traditionally attributed to Sīmandharasvāmin, a Tīrthaṅkara existing in Mahāvideha.

348 Cf. Sthānāṅga (X).

'You like wine, liquor, spirits, and honey; I have been made to drink burning fat and blood. (70)'

'Always frightened, trembling, distressed, and suffering, I have experienced the most exquisite pain and misery. (71)'

I believe these *āgamika* citations will suffice to convince a reader that Jainism prohibits flesh-eating. All the same, I shall refer to two incidents connected with the life of Hemacandra Sūri, an encyclopaedic author. When he accompanied Siddharāja Jayasiṃha [235], a Cālukya king, to Somanātha, he advised the king to give up for the time being wine and meat as a practice of *brahmacarya* and not on the Jaina ground of its offending against the grand human principle of *ahiṃsā*.[349] Under the influence of this powerful Sūri, 'a latitudinarian in religious views', Kumārapāla not only gave up meat-eating but promulgated the principle of *ahiṃsā* throughout his kingdom. Furthermore, Kumārapāla according to his advice abstained from taking a certain unobjectionable article of food which reminded him of flesh, and in expiation of this sin, he built thirty-two *vihāras*.[350] This will show how reprehensible is the idea of flesh-eating to Jainism.

Reasons for the abstaining from eating flesh:

1 Flesh-eating is inconsistent with the life, a saint is expected to lead.
2 Flesh is very bad *vikṛti*.
3 To eat flesh leads to a birth in hell.
4 Flesh-eating is to be given up as it otherwise interferes with the practice of celibacy.[351]

Over and above these causes already referred to, a few more, are noted in the Jaina literature e.g.: (i) in Siddhasena Gaṇi's comm. (pp. 238–239) to Tattvārthādhigamasūtra (IX, 19); (ii) in Śīlâṅka Sūri's comm. to Sūtrakṛtāṅga (II, 6, 38–39); and (iii) in Siddhasena Sūri's comm. to Pravacanasāroddhāra (p. 58).

---

349 See Syādvādamañjarī (B.S. Series LXXXIII, p. XVI).

350 See Prabandhacintāmaṇi (pp. 147–148) published by the Forbes Gujarati Sabhā.

351 This view is emphasized in Praśnavyākaraṇa (sūtra 27, p. 132), the 10th aṅga, as well as in the Bhāṣya (p. 47) of Tattvārthādhigamasūtra (VII, 3) and ist comm. (p. 47). Furthermore, in the 10th aṅga, (sūtra 29, p. 150), flesh-eating is prohibited, while recommending control over the sense of taste, and thus cultivating *saṃyama*.

The dispassionate examination of the above remarks, I am sure, will lead us to declare that Jainism does prohibit flesh-eating. Consequently, it remains to be seen, if it allows it as an *āpad-dharma*, i.e. to say under circumstances when no other food is available to sustain life. I have not come across any passage or quotation in the sacred works of the Jainas which supports this view in an unchallengeable manner.

Let us see if it is quite safe to infer from Haribhadra Sūri's commentary to Daśavaikālikasūtra (V. 1, 73–74) that 'the monks in the days of the Sūtras did not have any objection to eat flesh and fish which were given to them by the house-holders'.

Firstly, it should be borne in mind that Haribhadra remarks [236] that the monks in times of famine, etc. had to take flesh and fish, in order to live; but he does not mention the name of a single monk of that type. On the contrary we come across a passage in Titthogāliya paiṇṇā, one of the Jain *āgamas*, which runs as under: when the Madhyadeśa was affected by famine, some saints went away to another province (*viṣaya*) and some who were afraid of violating their holy vows willingly gave up food and drink (and died).

Secondly, other commentators referred to by Haribhadra himself do not interpret the words *poggala* and *aṇimisa* as meaning flesh and fish but they consider them to signify varieties of fruits.

Thirdly, if flesh-eating were permissible as *āpad-dharma* will there be any place for *saṃlekhanā*,[352] recommended in Jainism? Has not Samantabhadra defined *sallekhanā* as giving up body for the sake of *dharma*, when it is not possible to abide by *dharma* in cases like a calamity, a famine, an old age and an incurable disease? Does not Jainism proclaim that body is to be cared for so far as it helps us in observing *dharma*? What is the earthly use of supporting body by auctioning *dharma*? Does not a country when its honour is at stake, expect its citizens to preserve it even at the cost of their life?

Lastly in this connection, it may be mentioned that even Prof. Jacobi who had formerly translated *māṃsa* and *maccha* occurring in Ācārāṅga as flesh and fish has now modified his opinion. As his letter[353] is likely to throw much light on this burning question, it is being fully reproduced as under:

---

352 For its explanation see the Bhāṣya (p. 95) of Tattvārthādhigamasūtra (VII, 17). In the Digambara works we have *sallekhaṇā* in place of *saṃlekhanā*, which should not be confounded with suicide as the latter is denounced in Jainism.

353 I have to thank Mr Motilal Ladhaji for the permission he has given me to utilize this letter addressed to him.

Dear Sir,[354]

Your letter dated 10-1-28 duly at hand. I have carefully gone over the passage of the Āchārāṅga Sūtra II 1.10.6 which refers to the eating of 'meat' and 'fish' by Jaina monks or nuns. The result at which I arrived forms the subject of this letter.

Let me begin with the origin of the controversy in about AD 1900. In my translation of the Āchārāṅga Sūtra (S.B.E., vol. XXII, Oxford, 1884) I have rendered in the passage under consideration, *maṃsa* and *maccha* by 'meat' and 'fish'; for, such is the original [237] or primary meaning (*mukhyārtha*) of *māṃsa* and *matsya*. The Jainas took offence at this rendering and complained about it to Professor Max Müller, the editor of the S.B.E. Series.

In order to justify my translation, I tried to make it probable that in ancient times the prohibition of animal food may not have been so rigorous as it notoriously was in more modern times. But my suggestion has not been accepted, and Mr Khimji Hirji Kayani communicated to me the following explanation of the passage in question by the high priest of the Jain community of Bombay:

'A monk or a nun on a begging tour is prohibited from receiving conserve of fruits containing a large portion of bark or an exterior covering of a fruit, and if inadvertently received then the monk or nun should bury underground the remaining portion of such conserve which cannot be eaten,' etc. A similar explanation was given to me by several *yatis* on my visit to India in the cold season of 1913–14. I duly took notice of their interpretation which I promised to publish when a second edition of my translation of the Āchārāṅga Sūtra should be issued, but I refrained from further discussing or disputing the point, and there the matter rested.

Now the point to be decided is whether *māṃsa* and *matsya* can be proved to have the meaning conserve of fruits assigned to them by the orthodox interpreters of the

354 See also the article by munis Nemivijaya and Ānandasāgara 2007: 12ff. with a Sanskrit letter by Jacobi on p. 20f. and their reply to Jacobi on p. 22f. On my request for a copy of this letter of Jacobi Muni Śīlacandravijaya answered me that the letter could not be found (WB).

passage under consideration. In proof of this assertion no evidence has been brought forward either from Sanskrit Literature or from glossaries (*koṣas*).[355] It is true that *matsya-phalā* and *māṃsa-phalā* are names of certain plants, but not the words *matsya* and *māṃsa* by themselves; and even that meaning would not suit the requirement of our case. *Maṃsa* and *maccha* occur only once more in the Piṇḍesaṇā (1, 9, 3) and there they must be taken in their primary sense of 'meat' and 'fish.' That passage has reference to a meal which is being prepared for a guest or a sick person. After the usual opening words we read *maṃsaṃ vā macchaṃ vā majjijjamāṇaṃ pehāe*. The attribute *majjijjamāṇaṃ* 'being fried or roasted' shows that by *maṃsa* and *maccha* 'conserve of fruits' cannot be meant. [238] The householder who makes those preparations for the reception of a guest, need not be a Jaina layman; it is, therefore, not to be wondered at that he has meat or fish roasted for the guest. It will thus be seen that the exegetical rules of philology oblige us to attribute to the words *maṃsa* and *maccha*, in the doubtful passage, their primary meaning 'meat' and 'fish.' But how are we to reconcile this result with the prohibition of animal-food? Even if it be granted that this prohibition had not been as strictly observed of old as in historical times, still we cannot suppose that at any time a Jaina monk should explicitly admit that under certain conditions he was ready to accept as alms 'meat' and 'fish'; for, that would be the meaning of the passage if understood in its literal sense. I think I can suggest a way out of the dilemma, without either putting an inadmissible practice to the ancient Jaina monks. For, two Sanskrit passages, one in the Mahābhāṣya of Patañjali and the other in the Tātparya-ṭīkā of Vācaspati-miśra seem to me to throw some light on the quotation in

355 In order that a learned reader may argue out this case, I may state the following particulars:

(i) In Suśrutasaṃhitā (p. 642) we have: *'cūta-phale 'paripakve keśara-māṃsāsthi-majjā na pṛthag dṛśyante.'*

(ii) Carakasaṃhitā (p. 1028) remarks: *'kharjūra-māṃsānyatha nārikelam.'*

(iii) Hemacandra Sūri observes in his Anekārthasaṃgraha: *'tiktāriṣṭā kaṭur-matsyā cakrāṅgī śakulādanī.'*

(iv) Prajñāpanā declares that thereare several plants, etc. which bear the names of animals.

hand. In discussing a Vārttika ad Pāṇini (III, 3, 9) Patañjali illustrates the meaning of *nāntarīyakatva* by the following example: *'kaścit māṃsārthī matsyān sa-śakalān sa-kaṇṭakān āharati nāntarīyakatvāt. sa yāvad ādeyaṃ tāvad ādāya śakala-kaṇṭakāny utsṛjati. evam ihâpi'*, etc. (The same passage is repeated verbatim in the Mahābhāṣya ad IV. 1, 92).

Vācaspatimiśra in commenting on Nyāyasūtra IV 1, 54 says: *'tasmān māṃsārthīva kaṇṭakān uddhṛtya māṃsam aśnann ānarthaṃ kaṇṭaka-janyam āpnotīty evaṃ prajñāvān duḥkham uddhṛtyendriyādi-sādhanaṃ sukhaṃ mokṣyate.'* Patañjali and Vācaspatimiśra are separated by nine centuries: during all this time (and probably much longer) the standard example of an object containing the substance which is wanted in intimate connection (*nāntarīyaka*) with much that must be rejected, was 'fish' of which the flesh may be eaten, but the scales and bones must be taken out. By being generally understood in this way, and having become proverbial, as it were, the expression 'fish with many bones' came to be properly used, I assume, to denote metaphorically any substance similarly constituted. In this metaphorical sense, I believe, *bahu-aṭṭhiyeṇa maṃseṇa vā maccheṇa vā bahu-kaṇṭhaeṇa* has been used in the passage of Āchārāṅga Sūtra under consideration. A close examination of that passage is very much in favour of my supposition. It runs thus:

> *se bhikkhū vā jāva samāṇe siyā ṇaṃ paro bahu-aṭṭhieṇa maṃseṇa maccheṇa vā bahu-kaṇṭhaeṇa uvanimantejjā* | *āusanto samaṇā abhikaṅkhasi bahu-aṭṭhiyaṃ maṃsaṃ paḍigāhettae* | *etappagāraṃ nighosaṃ soccā* [239] *nisamma se puvvām-eva āloejjā* | *āuso ti vā bhaiṇī ti vā no khalu kappai me bahu-aṭṭhiyaṃ maṃsaṃ paḍigāhettae* | *abhikaṅkhasi me dāuṃ jāvatiyaṃ tāvatiyaṃ poggalaṃ dalayāhi, mā aṭṭhiyāiṃ* | etc.

The layman asks the monk whether he will accept 'meat with many bones'. Now if the alms-giver had actually offered meat, the answer of the monk would of a certainty have been: 'No, I am no flesh-eater.' Instead of this refusal he says: 'It is against our rules to accept "meat with many bones": "if you desire to make me a gift, give me as much of the substance as you like, but not the bones."' It is worthy of remark that the monk makes use of the (popular) phrase 'meat with many bones' when declining the offer, but not when he states that he will accept; there he uses not a metaphorical expression, but the direct designation *poggala*, substance. This change of appellation is due to the consciousness that the first expression is metaphorical and open to misunderstanding.

This meaning of the passage is, therefore, that a monk should not accept as alms any substance of which only a part can be eaten and a great part must be rejected. The same principle governs the preceding paragraphs of the 10th *uddesao*. In 4 some such substances are mentioned by name viz. different parts of sugarcane, etc. and in 5 we find *maṃsa* and *maccha* which expression, if I am right, comprises all the remaining substances of a similar description which have not been mentioned in the preceding paragraph.

Bonn, Yours faithfully,

14 February 1928. H. JACOBI